Civil War Battlefields
A Touring Guide

973.7

by David J. Eicher

Maps by John H. Eicher

Foreword by James M. McPherson

D0964936

TAYLOR TRADE PUBLISHING

Dallas • Lanham • Boulder • New York • Toronto • Oxford

Copyright © 1995 by David J. Eicher
Updated edition 2005

This Taylor Trade Publishing paperback edition of *Civil War Battlefields* is published by arrangement with the author.

Published by Taylor Trade Publishing
An imprint of The Rowman & Littlefield Publishing Group, Inc., 4501 Forbes Boulevard, Suite 200, Lanham, Maryland 20706

Distributed by NATIONAL BOOK NETWORK

Library of Congress Cataloging-in-Publication Data

Eicher, David J., 1961–
    Civil War Battlefields : a touring guide/by David J. Eicher: maps by John H. Eicher: foreword by James M. McPherson.
        p.   cm.
    Includes index.
    ISBN 1-58979-181-9 (pbk. : alk. paper)
        1. United States—History—Civil War, 1861–1865—Battlefields—Guidebooks.   2. United States—Guidebooks.   3. Battlefields—United States—Guidebooks.   4. Historic Sites—United States—Guidebooks.   I. Eicher, David J. 1961–.
    II. Title.
    E641.E33   1995
    973.7—dc20   94-38905

∞ ™ The paper used in this publication meets the minimum requirements of American National Standard for Information Sciences—Permanence of Paper for Printed Library Materials, ANSI/NISO Z39.48-1992.

Manufactured in the United States of America.

For Darius Wetzel, Private, Co. E,
74th Ohio Veteran Volunteer Infantry,
survivor of First Bull Run, Shiloh,
Corinth, Stones River, Chickamauga,
Chattanooga, Atlanta,
and the March to the Sea.

Contents

★ ★ ★

List of Maps

Foreword

If this book had existed twenty years ago, my job as a Civil War historian would have been much easier. In 1975 I signed contracts to write books that required a good working knowledge of Civil War military campaigns and battles (the books were *Ordeal by Fire* and *Battle Cry of Freedom*). Until that time my writings had focused on the political and social history of the Civil War era. To turn myself into a military historian, I read hundreds of books and articles. But there is nothing like seeing the ground on which these battles were fought, so I decided to tour as many battlefields as possible. In the summer of 1976 I embarked on the first of several tours that took me around most of the principal battlefields and related sites by automobile, by bicycle, and on foot.

Some of these battlefields are national parks with maps and self-guiding brochures or booklets to help one tour them. A few others are state parks. But a good many are in private hands. Scarcely any satisfactory guidebooks or maps were then available to help me locate or tour many of those sites—including portions of major battlefields that lie outside the boundaries of national or state parks. Thus I missed seeing some important things on those early tours.

If David Eicher's *Civil War Battlefields* had been available, I would not have missed them. It is a marvelous guidebook for the beginner. What makes it so useful, however, is its value even for veteran visitors to battlefields. Although I have been to some of them many times, reading Mr. Eicher's detailed directions on how to reach significant parts of these sites makes me realize that there is still more to see. It whets my desire to pack up my walking shoes and bicycle and head south yet again to those hallowed fields where the nation's fate was decided 130 years ago.

This book provides detailed, easy-to-follow, and up-to-date information. The maps enable one to use the modern road system to find and identify historical landmarks and sites. The text and maps together cover twenty-two campaigns that embrace approximately forty separate battles. Most of the important campaigns and battles east of the Mississippi are here. Those who use this book will eagerly await volume II, to cover the campaigns not included here. The certain success of the present volume will surely generate a demand for a second one covering other campaigns. In the meantime, I envy those of you who will be touring Civil War battlefields for the first or second times with this volume in hand. A whole new and exciting world awaits you. You may encounter me also with the book in hand. For I eagerly anticipate experiencing again the sense of awe that overcomes me every time I visit these battlefields.

James M. McPherson

Preface

Reading is an essential, primary means of experiencing the Civil War today. Yet in books, the Civil War is a distant, hazy memory locked in the past and visited only through ink on paper. The most powerful and moving way to appreciate the Civil War is to visit a few of the many places where it happened. Among my earliest memories is playing on the ramparts of Fort Stevens, outside Washington, D.C., while my family lived in Washington for a summer. When I was four, the place seemed pretty plain. Only later would I discover that behind these same ramparts, in 1864, Abraham Lincoln watched a Confederate raid threaten Washington, and a young soldier named Oliver Wendell Holmes, Jr.—at least according to Lincoln's secretary John Hay—admonished the President for exposing himself to fire, shouting, "Get down, you damned old fool!"

As an older boy, I was lucky enough to see many of the nation's great historical sites because my father was a professor and could take the family on lengthy summer vacations. I vividly remember the first time I explored Gettysburg, during a rainy summer weekend in 1972. The most lasting image—apart from real Civil War stuff for sale in the town's shops—came on a Saturday when my father and I tramped up Culp's Hill. The day was misty and cool, and the hill deserted, but about halfway up we saw a reenactor dressed in Confederate garb walking down the road as he shouldered a Springfield musket. After we reached the top of the hill, a rainstorm unleashed itself, and my father and I ran down the hill as fast as we could. For an impressionistic eleven-year-old, it was a surrealistic day.

Later, these experiences came back to me with more force when I was given war papers and relics owned by my great-great-grandfather Darius Wetzel, a private in the 74th Ohio Volunteer Infantry. That was all it took for me to become a Civil War buff.

During the 1980s and early 1990s my father and I traveled to all of the Civil War battlefields we could, as often as we could. We photographed and studied everything we had read about in our Civil War libraries, gaining familiarity with the greatest sites of the war. Despite the 50,000 books on the war, not one provided a detailed guide to what could be seen at the major Civil War sites. This struck us as particularly strange. To be sure, you can obtain literature at most battlefield sites, and that provided at National Park Service sites is quite well done. These brochures are a good starting point: they provide a brief introduction to the battles and information on a few stops at each park. But to gain an appreciation of what occurred on these fields you need a more complete guide. Several Civil War travel guides have been produced, but they either focus on the battles themselves rather than what can be seen at the parks, or they lack detail or specific touring advice and are badly outdated.

Civil War Battlefields takes you on a substantially more meaningful tour of the grounds, houses, monuments, cemeteries, and structures at twelve Civil War battlefield areas with large numbers of attractions extant. The book describes the battles, in brief, and 1,353 specific features of interest. Because battlefields often cover more ground than the parks contain, and because the parks are growing slowly in size, we include features owned by the federal government, state and local governments, and private owners. The term "site" refers to the position of a feature no longer extant. The term "Civil War interment" means Civil War soldiers buried within a given cemetery. The battlefield areas are Antietam, South Mountain, Harpers Ferry (Maryland and West Virginia, 79 features described); Bull Run (Virginia, 57 features); Chattanooga (Tennessee, 79 features); Chickamauga (Georgia, 146 features); Fredericksburg, Chancellorsville, The Wilderness, Spotsylvania (Virginia, 115 features); Gettysburg (Pennsylvania, 168 features); Petersburg, Five Forks, Appomattox Court House (Virginia, 121 features); Richmond and City Point (Virginia, 131 features); the Shenandoah Valley (Virginia, 128 features); Shiloh (Tennessee, 99 features); Stones River, Franklin, Spring Hill (Tennessee, 56 features); and Vicksburg (Mississippi, 174 features). The text provides a point-by-point description of how to see dozens of features at each battlefield and a brief summary of what occurred there. Forty-one maps based on extensive on-site study show you how to travel the fields efficiently. One hundred twenty-nine photographs highlight important features at each battlefield site. With the exception of one photograph credited in chapter 1, all photos are by the author.

Any work of this scope requires acknowledgments. My father John Eicher spent countless hours combining our own data with numerous historical base maps and U.S. Geological Survey base maps to produce the new battlefield maps in this book. He also proofread the work and offered many helpful suggestions.

The maps are unique. They offer information not found elsewhere. We included area maps to show the battlefield locations (indicated by dashed rectangles or squares) with respect to nearby cities and towns, and the principal highways providing access to the parks.

The detail maps include the major battle locations and/or adjacent cities, but do not indicate boundaries of the battlefield park lands. This is the case for two reasons. First, the National Park Service lands were acquired by gift or by the purchase of either parcels of land (as at Chickamauga and Gettysburg) or dedicated strips of land along roads, rivers, or topographical points of interest (as at Antietam and Vicksburg). Sometimes federal land ownership was established by a combination of methods. Second, throughout a century of acquisition, federal holdings have frequently been changed. The detail maps therefore cover the main battle areas including both public and private lands. Because of the physical size of this book, the maps pack lots of detail into a small space. You may wish to enlarge the maps by photocopying them to explore minute details with greater ease.

The rectangular detail maps as well as the square city maps are based primarily on the geographical and operational maps contained in the *Atlas to Accompany the Official Records of the Union and Confederate Armies* (U.S. Government Printing Office, Washington, 1891–1895). These were augmented by comparison with the appropriate United States Geological Survey quadrangle maps (1:24,000 scale) and the Army Map Service sheets (1:25,000 scale). Department of the Interior battlefield maps, historical base maps, special survey maps, general development plan maps, and National Park Service maps were also consulted for clarification of the principal roads, trails, and points of interest.

During the extensive checking and counterchecking of maps, however, we found that in many cases up-to-date maps of some of the areas simply did not exist (even in the vast government holdings). For example, the most current map of monuments at the Vicksburg National Military Park dates from 1903, and many changes have occurred since then. Checking and accurately plotting the locations of many features, particularly the locations of principal and unusual monuments, had to be done by on-site inspection.

My wife Lynda helped out in many ways, from copy editing to checking facts. My sister Nancy helped out with photography at selected sites. Michael Emmerich and Robert Burnham offered useful suggestions. Mike Danneman kindly allowed the use of a photo.

In addition, many devoted historians at parks and cemeteries supplied valuable information. They are Ted Alexander (Historian, Antietam National Battlefield, Sharpsburg, Maryland), Stacy Allen (Historian, Shiloh National Military Park, Shiloh, Tennessee), Gilbert Backlund (Historian, Stones River National Battlefield, Murfreesboro, Tennessee), Ray Brown (Cultural Resources Management Specialist, Manassas National Battlefield Park, Manassas, Virginia), Paul Brown (Manager, Prospect Hill Cemetery, Front Royal, Virginia), Kendall Clark (Administrative Assistant, Hollywood Cemetery, Richmond, Virginia), Martha Doss (Director, Lexington Visitor's Bureau, Lexington, Virginia), Barbara Harris (National Park Service Denver Service Center, Denver, Colorado), Scott Hartwig (Historian, Gettysburg National Military Park, Gettysburg, Pennsylvania), Greg Mertz (Supervisory Historian, Fredericksburg and Spotsylvania National Military Park, Fredericksburg, Virginia), Richard Miller (Historian, Stones River National Battlefield, Murfreesboro, Tennessee), Illona Ramsey (Program Assistant, Culpeper National Cemetery, Culpeper, Virginia), Charles Spearman, (Historian, Chickamauga and Chattanooga National Military Park, Chattanooga, Tennessee), Ramona Vaughn (Director, Richmond National Cemeteries Complex, Richmond, Virginia), and Terry Winschel (Historian, Vicksburg National Military Park, Vicksburg, Mississippi).

I thank them for their generous assistance and hope that you will have great fun exploring the battlefields of the Civil War with this book.

Dave Eicher

Chapter 1

✪   ✪   ✪

Antietam, South Mountain, and Harpers Ferry

In a second the air was full of the hiss of bullets and the
hurtle of grape-shot. The mental strain was so great that I saw at that
moment the singular effect mentioned, I think, in the
life of Goethe on a similar occasion—the whole landscape
for an instant turned slightly red.

—Pvt. David Thompson, 9th New York Volunteer Infantry,
describing the counterattack of A. P. Hill's Light Division at Antietam,
September 17, 1862.

We approached quietly from the north. The drive carried us across long stretches of farmland, open fields punctuated by occasional side roads, barns, houses, and gates. The landscape must have looked quite similar long ago, in the days of the Civil War. In what seemed like rapid succession, we crossed the Maryland border, passed through quiet Hagerstown, and found Maryland State Route 65 heading south. This was the road that would take us to the village of **Sharpsburg** (population 659), nestled near the small meandering creek called Antietam.

It was midsummer 1988, hot, sweltering in fact, and the air was still and thick. Having spent several years becoming die-hard Civil War buffs, my father John and I had decided it was high time to again make a sweep of the eastern battlefields, and Antietam was a special favorite. We would arrive at **Antietam National Battlefield**, Maryland, early in the morning, and have a full day to survey the

sights—structures, fields, and monuments—that commemorate America's most terrible single day. The following morning we would head to South Mountain to see associated sites, then down to one of the prettiest historic towns in the world, Harpers Ferry, West Virginia. This coincided well with Gen. Robert E. Lee's 1862 Maryland campaign, one part of which included Maj. Gen. Thomas J. "Stonewall" Jackson's capture of Harpers Ferry and a nearly simultaneous set of skirmishes along the mountain gaps on South Mountain.

In the area north and east of Sharpsburg, the Union and Confederate armies fought the bloodiest one-day battle in North American history on Wednesday, September 17, 1862. Here General Lee brought his Army of Northern Virginia onto Yankee soil for the first time, hoping to gain a decisive victory, terrorize the northern spirit, gain diplomatic recognition from Europe, and sue for peace, ensuring the existence of the young Confederacy. Here, on the same day, Maj. Gen. George B. McClellan with his Army of the Potomac cautiously fought a large battle in fits and starts, not using the elite 5th Army Corps, and timidly allowing Lee to exercise his battle plan though a copy of it had been captured several days before. The Confederates invaded Maryland with about 51,800 men; the Union army consisted of approximately 87,100. When it was all over, 4,808 men lay dead on the fields and another 21,483 were wounded or missing. Lee's army limped southward across the Potomac unpursued, the Federal armies too depleted to harass the Confederates further. The battle was a tactical draw but a strategic loss for the South. The most significant outcome of Antietam was the issuance of the preliminary Emancipation Proclamation by President Lincoln, forever abolishing slavery throughout the states in rebellion.

Antietam Tour

We arrived in Sharpsburg, a grid enclosing about one-half square mile, and proceeded to the Antietam National Battlefield **Visitor Center**, located off Dunkard Church Avenue (Old Hagerstown Pike) just short of a mile north of town (you'll see signs as you approach Sharpsburg). Throughout the Antietam Tour see the Antietam detail map (page 4). Whether you approach as we did from Pennsylvania, via Frederick, Maryland, or from Winchester, Virginia, it's a good idea to stop at the visitor center before touring the battlefield. As with nearly all National Park Service centers, the museum contained within will orient you, provide a basic history of the battle, and display significant relics associated with the park. When finished with the museum, you may wish to take a look at the adjacent **Maryland**, **New York**, and **Ohio Monuments**. You'll come back to the little white church building across the pike later.

On that sleepy Wednesday morning in 1862, the Union army came from the north and east, the Confederates from the south and west.

Union officers spotted long Confederate columns in the cornfields by the bright metallic gleam of their bayonets. The battle that followed was in essence three separate engagements, the earliest occurring north of town in the North and West Woods around the visitor center and the church. The midday phase of the battle flared most heavily in the central part of the field, along a sunken farm road, near the farmhouses owned by the Mumma and Piper families, and the area immediately north of town. The final phase of the contest saw continued fighting in this central area and a major flare-up of action in the southern part of the field, chiefly around the Lower Bridge across the Antietam and the farmhouses owned by Rohrbachs, Sherricks, and Ottos.

If you travel north on Dunkard Church Avenue, note where you cross Cornfield Avenue. Just more than one-fourth mile from that spot, on the right side, you can see the **David R. Miller Farm**. The **Cornfield** south and east of the farm buildings marks the area of some of the heaviest fighting of the war, several official reports noting that the corn was cut down by small arms fire "as if by a scythe."

On the other side of the road, the rise left of the road visible after crossing Cornfield

THE BLOODIEST FIGHTING at Antietam took place in the presently serene cornfields on the David R. Miller Farm.

2

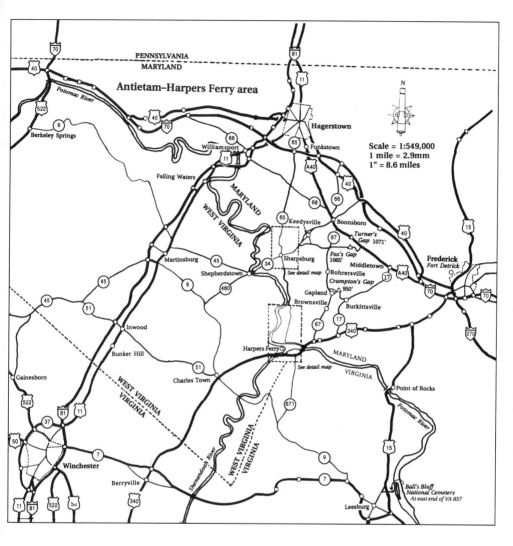

Antietam–Harpers Ferry area

Scale = 1:549,000
1 mile = 2.9mm
1" = 8.6 miles

Avenue is **Nicodemus Hill**, a commanding Confederate artillery position throughout the battle. Beyond the Miller Farm is the site of the **North Woods**. On the left of the road, you'll see the **Joseph Poffenberger Farm**, which served as Union Maj. Gen. Joseph Hooker's headquarters. Tremendous attacks originated from this area, beginning with Hooker's own 1st Corps moving south toward the Cornfield, where they met stiff Confederate resistance. On the roadside you will see a monument honoring Clara Barton, who nursed wounded soldiers at Antietam and later founded the Red Cross. Despite the marker's position, research shows that Barton occupied part of the grounds on the **Samuel Poffenberger Farm**, located three-fourths of a mile southeast of Hooker's headquarters.

To see the Samuel Poffenberger Farm and several other notable structures, turn right onto

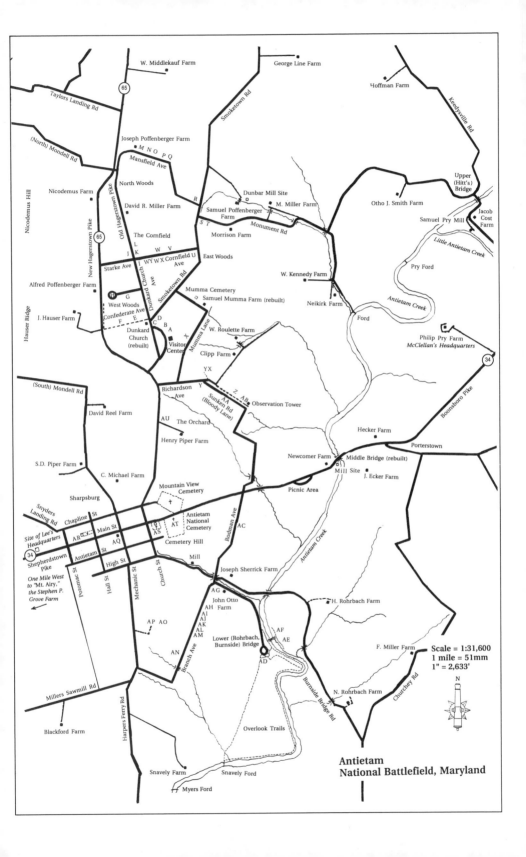

Antietam National Battlefield, Maryland

Scale = 1:31,600
1 mile = 51mm
1" = 2,633'

Key to Features on Antietam Detail Map

A 20th New York Infantry Monument
B New York Monument
C 5th, 7th, and 66th Ohio Infantry Monument
D Maryland Monument
E 125th Pennsylvania Infantry Monument
F 34th New York Infantry Monument
G William Edwin Starke Mortal Wounding Monument
H Philadelphia Brigade Monument
I Massachusetts Monument
J 124th Pennsylvania Infantry Monument
K New Jersey Monument
L Indiana Monument
M Clara Barton Monument
N 7th Pennsylvania Infantry Monument
O 4th Pennsylvania Infantry Monument
P 3rd Pennsylvania Infantry Monument
Q 8th Pennsylvania Infantry Monument

R 12th Pennsylvania Cavalry Monument
S Joseph King Fenno Mansfield Obelisk
T Joseph King Fenno Mansfield Mortal Wounding Monument
U 1st New Jersey Brigade Monument
V 137th Pennsylvania Infantry Monument
W 128th Pennsylvania Infantry Monument
WX Texas Monument
WY Georgia Monument
X Old Vermont Brigade Monument
Y 130th Pennsylvania Infantry Monument
YX 5th Maryland (U.S.) Monument
Z 132nd Pennsylvania Infantry Monument
AA George Burgwyn Anderson Mortal Wounding Monument
AB Israel Bush Richardson Mortal Wounding Monument
AC 50th Pennsylvania Infantry Monument
AD William McKinley Monument
AE 51st New York Infantry Monument

AF 51st Pennsylvania Infantry Monument
AG 45th Pennsylvania Infantry Monument
AH 100th Pennsylvania Infantry Monument
AI 28th Ohio Infantry Monument
AJ 51st Pennsylvania Infantry Monument
AK Durrell's Battery Monument
AL 48th Pennsylvania Infantry Monument
AM 23rd Ohio Infantry Monument
AN Lawrence O'Bryan Branch Death Monument
AO Isaac Peace Rodman Mortal Wounding Monument
AP Hawkin's 9th New York Zouaves Monument
AQ Jacob H. Grove House
AR St. Paul's Episcopal Church (rebuilt), ruins and cemetery
AS Lutheran Church (ruins) and cemetery
AT U.S. Soldier's Monument and Antietam National Cemetery
AU Army of Northern Virginia Monument

the Smoketown Road and then left onto Monument Road. After traveling 500 yards, you'll see the Poffenberger Farm on the left side of the road. Another 300 yards will bring you to the **M. Miller Farm** on the left of the road. From there a three-fourths-mile trip, bearing to the left, will bring you to the **Otho J. Smith Farm**, located to the right of the road. Continue on and you'll cross the **Upper Bridge**, known as Hitt's Bridge. By curving right, you can see the **Jacob Cost House** and the **Samuel Pry Mill**. Thousands of troops marched past these structures and across the Upper Bridge on their way to the battle.

If you return to the Smoketown Road, just before you reach it, you'll enter the **East**
Woods and see on the left side of the road a downturned cannon set in stone, the **Joseph King Fenno Mansfield Monument**. (Tradition on the Antietam battlefield dictates upturned cannon to mark headquarters locations and downturned cannon to signify sites of important deaths or mortal woundings.) This Union brigadier general led the 12th Corps into battle on the morning of the seventeenth and, before half an hour had passed, was mortally wounded, hit in the chest by a minié bullet. He died the following day at the **George Line Farm** in the extreme northern portion of the battlefield.

Continue south on the Smoketown Road about 150 yards, then turn right on Cornfield

Avenue. Traveling along Cornfield Avenue will afford you views of several regimental monuments and a better view of the Cornfield, this time from the south. If you cross Dunkard Church Avenue, you may view the monuments along Starke Avenue. Turning right (south) on Dunkard Church Avenue and traveling south 300 yards will lead you to a short road to the **Philadelphia Brigade Monument**, which is surrounded by a circle drive. You'll now be in what was the thick of the **West Woods**, ground viciously fought over by Brig. Gen. Oliver O. Howard's brigade of Pennsylvanians, among others. Due west, along the rising slope of ground, you can see **Hauser's Ridge**, an important Confederate artillery perch during

the early phase of the battle. Just south of the Philadelphia Brigade Monument lies the **William Edwin Starke Monument**, a down-turned cannon marking the position where the Confederate brigadier general was mortally wounded by three volleys. He died an hour after being shot.

Heading back toward Dunkard Church Avenue, turn right (south), and travel 300 yards. You will now see the white church building you passed earlier. This is the **Dunkard**

THE STORM CENTER of Antietam's first hours was the whitewashed Dunkard Church, a single-room assembly house on Dunkard Church Avenue. The reconstructed church's interior accurately depicts its simple furnishings (below and at right).

Church, the meeting house of a small sect of German Baptist Brethren who believed in fully immersing their converts, thus attaining the name Dunkers. The Dunkard Church was an important landmark in the early and middle stages of the battle. Prolonged, repeated attempts at capture came from both sides. High ground around the church was held by Confederate Maj. Gen. Stonewall Jackson. Heavy casualties lay scattered around the church and surrounding grounds in the wake of the battle. A violent storm in 1921 demolished the original church, but in 1962 the church was reconstructed using in part original materials.

More regimental monuments are scattered along Confederate Avenue, west of the Dunkard Church. The road is closed to automobile traffic, however, so you'll need to walk its length to see them. You may then want to view the monuments along Smoketown Road.

Head northeast on the Smoketown Road, and after 400 yards, turn right to see the **Samuel Mumma Farm**. Prominently located in the center of the battlefield, this farmhouse and its outbuildings burned during the battle after retreating Confederates set them ablaze to ward off Yankee sharpshooters. Only the Spring House is an original structure. Immediately northwest lies the **Mumma Cemetery**, a plot that contains about 165 graves of local citizens. About 500 yards southeast of the Mumma Farm are two more buildings fought around in the middle phase of the battle, the **W. Roulette Farm** and the **Clipp Farm**. Beyond these farms, you can follow the road until it joins Richardson Avenue. To reach the next point of interest, simply turn left, wind down the road, and park.

You have reached the most infamous ground of the Antietam battlefield, the **Sunken**

BURNED DURING THE BATTLE, the Samuel Mumma farmhouse occupies a central location on the field and offers tourists a glimpse of an adjacent family burying ground.

A MAKESHIFT RIFLE PIT, this sunken farm road acquired the nickname "Bloody Lane" after dozens of soldiers had perished within it. An observation tower now graces the eastern end of the preserved portion of the road.

North Carolina. At the southeast end of the lane, you'll see a similar marker, the **Israel Bush Richardson Monument**. Union Major General Richardson was also mortally wounded during the Sunken Road fight, dying nearly six weeks later in the Philip Pry House east of the battlefield. At the eastern end of the Sunken Road stands an **Observation Tower**, affording an excellent chance for climbers to see the terrain of the field.

Northwest of the tower lies the field you've already explored, south of the tower the battlefield sites to come. Southwest of the tower is the town of Sharpsburg, and about halfway to the town lies an isolated farmhouse. This is the **Henry Piper Farm**, a group of buildings squarely in the thick of the battle and used briefly for a council of war by Confederate Maj. Gens. James Longstreet, D. H. Hill, and Richard H. Anderson. The farmhouse, accessible from Dunkard Church Avenue, is now a bed and breakfast inn—the only historic structure where you can spend a night on a Civil War battlefield. East of the tower you'll see the long form of South Mountain.

If you head south on Rodman Avenue, you'll cross the Boonsboro Pike (State Route 34), the town's main east-west road. The

Road. This little farm lane etched in the landscape provided a natural rifle pit for Confederate troops who lay down inside it and fired on Union infantry attacking from the north. The Yankees finally pushed the Rebels south, out of the lane, but only after producing fearsome casualties on both sides. The bodies stacked inside the lane at day's end gave rise to the nickname "Bloody Lane."

As you walk down the lane from northwest to southeast, you'll see a number of regimentals and the **George Burgwyn Anderson Monument**, a downturned cannon. Confederate Brigadier General Anderson was hit by a ball in the foot as he watched the battle from the lane. He died a month later in Raleigh,

THE PIPER FARMHOUSE served briefly as a stopping place for Confederate Gens. James Longstreet, D. H. Hill, and Dick Anderson. It is now a bed and breakfast inn.

BATTERIES OF NAPOLEONS guarded the heights above the Joseph Sherrick Farm (background) from a Union advance from the east.

buildings you'll see to the left comprise the **Joseph Sherrick Farm**, around which Confederates defended the slopes below against a Federal attack toward the town. After crossing the overpass, turn left; the house you see on the right belongs to the **John Otto Farm**, another antebellum structure. Near the parking lot you'll see the **William McKinley Monument**, honoring the future President who as a nineteen-year-old sergeant made coffee for all the troops in the area. Follow the trail down to the **Lower Bridge**, which is variously called the Rohrbach Bridge and its most celebrated name, Burnside Bridge. This famous structure held the key to the Union assault. From the eastern side of Antietam Creek, Union troops attempted to cross the creek and push the Confederates toward Sharpsburg. Overcautious Union Maj. Gen.

Ambrose E. Burnside, commanding the 9th Corps, waited nearly all day before attacking the mostly Georgia troops who defended the slope west of the creek. Burnside sent numerous narrow columns of attackers across the bridge, many of whom were slaughtered by the crack-shot Georgians. Had he checked the Antietam's depth, he would have found it fordable.

Back on Rodman Avenue, you can turn left on what becomes Branch Avenue to view several regimental markers and, before the road jogs northwest, a downturned cannon, the **Lawrence O'Bryan Branch Monument**. During the latter part of the battle, Confederate Maj. Gen. A. P. Hill arrived with his "Light Division" from Harpers Ferry, substantially ruining the Union army's hopes of pushing the Confederates back into the town. Branch, a young

A STONE BRIDGE over the Antietam provided the means for Union soldiers to move toward Sharpsburg late in the day. Originally called the Rohrbach Bridge, the structure is now named for the timid Union commander who eventually crossed it, Ambrose Burnside.

brigadier general from North Carolina, was killed instantly by a sharpshooter while talking with Hill near this spot.

Continue on Branch Avenue until you reach Harpers Ferry Road, then turn right. If you drive 400 yards, you'll see an unpaved footpath that leads to the **Hawkins' Zouaves Monument**, honoring the 9th New York Infantry. Just east of this monument you'll find another down-turned cannon, the **Isaac Peace Rodman Monument**. Brigadier General Rodman was struck in the chest by a ball while leading an attack against Hill's Confederates. He died two weeks later.

Harpers Ferry Road (which becomes Mechanic Street) takes you into town. Turn left on Main Street. After crossing Potomac Street, on the right side of the road you'll find a marker on the site of the **General Headquarters, Army of Northern Virginia**. General Lee camped with his staff in tents set up on these grounds and directed the battle as it unfolded. Continue west on Main Street one mile until you see a prominent farm located on a rise on the left of the road. This is the **Stephen P. Grove Farm**, "Mount Airy," the 5th Army

Corps headquarters after the battle and the site of Lincoln's meeting with McClellan in the wake of the battle. A famous series of photographs of Lincoln with McClellan and other Union officers was made at this house on October 4, 1862.

You may wish to see two other wartime farm sites just north of the town, which you can do by turning north on Mechanic Street in the center of Sharpsburg. Both the **S. D. Piper Farm** and the **David Reel Farm** were used as staging areas and hospitals by Confederate troops during the battle. Union artillery demolished the Reel barn before wounded Confederates could escape. Many of them burned to death inside the barn.

Heading east on Main Street, which will become the Boonsboro Pike, will take you out of town. After traveling three miles turn left into a long, winding farm lane. This will bring you to the **Philip Pry House**, General Headquarters of the Army of the Potomac. Major General McClellan and staff watched the battle from this high ground about one and one-half miles from the center of the field, and on a clear day from the Pry House you can see much of the battlefield terrain.

You may wish to return to town on the Boonsboro Pike and note the modern highway bridge you cross when passing over Antietam Creek. This is the site of the **Middle Bridge**, originally a stone structure resembling the Lower Bridge, used by thousands of troops marching toward battle lines. One mile from the bridge, you can turn left into **Antietam National Cemetery**, a burying ground established in 1866 when thousands of temporary graves on the field were excavated and reinterred here. Some 4,695 soldiers lie within the cemetery's eleven acres. In the center of the cemetery, you'll see the **Private Soldier**, a monument nicknamed "Old Simon." Along with the graves of the battle casualties, you can see the grave of Bvt. Brig. Gen. Jacob E. Duryée. West of the cemetery you may find the ruins of the **Lutheran Church**, a Confederate sig-

McCLELLAN WATCHED THE BATTLE of Antietam from the Philip Pry dwelling, a large brick farmhouse situated one and one-half miles east-northeast of the center of the field.

nal station during the battle and Union hospital afterward. Also in town are the ruins of **St. Paul's Episcopal Church**, hit by Union artillery frequently during the battle.

South Mountain Tour

If your schedule permits you may want to visit **South Mountain**, site of the engagements prior to Antietam. Throughout the South Mountain Tour see the Antietam-Harpers Ferry area map (p. 3). Head east out of Sharpsburg on the Boonsboro Pike, past Keedysville, to the small town of **Boonsboro** (pop. 1,900)—a six-and-three-fourths-mile drive. Here you'll pick up U.S. Alt. 40, a road that leads after two and one-half miles to the first of three South Mountain sites, **Turner's Gap**. On September 14, 1862, as the armies felt their way toward each other,

Maj. Gen. D. H. Hill's Confederates stubbornly defended Turner's Gap, hoping to prevent Union escape from the besieged Harpers Ferry and block the mountain pass. Along U.S. Alt. 40, the old National Road, Major General Hooker's Federals pursued the Rebels. The ground surrounding the **Mountain House**, located at Turner's Gap, afforded Hill a position to see the Federal army approaching. By noon on the fourteenth Union troops under Brig. Gen. Jacob D. Cox had pushed the Confederates to **Fox's Gap**, one mile south.

To reach Fox's Gap from the Mountain House, travel three-fourths mile southeast on U.S. Alt. 40 and turn right on Fox's Gap Road. This road winds south for nearly a mile before reaching Reno Monument Road, where you should turn right. At this junction, on the right side of the road, is the **Reno Oak Site**. A mighty oak once stood here, under which Union Maj. Gen. Jesse Lee Reno, mortally wounded at Fox's Gap, expired. Continue northwest on Reno Monument Road for three-fourths mile and you will see on the left side of the road the **Jesse Lee Reno Monument** enclosed in a small stone wall. This marks the spot where Reno was wounded and also the height of the action at Fox's Gap. After a bloody struggle, the Confederates withdrew.

The final site associated with South Mountain is **Crampton's Gap** four and one-half miles south of Fox's Gap. To reach it, continue west on Reno Monument Road until you reach State Route 67. At Mt. Carmel Church turn left and take 67 south past tiny Rohrersville. Turn left on Gapland Road and drive one and one-fourth miles to the **War Correspondents' Arch** at **Gathland State Park**, located at Crampton's Gap.

A LONE MONUMENT at Fox's Gap marks the spot where Federal Maj. Gen. Jesse Reno was mortally wounded while leading his troops in the battle of South Mountain.

As the action unfolded to the north at Fox's and Turner's Gaps, Confederate Maj. Gen. Lafayette McLaws defended this gap against the Federal 6th Corps under Maj. Gen. William B. Franklin. The state park was established around the home and grounds of George Alfred Townsend, influential war correspondent for the *New York Herald.* After the war Townsend's home on lofty Crampton's Gap housed meetings of veterans—Union and Confederate alike—who recounted their wartime experiences. The arch is the memorial to all correspondents—the "bohemian brigade" that brought the war to the home front each day. On September 14, 1862, the Confederates retreated from Crampton's Gap and the prelude to Antietam was over.

Harpers Ferry Tour

Whether or not you find time for South Mountain, you shouldn't pass up the chance to spend at least half a day in **Harpers Ferry National Historical Park** in West Virginia. One of the most beautiful and well-preserved antebellum towns, **Harpers Ferry** (pop. 361) is situated in the Blue Ridge Mountains at the northern tip of the Shenandoah Valley at the point where the Potomac and Shenandoah Rivers join. The site of a U.S. arsenal and gun factory since 1801, Harpers Ferry witnessed abolitionist John Brown's abortive raid in 1859 in which he attempted to incite a slave rebellion. Though an utter failure (Brown was hanged shortly thereafter in nearby Charles Town), the raid sent shock waves throughout both South and North and helped spark the inevitable conflict. The arsenal was also a casualty, burned by Union troops in 1861 so it would not be a military objective of the Confederates. During the Antietam campaign, Maj. Gen. Stonewall Jackson captured the town and forced the Federals to flee again.

Throughout the Harpers Ferry Tour see the Harpers Ferry detail map (p. 14). Individual buildings within the park are not shown on the

HARPERS FERRY SITS some three-fourths mile away as viewed from a rock outcrop on Maryland Heights, northeast of the historic town. Fog blankets the town and the confluence of the Potomac and Shenandoah rivers. Photo by Mike Danneman.

map due to scale but can be found by following the written directions. Reaching Harpers Ferry is relatively easy. From Crampton's Gap, proceed south on State Route 67 past Brownsville, a total of five miles, to U.S. 340. Take U.S. 340 southwest another five miles, crossing the Potomac, winding west for about a mile, and crossing the Shenendoah River before reaching the park entrance. From Sharpsburg, take the Harpers Ferry Road (Mechanic Street) south out of town for a distance of seven and one-half miles; when you reach the Potomac, the road curves southeast along the river, becomes Sandy Hook Road, and joins U.S. 340 a mile east of town. Along the way, you may want to see the **Dr. Booth Kennedy Farm**, the house where John Brown and his raiders hid out and began their attack on Harpers Ferry. To reach the farm from Sharpsburg, travel south on the Harpers Ferry Road for three miles to reach the town of Antietam, another three and one-half miles to Dargan, and half a mile farther to Samples Manor. At Samples Manor you'll see Bethel Church and its cemetery; turn left here onto Chestnut Grove Road. Proceed about three-fourths mile and you'll see the Kennedy Farm on the left of the road.

When you reach Harpers Ferry itself, you may wish to enter the park and take a brief look at the **Visitor Center**, located near the main gate. A shuttle bus can transport you into the town itself, taking you one and one-fourth miles down a winding road, past the site of the **Hall Rifle Works** (now ruins), a government contract plant destroyed at the start of the war; past

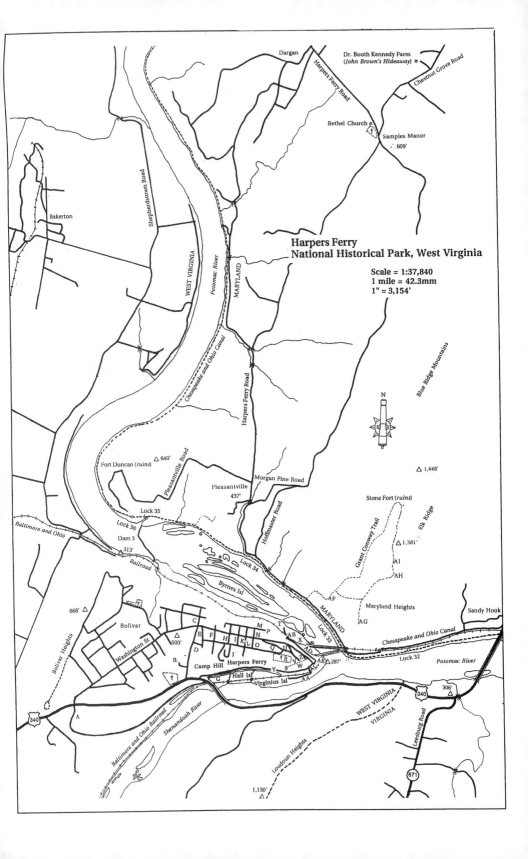

Harpers Ferry
National Historical Park, West Virginia

Scale = 1:37,840
1 mile = 42.3mm
1" = 3,154'

Virginius Island in the Shenandoah; and to a parking lot near the southernmost part of Harpers Ferry, the Lower Shuttle Bus Station.

Walking eastward down Shenandoah Street, check out the **Blacksmith Shop**, **Museum**, and **John Brown Museum**, all of which contain superb displays. Walk to the southeast end of the street and you can see **John Brown's Fort** (the Arsenal-Armory Firehouse), the reconstructed and relocated stucture in which Brown holed up and was captured during his raid. Walk up a path toward **the Point**, land's end that reaches out toward the confluence of the rivers, and you'll see an obelisk marking the original site of the Brown enginehouse. Gaze northwest along the Potomac River and you'll see the site of the **U.S. Arsenal and Armory.**

Note the present Baltimore & Ohio railroad bridge that spans the Potomac and enters a tunnel into Maryland. Parallel to the railroad bridge is a footpath that allows you to walk across to Maryland along a piece of the Appalachian trail. Note also the rock bridge piers that protrude from the river south of the railroad bridge.

These are remnants of the antebellum bridge wrecked by besieging Confederates. The massive swell of ground on the Maryland side is **Maryland Heights**, a strategic overlook that offered defenders a commanding artillery position. Ruins of the stone forts built on Maryland

JOHN BROWN'S FORT, although moved from its original location and substantially rebuilt, resembles the enginehouse in which Brown and followers attempted to incite a slave rebellion.

STONE PIERS spanning the Potomac once supported a railroad bridge wrecked by Confederate troops during the Antietam campaign. The present bridge carries a piece of the Appalachian trail.

SHENANDOAH STREET offers a taste of Harpers Ferry as it was at the time of the Civil War. Numerous antebellum and wartime buildings stand within the park, although the U.S. arsenal was destroyed during the war.

Heights by Civil War soldiers exist, but they are anything but easily accessible. As you look across the Shenandoah, the rise across the way in West Virginia is **Loudoun Heights**, another key artillery position. The high ground above the town to the west is **Bolivar Heights**, which you may wish to visit to see well-preserved entrenchments.

Back on Shenandoah Street you can check out the buildings on the south side of the street. These include the **Provost Office, Dry Goods Store**, and **Master Armorer's House**. Next, walk north along High Street to find the **Pharmacy**, the **Confectionery**, and **Civil War Museums** buildings, which offer more exhibits depicting life in Harpers Ferry. Behind these structures you'll find the **Stone Steps**, a natural walkway cut into the hillside at the beginning of the nineteenth century. To see the **Harper House**, walk up the steps and view the homestead of the town's namesake, Robert Harper. Continue on past **St. Peter's Catholic Church** (on your left) and past the ruins of **St. John's Episcopal Church** (on your right). When you come to **Jefferson's Rock**, an overlook where Thomas Jefferson proclaimed the

view magnificent, you may agree as you soak in the valley below.

You've now seen the entire Antietam-South Mountain-Harpers Ferry triangle, a feat that not even all eastern theater Civil War combatants managed to pull off.

JEFFERSON'S ROCK marks the spot in Harpers Ferry where Thomas Jefferson declared the valley below the most beautiful he knew of in Virginia.

Antietam National Battlefield

Mailing address: P.O. Box 158, Sharpsburg, Maryland 21782-0158
Telephone: (301) 432-5124
Park established: August 30, 1890
Area: 3,244.1 acres

Antietam National Cemetery

Established: 1866
Area: 11.4 acres
Civil War interments: about 4,695

Harpers Ferry National Historical Park

Mailing address: P.O. Box 65, Harpers Ferry, West Virginia 25425
Telephone: (304) 535-6029
Park established: June 30, 1944
Area: 2,501 acres

Antietam accommodations

Sharpsburg has two bed and breakfast inns, including one near the center of the battlefield. On State Route 34 across the Potomac in Shepherdstown, West Virginia, travelers can find one motel about five miles southwest of the park. Other accommodations are available in Hagerstown and Frederick, Maryland, and Winchester, Virginia.

Harpers Ferry accommodations

Harpers Ferry has two motels, one adjacent to the park entrance. Charles Town, West Virginia, six miles west on U.S. 340, offers two motels. Plentiful accommodations are available in Hagerstown and Frederick, Maryland, and Winchester, Virginia.

Chapter 2

✪   ✪   ✪

Bull Run

There is Jackson, standing like a stone wall.

—Brig. Gen. Barnard Elliott Bee,
during the first battle of Bull Run, Manassas,
Virginia, July 21, 1861.

The battlefield of **Bull Run**, Virginia, located just twenty-four miles from downtown Washington, has the distinction of being the site of not one but two major Civil War battles. The first important engagement of the war occurred on the pastoral farmlands, hills, and ravines around this spot. A year later, a larger, bloodier fight ravaged over the same land, past the same houses, across the same creeks. Few places in America have witnessed such a double shot of carnage.

As my father and I drove west from Washington's parks and government, the landscape transformed into bustling suburbia, then slowly dissolved into a peaceful countryside reminiscent of times past. We made our way on U.S. 29 through Arlington (where many veterans of the Bull Run battles are entombed) past Falls Church, Fairfax, and Centreville, strategically important towns in Civil War days. Following the route of the Union army during the first major campaign of the war, we traveled a few miles past Centreville and arrived at the crossroads of U.S. 29 and Virginia 234, the center of the Bull Run battlefield. The place can be reached easily from Washington, from Richmond to the south, from Dulles International Airport to the north, or from the small towns scattered through the Shenandoah Valley to the west.

Bull Run, or Manassas, rang as the great watch word of the war during its first long, hot summer. Following the bombardment and evacuation of Fort Sumter in April 1861, both armies spent weeks recruiting, organizing, equipping, drilling, and marching—readying themselves for the battles to come. The Confederate strategy dictated a defensive war, one in which the chief goal would be to protect their homelands from the "foreign invaders." The Union strategy necessitated a more ambitious offensive war, one in which the Federal armies would march "On to Richmond" and capture the Rebel capital, ending the war in a matter of ninety days.

On July 16, 1861, forced into action by public pressure, Brig. Gen. Irvin McDowell led his 35,000 troops out of Washington and on toward the vital rail center of Manassas Junction. McDowell faced Confederate Brig. Gen. Pierre Gustave Toutant Beauregard, the Confederate hero of Fort Sumter, who commanded 20,000 men in the vicinity of Manassas, and Gen. Joseph Eggleston Johnston, whose 18,000 troops, situated in the Shenandoah Valley near Winchester, would arrive at the battlefield before heavy fighting commenced.

On July 21, 1861, the armies clashed. The Union troops came from the north and east, the Confederates from the south and west. Intense fighting flared through several points along Bull Run, around Henry House Hill, Bald Hill, and Chinn Ridge. The battle started well for the Federals, whose sweeping flank attack from the north pushed the Confederates back, but a Rebel stand on Henry House Hill thwarted McDowell's piecemeal attacks. The Confederate troops counterattacked and, by late afternoon, had the Union army in withdrawal toward Washington. The Confederates were too bloodied to pursue the Federal army, and although they retained the field, soon went south. Although First Bull Run was not a substantial victory for either side, the battle stunned those Yankees who expected their boys would easily whip the Rebels. When it was over, of the 28,452 Federals and 32,232 Confederates engaged, 805 were killed and 3,821 were wounded or missing.

War again touched Bull Run in August 1862 during Union Maj. Gen. John Pope's Virginia campaign. The Federal Army of Virginia employed those forces that had failed to rout Maj. Gen. Thomas J. "Stonewall" Jackson in the Shenandoah Valley. As Maj. Gen. George B. McClellan's Army of the Potomac marched toward Richmond on the Virginia peninsula, Pope's army of 47,000 was assigned to apply pressure on the valley, protect Washington, and draw Gen. Robert E. Lee away from his Richmond defenses. The plan worked only in part.

On July 12 Lee sent Jackson to secure the junction at Gordonsville, south of Manassas. In early August, Lee gambled on McClellan's continuous inactivity and sent reinforcements to Jackson. An engagement took place at Cedar Mountain on August 9, a battle executed in sloppy fashion on both sides. The outcome convinced Lee that Jackson should be heavily reinforced and strike Pope before McClellan's retreating army could arrive. This decision established the situation for the second battle of Bull Run. On August 27 Jackson captured trains filled with stores at Manassas Junction, made use of everything he could, and burned the rest. Meanwhile Confederate Maj. Gen. James Longstreet's corps moved north to unite with Jackson.

On the afternoon of August 28, Pope attacked Jackson in retaliation for the supply raid, and a bloody engagement occurred on John C. Brawner's Farm. Jackson moved to Groveton and spread his forces along an unfinished railroad grade, where he was assaulted by Pope's army on the twenty-ninth. Piecemeal attacks erupted along the railroad and swayed back and forth inconclusively. The next morning Pope ordered his army forward, believing that Lee and Jackson were retreating. Instead, the battle raged out of control. Confederate counterattacks demolished many Union regiments. Federal troops made stands on Chinn Ridge and Henry House Hill, the heart of the old Bull Run battlefield, and prevented the battle from becoming a Union disaster. After dark, Pope's battered army withdrew toward Washington, in a haunting repeat of the march made a year earlier. After the smoke cleared, of the 75,696 Union and 48,527 Confederate troops engaged at Second Bull Run, 3,205 men lay dead and another 22,046 were wounded or missing. As Pope retreated, Lee lashed out at the army's rear guard, and a battle took place at Chantilly, lasting until nightfall on September 1. This battle produced an additional 2,200 casualties.

Bull Run Tour

The complex, separate but overlapping stories of First and Second Bull Run seemed overpowering as we approached the old battlefield. We turned south from U.S. 29 onto Virginia 234, the Manassas-Sudley Road, and proceeded into the **Manassas National Battlefield Park** entrance on **Henry House Hill**, parked, and began to explore the **Visitor Center**. The drama of those two bloody battles began to come alive in the superb museum contained within the center. When finished with the museum, you may wish to take a walking tour of Henry House Hill, the ground on which Con-

federates made a stand during the first battle and Federals made a stand during the second battle. On the hill you'll find the **Barnard Elliott Bee Monument** marking the spot where this Confederate brigadier general, a South Carolina native, was mortally wounded. Shortly before his wounding, Bee uttered the famous words immortalizing Jackson, who "stood like a stone wall." Whether Bee meant Jackson was gallantly holding up against Union attacks or whether he meant Jackson was uselessly blocking Bee's troops who wanted to attack is a question of fierce debate among historians. Whichever way you see it, just north of the Bee monument stands the **Thomas Jonathan "Stonewall" Jackson Monument**, a superb equestrian statue that graces the ridge running along Henry House Hill.

THE BULL RUN MONUMENT, erected by Union soldiers in 1865 near the Judith Henry House, is among the first memorials to the Civil War.

"JACKSON STOOD LIKE A STONE WALL"
on Henry House Hill, in the words of
Confederate Brig. Gen. Barnard E. Bee. The
implication of Jackson's sobriquet, which is
recorded on his equestrian statue, is still
debated among historians.

Other monuments and structures adorn
Henry House Hill. Near the Jackson and Bee
monuments, you'll see the **Francis Stebbins
Bartow Monument**, a stone honoring the
Georgia colonel who was killed near this spot
while leading his brigade at First Bull Run. From
the Bartow monument, you may wish to walk
west to the white house, the **Judith Carter
Henry Farmhouse**, or "Spring Hill." Blown
apart and burned during the first battle, the
structure was rebuilt using in part original materials. Sadly, the eighty-five-year-old widow, an
invalid, was mortally wounded by a shell during the afternoon of July 21, 1861, and died
before nightfall.

Immediately west of the house you can see
the **Henry Cemetery**, which contains Judith
Henry's grave. On the other side of the house
you'll spot the **Bull Run Monument**, one of
the earliest memorials to Civil War soldiers.
Union troops in Brig. Gen. William Gamble's
brigade erected this obelisk in 1865 to remember the "patriots who fell at Bull Run, July 21,
1861." Several small markers are scattered
between the Henry Farmhouse and the Manassas-Sudley Road, marking the positions
where Confederate Col. Wade Hampton was
wounded, Federal First Lt. Douglas Ramsay was
killed, and Frank Head, color bearer of the 84th
New York (14th Brooklyn Militia) Volunteer
Infantry, was killed. You may see a headstone-
like marker nearby. This is the **7th Georgia
Infantry Monument**, one of at least six such
stones placed by veterans of the 7th Georgia
sometime after 1903 to mark the positions
where they captured a Federal battery. You may
wish to walk to the other major structure on
Henry House Hill, the rebuilt **James Robinson
House**, located 500 yards northeast of the
Henry House. Robinson was a free black whose
house marks the area where Wade Hampton
led his Confederate regiment into battle.
Regrettably, this house burned in 1993 and is
being restored. If you walk back to the visitor
center from the Robinson House, you'll see cannon marking the position of the Confederate
batteries that held the hill during the first battle.

From the visitor center you may wish to
drive across the Manassas-Sudley Road along
the base of **Bald Hill**, a position held by Confederates during the first battle and captured
by the great Confederate attack during Second
Bull Run. If you follow the road, you'll curve
left after crossing **Chinn Branch** and soon
come to a small enclosed structure, the **Hooe
Cemetery**, a local burying ground. Turning
right at this junction will bring you up onto
Chinn Ridge, an area of the most severe combat during Second Bull Run. After 250 yards
you'll see on the left of the road the ruins of
the **Benjamin T. Chinn Farmhouse**, "Hazel
Plain." In this area during the first battle, the
Confederate attack crushed the Union right
and started the Federals in retreat. During
the second battle, at 5 P.M. on August 30,
Longstreet's rebels passed along both sides of
this house as they pushed Pope's soldiers

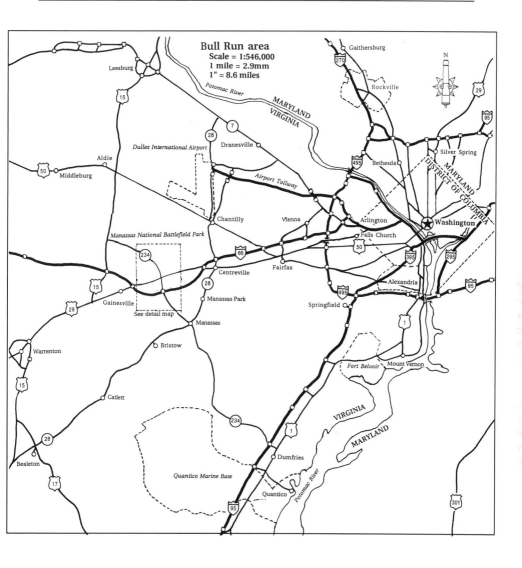

Bull Run area
Scale = 1:546,000
1 mile = 2.9mm
1" = 8.6 miles

eastward. Continuing on the road 400 yards will bring you to the **Fletcher Webster Monument** located on the right side of the road. Son of Daniel Webster and colonel of the 12th Massachusetts Volunteer Infantry, Webster was killed during Second Bull Run while leading his men into battle.

Returning to the Manassas-Sudley Road on the same road, turn south (right) and travel past the campus of the Northern Virginia Community College. Shortly before you reach Interstate 66, turn east (left) onto Infantry Ridge Road, pass through a housing development, and turn north (left) onto Vandor Lane. After one-third mile, the road degrades into an unpaved lane. At this point you may wish to park and take the footpath to the east, which leads to the **M. Lewis Farm Site**, "Portici." Here Gen. Joseph

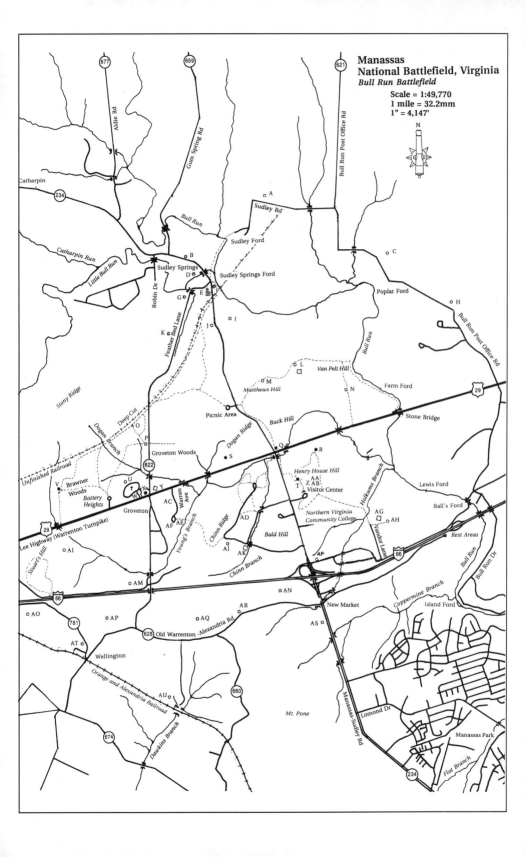

Key to Features on Bull Run Map

A Cushing Farm Site, "Sudley Mansion"
B Red Hill Farm Site
C Weir Farm Site
D Sudley Mill Site
E Sudley United Methodist Church (rebuilt) and cemetery
F Benson Farm Site, "Christian Hill"
G Cushing Farm Site
H George W. Lee Farm Site
I Newman Farm Site
J Dean Farm Site
K Wilkins Farm Site
L Carter Farm Site, "Pittsylvania"
M Matthews Farm Site
N Van Pelt Farm Site, "Avon"
O Groveton Monument
P Groveton School Site
Q Henry P. Matthew Farmhouse, "Stone House"
R James Robinson Farmhouse (rebuilt)

S John Dogan Farmhouse (rebuilt), "Rosefield"
T Judith Carter Henry Farmhouse (rebuilt), Henry Cemetery, and Bull Run Monument
U Peach Grove Farm (ruins)
V John C. Brawner Farm (rebuilt, ruins)
W Stonewall Memory Gardens Cemetery
X Lucinda Dogan Farmhouse (rebuilt)
Y Groveton Confederate Cemetery
Z Francis S. Bartow Monument
AA Thomas J. "Stonewall" Jackson Monument
AB Barnard E. Bee Monument
AC 14th New York Infantry Militia Monument
AD Fletcher Webster Monument
AE 5th New York Infantry Monument
AF 10th New York Infantry Monument
AG Ball Cemetery

AH M. Lewis Farm Site, "Portici"
AI J. W. Cundiffe Farm Site
AJ Benjamin T. Chinn Farmhouse (ruins), "Hazel Plain"
AK Hooe Cemetery
AL Conrad Farm Site
AM William M. Lewis Farm Site
AN Wheeler Farm Site
AO Monroe Farm Site
AP Britt Farm Site
AQ Rev. A. Compton Farm Site
AR Gaskins Farm Site
AS Smith Farm Site
AT Hampton Cole Farm Site
AU Joseph Nickerson Farm Site
AV Battlefield Parkway (Battleview Parkway)
AW Infantry Ridge Road

✪   ✪   ✪

E. Johnston set up headquarters for the Confederate command during First Bull Run. Some 100 yards northwest of the Portici site you may spot the **Ball Cemetery**, a local graveyard.

Back on the Manassas-Sudley Road, consider turning north (right) and traveling one mile until you meet U.S. 29, the Lee Highway (Warrenton Turnpike). Turn left and proceed slowly. After 750 yards you'll see on the right side of the road the rebuilt **John Dogan Farmhouse**, "Rosefield." You'll cross two streams, **Young's Branch** and **Dogan Branch**, and then you may wish to turn left onto a park road. Here you'll find three New York regimental monuments, the **84th New York (14th Brooklyn Militia) Infantry Monument**, the **5th New York Infantry Monument**, and the **10th New York Infantry Monument**. Across the Lee Highway you may want to explore the **Groveton Confederate Cemetery**, the final resting place for about 260 Confederate dead from the two battles, almost all of whom are

unknown. Just west of the cemetery, at the crossroads of the Lee Highway and Virginia 622, you'll find the **Lucinda Dogan House**, a rebuilt structure that is the only house remaining in the village of Groveton. You're now in the heart of the Confederate positions

THE LUCINDA DOGAN HOUSE is the only remaining structure of Groveton, around which fierce fighting occurred during Second Bull Run.

GROVETON CONFEDERATE CEMETERY contains the graves of more than 260 soldiers, only a few with recorded identities.

held early in the second battle. Continuing west on the Lee Highway, you'll see the **Stonewall Memory Gardens Cemetery**, a postwar burying ground established in front of the ruins of a wartime farmhouse, "**Peach Grove.**" Some 500 yards west of the cemetery, you'll spot a park road on the right side of the Lee Highway. This leads to **Battery Heights**, site of the opening fighting at Second Bull Run. Here Jackson's troops battled Federal units spearheaded by the Iron Brigade. The fighting swirled around the **John C. Brawner Farm**, located 750 yards to the northwest. Several long footpaths wind through the woods and lead to the ruins of Brawner Farm, the shortest of which starts on the Lee Highway directly south of the farm.

Having seen Battery Heights, you may wish to head east on the Lee Highway and turn north

(left) on Virginia 622. You'll come back to the stone house at the intersection later. Continuing north, you'll cross Dogan Branch and, after another 500 yards, you'll come to the **Groveton School Site** on the left side of the road. Nothing remains of this early schoolhouse. Proceed another 500 yards and you'll spot a parking lot on the right side of the road. You've now reached a critical area of both battles, the **Unfinished Railroad**. You may hike along a path that follows the railroad bed. The center of Jackson's line occupied this area during much of Second Bull Run, and heavy fighting occurred throughout the grade, which served as a natural breastwork for Jackson's Confederates. If you walk 400 yards down the path, you'll reach two important landmarks of the second battle. On the morning of August 30, 1862, Pope's advance toward Jackson's line centered on the area about 200 yards down the railroad bed. The region, called the **Deep Cut,** was an overgrown wilderness, as thick and unmanageable today as it was during the war. More than 5,000 Union men under Maj. Gen. Fitz John Porter assaulted Jackson's line several times in this area but failed to make any permanent gains. When ammunition ran low on both sides, soldiers resorted to hurling rocks at oncoming attackers. If you continue another 200 yards, you'll come to the **Groveton Monument,** an obelisk built by Gamble's cavalry in 1865 that, along with the similar monument on Henry House Hill, is one of the first memorials to Civil War soldiers.

Returning to your car and continuing north on Virginia 622 will carry you past the **Wilkins Farm Site** and the **Cushing Farm Site,** just before **Little Bull Run**. You're now entering the hamlet of **Sudley Springs,** a tiny community built around the reconstructed **Sudley United Methodist Church,** which you'll see on the right of the road just before the intersection with the Manassas-Sudley Road. This area marks the position of several savage attacks on August 29, 1862, during which Union troops tried to destroy the far left of Jackson's line. Across the Manassas-Sudley

ERECTED IN 1865, the Groveton Monument records the "memory of the patriots who fell at Groveton, Aug. 1862." The Union memorial is a virtual twin with that on Henry House Hill.

Road is the **Benson Farm Site,** "Christian Hill," around which heavy fighting flared. A few hundred yards north on the Manassas-Sudley Road are the **Sudley Mill Site** and the **Red Hill Farm Site,** two wartime structures no longer extant.

Traveling south on the Manassas-Sudley Road will take you past the **Newman Farm Site** and the **Dean Farm Site,** of which nothing is left, and after a mile, to a picnic area parking lot on the right side of the road. You may want to park here and cross the road to explore **Matthews Hill,** an area affording an excellent overview of the Bull Run battlefield. The cannon you see lined up on Matthews Hill mark the position of a bloody engagement between the Union troops of Col. Ambrose Burnside and ranks of Confederate Col. Nathan G. Evans early in First Bull Run. During the second battle, Federal guns commanded the position until the chaotic retreat of the Union army. The path along the ridge on Matthews Hill leads to the **M. Matthews Farm Site,** the **L. Carter Farm Site,** known as "Pittsylvania," and to the **Van Pelt Farm Site,** "Avon," on **Van Pelt Hill.** All are merely ruins covered by brush.

Continuing south on the Manassas-Sudley Road will bring you back to the intersection where you earlier saw the conspicuous stone house. This is the **Henry P. Matthew Farmhouse,** known simply as "Stone House," a prominent landmark during both battles. Placed at the base of **Buck Hill,** Stone House was struck by artillery during both engagements and served as a hospital following each battle. Anchored by modern mortar, a cannonball and shell are visible on the southern face of the building. During Second Bull Run, Pope's headquarters were established directly behind this structure.

Traveling east on the Lee Highway a distance of just over a mile will bring you to the final Bull Run landmark, the **Stone Bridge** over **Bull Run** itself. Substantially blown apart at First Bull Run and several times reconstructed, the bridge carried the weight of thousands of

THE STONE BRIDGE over Bull Run is a reconstruction of the edifice over which the Union army retreated to Washington after First Bull Run.

Union troops as they marched toward the battles and subsequently retreated to Washington. A long, winding trail along the western side of the creek leads to **Farm Ford**, the crossing where a little-known Union colonel named

William Tecumseh Sherman led his brigade on an attack that helped push the Confederates back to Matthews Hill.

Having seen Bull Run, you may wish to travel eight miles to see what remains of the **Chantilly Battlefield**, site of the fierce engagement that followed Second Bull Run. To reach Chantilly from Bull Run consult the Bull Run area map (p. 23), take U.S. 29 east to Centreville, then travel on Virginia 28 to its junction with U.S. 50. Turn right on U.S. 50 and proceed four and one-quarter miles to West Ox Road, where you'll turn right. Continue on about 700 yards and turn right onto a residential street. After traveling 350 yards, stop on a slight rise. The small hill just south of the sidewalk contains the **Philip Kearny Monument** and the **Isaac Ingalls Stevens Monument**, adjacent stones in a small grove that mark a spot just east of the center of the Chantilly battlefield. On September 1, 1862, Federal Major General Kearny

THE HENRY P. MATTHEW HOUSE, known as "Stone House," served as a hospital in the wake of both battles at Bull Run. During the battles the structure was hit by artillery.

STONE MARKERS AT CHANTILLY mark the area where Federal Maj. Gen. Philip Kearny and Brig. Gen. Isaac I. Stevens were killed during the intense battle. Nothing more is left of the battlefield.

was killed instantly when he inadvertently rode into the Confederate lines. His fellow officer Brigadier General Stevens was also killed instantly during the battle, hit in the temple by a minié bullet. Their monuments are all that remain of the Chantilly battlefield, an historic field devastated by the surrounding commercial development.

Manassas National Battlefield Park
Mailing address: 12521 Lee Highway, Manassas, Virginia 20109-2005
Telephone: (703) 361-1339
Park established: May 10, 1940
Area: 5,071.6 acres

Groveton Confederate Cemetery
Established: April 27, 1867
Area: 0.9 acre
Civil War interments: about 260

Bull Run accommodations
Manassas, the town closest to the battlefield park, has three motels. Travelers can find accommodations in nearby Fairfax, Falls Church, Springfield, and in the region surrounding Dulles National Airport.

Chapter 3

✪   ✪   ✪

Chattanooga

At twenty minutes before four the signal guns were fired.
Suddenly twenty thousand men rushed forward, moving in line of battle
by brigades, with a double line of skirmishers in front,
and closely followed by the reserves in mass. The big siege guns in
the Chattanooga forts roared above the light artillery and musketry
in the valley. . .There was a halt of but a few minutes, to take breath
and to re-form lines; then, with a sudden impulse, and without orders,
all started up the ridge. Officers, catching their spirit,
first followed, then led.

—Lt. Col. Joseph Scott Fullerton describing the assault on Missionary Ridge,
November 25, 1863.

The city of **Chattanooga**, Tennessee (pop. 152,466), is topographically the most varied and unusual of any Civil War battlefield. During the summer of 1863, this vital rail center linking Union-occupied central Tennessee with the deep South became a focus for Federal military occupation. Confederate Gen. Braxton Bragg and his Army of Tennessee and Union Maj. Gen. William S. Rosecrans and his Army of the Cumberland prepared for an inevitable engagement.

The battle did not occur at Chattanooga, however, but twenty miles south at Chickamauga Creek, Georgia (see chapter 4), on September 19 and 20, 1863. The Confederate victory drove the Union army back into Chattanooga, which Bragg then invested. Rosecrans was in poor position for resupply and by late October his troops were completely demoralized. On October 19 Maj. Gen. George H. Thomas, hero of Chickamauga, succeeded Rosecrans in command of the Army of the

Cumberland. Thomas's orders were that Chattanooga must be held. To make matters worse for Thomas, Bragg's Confederates held the high ground around the city. Confederate positions on Lookout Mountain, a lofty peak southwest of the city, and Missionary Ridge, a long north-south mountain stretching from east of the city south into Georgia, offered artillery positions that commanded the town below.

Nonetheless, little action took place during October excepting an occasional Confederate shell Bragg lobbed into the city. Meanwhile, Thomas, now supervised in person by U. S. Grant, who arrived on the twenty-third, desperately needed to open a proper supply line into the city. On October 26 he detached Brig. Gen. William B. Hazen to capture Browns Ferry on the Tennessee River, a crucial point from which the supply line could move eastward across a curve in the river called Moccasin Bend. Under the direction of Thomas's chief engineer, Brig. Gen. William F. "Baldy" Smith, the delicate and lengthy supply route called the "cracker line" was opened. Furthermore, on November 15, Maj. Gen. William T. Sherman's army arrived from Vicksburg with orders to drive the Confederates from Tunnel Hill and, assisted by Thomas, move southward to capture Missionary Ridge.

The Union plan also necessitated the capture of Lookout Mountain by Maj. Gen. Joseph Hooker, who had joined Grant with the 11th and 12th Corps detached from the Army of the Potomac. On November 23 the plan got under way. Grant ordered Thomas eastward in a small-scale attack that took place in broad daylight and at first appeared to be a drill, in plain view of the Confederate army. As the "drill" unfolded, Thomas's men scurried toward Missionary Ridge and captured a rise east of the city known as Orchard Knob after brief but intense fighting.

The following day Hooker and Sherman attacked. By noon the Union troops under Hooker had placed themselves between the river and Lookout Mountain and started their movement uphill. They halted by mid-afternoon due to a shortage of ammunition and a blinding fog. (The action was known thereafter as the "battle above the clouds.") Sherman moved eastward but before nightfall gave the Confederates under Maj. Gen. Patrick R. Cleburne time to entrench. During the night the Confederates remaining on Lookout Mountain, their numbers diminished by the withdrawal of Longstreet's Corps—which Bragg had ordered to Knoxville—abandoned the position.

November 25 proved the crucial day for the Chattanooga campaign. With Lookout Mountain in Union hands, the full force of the combined armies turned to Sherman's leading attack toward Missionary Ridge. Grant, Thomas, Maj. Gen. Gordon Granger, Quartermaster Gen. Montgomery C. Meigs, Brig. Gens. John A. Rawlins, Baldy Smith, and Thomas J. Wood, and Asst. Secy. of War Charles A. Dana watched the action from Grant's command post on Orchard Knob. By late afternoon Grant was

alarmed by Hooker's delay in coordinating his advance with that of Sherman's and by Sherman's apparent inability to break through the Confederate line. Grant ordered Thomas's men forward toward the base of Missionary Ridge, hoping they might be used as a diversion.

In one of the great moments of the war, Thomas's men not only seized the rifle pits at the mountain's base, but fought their way up the steep mountain, though exposed to heavy fire from above. The attack surprised everyone who saw it. The western face of the mountain sprouted dots and rows of Union blue. Confederate cannon on Missionary Ridge could not be trained low enough to fire on the attackers, and sheer panic in the Confederate lines when hit by the unbelievable frontal attack caused the defenders to break and scatter in chaos. By 4:30 P.M. the Confederate lines were shattered and the defenders had fled in disarray.

Chattanooga and its environs were in Union hands, the mistakes of Chickamauga corrected. But the cost had been high: from a total of 56,359 Union and 64,165 Confederate troops engaged in the campaign, 1,114 were killed, 6,882 wounded, and 4,495 missing. Grant's collected armies had now paved the way for Sherman's daunting Atlanta campaign and the subsequent March to the Sea.

Chattanooga Tour

Chattanooga's location on interstate highways between Knoxville, Nashville, and Atlanta makes it convenient to reach. The city contains three major components of the **Chickamauga and Chattanooga National Military Park**, whose headquarters exist on the Chickamauga battlefield. Several ancillary sites lie scattered within and around the city.

Before exploring the city, we approached from the north and went to **Signal Mountain** overlooking the Tennessee River (consult the Chattanooga area map on page 35). About nine miles north of the city on Signal Mountain, you'll find **Signal Point Reservation**, which overlooks the north bank of the river. To reach it, take U.S. 127 to Signal Mountain Boulevard and head west one and one-half miles. This area served as an important signal position for both armies during the Chattanooga and Chickamauga campaigns.

Throughout the Lookout Mountain tour, see the Lookout Mountain detail map (p. 36). The first major area to explore is **Lookout Mountain**, captured by Hooker's forces on November 24. Take U.S. 27 south across the Tennessee, into the city, then head south on Broad Street (Tennessee 17). The mountain looms large above the city and has an elevation of 2,146 feet at its summit, so drive up the mountain roads cautiously—they are fairly narrow and wind through sharp curves. Approach the mountain along the south bank of the Ten-

nessee on West Lee Highway, and turn south on Lookout Mountain Scenic Highway (Tennessee 148). Slowly work your way higher in elevation. You'll want to turn northwest soon after the road crosses the Incline Railroad. A short drive leads to the **Robert Cravens House,** the only principal structure remaining from the Lookout Mountain battlefield.

The reconstructed Cravens House stands on a flat area of the mountain known before the war as the bench. In many battle reports, soldiers and officers called the Cravens House the "white house on the bench." The structure was heavily defended by Confederate soldiers under Maj. Gen. Edward C. Walthall when the battle of Lookout Mountain began. Indeed, the structure served for a time as Walthall's headquarters. Brisk fighting erupted around the

MOCCASIN BEND in the Tennessee River, as seen from Lookout Mountain, skirts the city of Chattanooga. Here, in 1863, Grant opened his "cracker line" of supplies that helped push the Confederates into Georgia.

LOOKOUT MOUNTAIN looms over Chattanooga as seen from the National Cemetery. On November 24, 1863, the "battle above the clouds" erupted on Lookout Mountain and Hooker's army secured the strategic heights.

Cravens House on November 24 as Union attackers made their way uphill and eventually captured the position. The Confederates retreated uphill and briefly concentrated their forces at the summit before abandoning the mountain. On the grounds surrounding the Cravens House, you can see two large state memorials, the **New York Monument** and the

THE ROBERT CRAVENS HOUSE on Lookout Mountain briefly served as Confederate Brig. Gen. Edward C. Walthall's headquarters before the rebels abandoned the position.

Ohio Monument, and smaller regimentals, the **75th**, the **84th**, the **92nd**, and the **104th Illinois Infantry Monuments**. A small spur road below the Cravens House leads to the **Iowa Monument**.

Now return to the Scenic Highway and continue south, rising in height as you go. Turn north (right) on East Brow Road and, after traveling one mile, you'll come to **Point Park** at the mountain's summit. At this position Confederate batteries guarded the strategic overlook from Hooker's Union men until the position became untenable and the Confederates escaped southward. Enter the park through the **U.S. Engineers' Gate**. Across the road from this entrance, you'll see the National Park Service **Visitor Center**, containing exhibits on the "battle above the clouds." Inspecting the cannon in the park—especially the northernmost batteries—affords a great overlook view of Chattanooga. Looking north, you can see not only the city but **Moccasin Bend** in the Tennessee River and **Moccasin Point**, the peninsula of land crossed by the Union supply line. The central monument on the mountain's summit is the **New York Peace Memorial**. You may also see the **96th Illinois Infantry Monument**.

A short trail through the woods north of the Peace Memorial leads to the **Adolph S. Ochs Museum**, which contains a small collection of relics and historical memorabilia. Nearby stands **Umbrella Rock**, a famous outcrop perched above a near vertical drop to the valley below. Many soldiers sat or stood on Umbrella Rock and had their pictures taken, including Major General Hooker. Do not climb out onto Umbrella Rock, however. It is very dangerous. Along the trail you may also see **Roper's Rock**, an equally dangerous perch where a soldier named Roper gained immortality during the war by falling to his death. If the day is clear and free of haze, you can get a spectacular view of Chattanooga, Lookout Valley, and Missionary Ridge from the area of the Ochs Museum.

Chattanooga-Chickamauga area

Scale = 1:549,000
1 mile = 2.9mm
1" = 8.6 miles

The Lookout Mountain battlefield spreads south several miles into Georgia, but few monuments or markers exist apart from those in Point Park. Several other sites are scattered west and north of Lookout Mountain, but some are difficult to reach. Returning to the base of Lookout Mountain, take West Lee Highway northwest, cross Lookout Creek, and head north on Browns Ferry Road. After one and one-third miles, you'll come to **Browns Tavern**, a structure established in 1803 that appears now much as it did during the Chattanooga battles. About three-fourths mile farther north on the road, and east along the river, is the site of **Browns Ferry**, which is no longer accessible. This was the critical point at which Union Brig. Gen. Baldy Smith began constructing the "cracker line" over Moccasin Bend. Brig. Gen. William B. Hazen's small band of men assaulted the Confederate position at Browns Ferry by

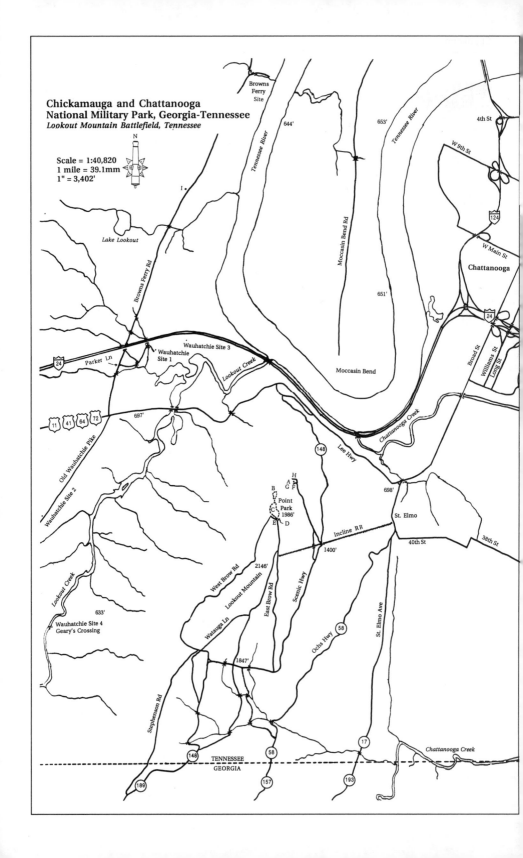

Chickamauga and Chattanooga
National Military Park, Georgia-Tennessee
Lookout Mountain Battlefield, Tennessee

Scale = 1:40,820
1 mile = 39.1mm
1" = 3,402'

N

Browns
Ferry
Site

644'

653'

Tennessee River

4th St

W 9th St

I-124

Moccasin Bend Rd

W Main St

Chattanooga

Lake Lookout

Browns Ferry Rd

651'

24

Wauhatchie Site 3

Wauhatchie
Site 1

Parker Ln

Lookout Creek

Broad St

Williams St

Long St

24

Moccasin Bend

11 41 64 72

697'

Old Wauhatchie Pike

148

Lee Hwy

Chattanooga Creek

698'

H
A
G
F

B

St. Elmo

Wauhatchie Site 2

Point
Park
1986'

Incline RR

C

E   D

40th St

38th St

1400'

West Brow Rd

2146'

Lookout Creek

633'

Wauhatchie Site 4
Geary's Crossing

Watauga Ln

Lookout Mountain

East Brow Rd

Scenic Hwy

Ochs Hwy

St. Elmo Ave

58

1847'

17

Chattanooga Creek

148

TENNESSEE

58

189

GEORGIA

157

193

THE NEW YORK PEACE MEMORIAL in Point Park near the summit of Lookout Mountain marks the spot where Union attackers captured Confederate batteries stationed on the lofty mountain.

boat on October 27. The strategic position was in Federal hands after a half hour skirmish, and this greatly helped the Federal drive to recapture the area.

Four so-called Wauhatchie Sites lay scattered across the Lookout Valley south of Browns Ferry and west of Lookout Mountain. Two of

these sites can be reached today, and two are inaccessible. They mark the positions of crossings and skirmishes in late October between mostly New York troops in Major General Hooker's army and Confederates blocking their approach from Wauhatchie.

If you head south on Browns Ferry Road, cross Interstate 24 and proceed 200 yards to a small road that leads eastward. After 600 yards you'll come to **Wauhatchie Site One**, which contains the **1st New York Artillery Monument**. About 400 yards northeast of this spot is **Wauhatchie Site Three**, which marks the position of New York artillery units and cannot conveniently be reached. Continuing south on Browns Ferry Road, which becomes the Old Wauhatchie Pike, a distance of one and one-third miles brings you to **Wauhatchie Site Two**, containing the **78th, 137th, and 149th New York Infantry Monument**. About three-fourths mile south of this position on Lookout Creek is the difficult to reach **Wauhatchie Site Four**, known as the Old Mill Dam or Geary's Crossing. At this spot Brig. Gen. John W. Geary held his division as a rear guard while Hooker's army continued the northward march from Wauhatchie.

At this point, switch to the Missionary Ridge detail map (p. 39). One of the least-visited Civil War sites in the city stands between Third and Fifth Streets just north of the University of Tennessee at Chattanooga campus. The **Confederate Cemetery** occupies the northeast corner of Chattanooga's Citizens Cemetery. About

Key to Features on Lookout Mountain Map

A Robert Cravens House, "the White House on the bench"
B Adolph S. Ochs Museum and Umbrella Rock
C New York Peace Memorial
  96th Illinois Infantry Monument
D U.S. Engineers' Gate
E NPS Visitor Center and Museum
F Ohio Monument
G New York Monument
  75th Illinois Infantry Monument
  84th Illinois Infantry Monument
  92nd Illinois Infantry Monument
  104th Illinois Infantry Monument
H Iowa Monument
I Browns Tavern

1,000 Confederate soldiers lie buried in this plot, which consists of mass burial trenches.

Continue east on Third Street, turn south (right) on Hawthorne Street, and travel one block to reach the **Orchard Knob Reservation**. This hill is the strategic position captured by Union Major General Thomas during the "drill" of November 23. After brief but intense fighting, the Confederates evacuated the position and the hill became a Federal command post. Here Grant and his generals watched the incredible assault up Missionary Ridge, plainly visible to the east. Near the summit of Orchard Knob, you can see the **Illinois Monument**, the **Maryland Monument**, the **New York Monument**, and the **New Jersey Monument**. The **Wisconsin Monument** stands toward the southern end of the knob. Ten regimentals are scattered along the perimeter of the reservation, including the **109th Pennsylvania Infantry Monument**, the **1st Michigan Engineers Monument**, the **10th Michigan Infantry Monument**, the **27th Pennsylvania Infantry Monument**, the **46th Pennsylvania Infantry Monument**, and the **8th Kansas Infantry Monument**.

As a follow-up to Orchard Knob, you may wish to drive along Missionary Ridge to see the corresponding view of the Confederate defenders. From Orchard Knob head southeast on Third Street and turn northeast (left) on Dodson Avenue, then east (right) on Glass Street. At the intersection of Glass and Campbell Road, you'll come to the first site along the base of

---

Key to Features on Missionary Ridge Map

A Confederate Cemetery (within Citizens Cemetery)
B Chattanooga National Cemetery
C Orchard Knob
  New York Monument
  Maryland Monument
  Illinois Monument
  New Jersey Monument
  Wisconsin Monument
  5th and 20th Connecticut Infantry Monument
  8th Kansas Infantry Monument
  2nd and 33rd Massachusetts Infantry Monument
  10th Michigan Infantry Monument
  1st Michigan Engineers Monument
  27th, 46th, 75th, and 109th Pennsylvania Infantry Monument
  Knap's Battery Pennsylvania Artillery Monument
D William T. Sherman Reservation
  40th Illinois Infantry Monument
  55th Illinois Infantry Monument
  56th Illinois Infantry Monument
  63rd Illinois Infantry Monument

93rd Illinois Infantry Monument
103rd Illinois Infantry Monument
116th Illinois Infantry Monument
127th Illinois Infantry Monument
6th Missouri Infantry Monument
8th Missouri Infantry Monument
Iowa Monument
E 73rd Pennsylvania Infantry Reservation
  73rd Pennsylvania Infantry Monument
  26th Illinois Infantry Monument
  90th Illinois Infantry Monument
F Edward H. Phelps Monument
G DeLong Reservation
  2nd Minnesota Infantry Monument
H John B. Turchin Reservation
I 25th Illinois Infantry Monument
  35th Illinois Infantry Monument
  89th Illinois Infantry Monument
  8th Kansas Infantry Monument
J Ohio Reservation
  Ohio Monument
K 100th Illinois Infantry Monument
L Braxton Bragg Reservation
  Illinois Monument
  18th Illinois Infantry Monument
  27th Illinois Infantry Monument
  36th Illinois Infantry Monument
  42nd Illinois Infantry Monument

44th Illinois Infantry Monument
51st Illinois Infantry Monument
73rd Illinois Infantry Monument
79th Illinois Infantry Monument
2nd and 15th Missouri Infantry Monument
3rd Missouri Infantry Monument
12th Missouri Infantry Monument
17th Missouri Infantry Monument
29th Missouri Infantry Monument
31st Missouri Infantry Monument
32nd Missouri Infantry Monument
97th Ohio Infantry Monument
M 24th Wisconsin Infantry Monument
N 88th Illinois Infantry Monument
O 74th Illinois Infantry Monument
P 19th Illinois Infantry Monument
Q 11th Michigan Infantry Monument
R 104th Illinois Infantry Monument
S 60th, 102nd, 137th, and 149th New York Monument
T 3rd, 12th, 17th, 27th, 29th, 31st, and 32nd Missouri Infantry and 2nd Missouri Artillery Monument
U Iowa Reservation
  Iowa Monument
V John Ross House (rebuilt and relocated)

38

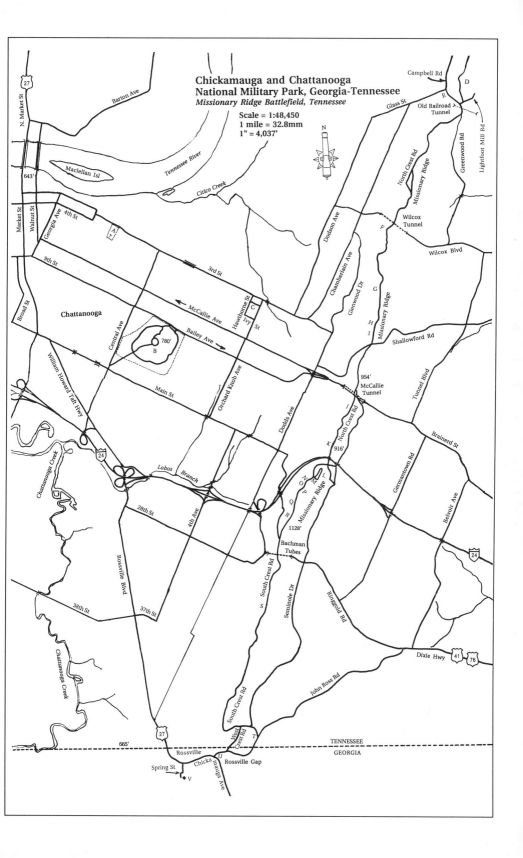

ORCHARD KNOB is a hill in Chattanooga captured by the Yankees on November 23, 1863. From this hill the Federal high command—including Grant, Maj. Gen. George H. Thomas, Maj. Gen. Gordon Granger, and Asst. Secy. of War Charles A. Dana—watched the surprising charge up Missionary Ridge.

Missionary Ridge, the **73rd Pennsylvania Infantry Reservation**. Here you'll see the **73rd Pennsylvania Infantry Monument**, the **26th Illinois Infantry Monument**, and the **90th Illinois Infantry Monument**.

If you turn south (right) on Campbell Road and then east (left) on Lightfoot Mill Road, you'll soon reach the **Sherman Reservation**, the largest park area on Missionary Ridge. This high ground was occupied during the battle of Missionary Ridge by Sherman's Army of the Tennessee as it moved slowly from the north to try to capture the old railroad tunnel at **Tunnel Hill** south of the Sherman Reservation. Although Sherman made slow progress southward, Thomas's frontal attack would be the decisive maneuver to break the Confederate defenses on the ridge. The Sherman Reservation contains many monuments, cannon, and remnants of entrenchments made by Sherman's troops. On a clear day you can gain a panoramic view of the city and of Lookout Mountain from this area. Among the monuments are the **Iowa Monument**, the **40th Illinois Infantry Monument**, the **55th Illinois Infantry Mon-**

ument, the **103rd Illinois Infantry Monument**, and the **6th Missouri Infantry Monument**.

As you leave the Sherman Reservation on Lightfoot Mill Road, turn south (left) on North Crest Road to see the rest of Missionary Ridge. Shortly after the turn, you'll pass over the abandoned railroad tunnel that was Sherman's objective during the early part of the battle. After traveling one and one-fourth miles, you'll cross over the Wilcox Tunnel and shortly thereafter come to the **Edward H. Phelps Death Monument** on the west side of the road. (Practically all of the Missionary Ridge monuments were erected on the side of the crest from which the attack came.) This area marks one of the heavily used approaches of Thomas's frontal attack. Thousands of Union soldiers ascended the heights along these draws and startled the Confederates into a confused retreat, gaining control of the ridge. At this spot Colonel Phelps, commanding the Third Brigade in the 12th Corps's Third Division, was killed leading a column toward the crest.

Continuing south one-half mile will take you to the **DeLong Reservation**, also on the west side of the road. This small preserve contains a single monument, the **2nd Minneso-**

ON MISSIONARY RIDGE the DeLong Reservation holds the 2nd Minnesota Infantry Monument, commemorating this regiment's participation in the Missionary Ridge attack.

ta Infantry Monument, honoring one of the first regiments to reach the crest of the ridge. Scattered south of the DeLong Reservation are several regimentals including the **25th Illinois Infantry Monument**, the **35th Illinois Infantry Monument**, the **89th Illinois Infantry Monument**, and the **8th Kansas Infantry Monument**.

Slightly over one-half mile farther south, after crossing over the McCallie Tunnel, you'll find the **Ohio Reservation** west of the road. The impressive **Ohio Monument** honors a number of Ohio regiments that reached the crest of the ridge during Thomas's attack. About 600 yards south of the Ohio Reservation stands the **100th Illinois Infantry Monument**, also on the west side of the road. As you head south, you'll cross over Interstate 24 and continue on what is now South Crest Drive.

The next objective is the **Braxton Bragg Reservation**, the primary park unit on the southern half of Missionary Ridge. This area served as Bragg's headquarters during the siege of Chattanooga and was a key position of attack during the Missionary Ridge battle. On the

THE BRAGG RESERVATION on Missionary Ridge contains several monuments and cannon placed along the southern end of the Federal attack.

grounds here, you'll find the **Illinois Monument** and more than a dozen regimentals including the **18th Illinois Infantry Monument**, the **2nd and 15th Missouri Infantry Monument**, and the **97th Ohio Infantry Monument**.

The area just south of the Bragg Reservation holds several noteworthy monuments. The first you'll see is the **24th Wisconsin Infantry Monument**, followed by the **88th Illinois Infantry Monument**, the **74th Illinois Infantry Monument**, the **19th Illinois Infantry Monument**, the **11th Michigan Infantry Monument**, and the **104th Illinois Infantry Monument**. Each of these regimentals commemorates these units for their part in the assault on Missionary Ridge.

Continuing south three-fourths mile and passing over the Bachman Tubes brings you to another monument west of the road, the **60th, 102nd, 137th, and 149th New York Infantry Monument**. You may now travel south just over one mile to a point where the road bends eastward. Carry on another 500 yards to an intersection to see the **3rd, 12th, 17th, 27th, 29th, 31st, and 32nd Missouri Infantry and 2nd Missouri Artillery Monument**. At this intersection, head south down the mountain a distance of 750 yards to the **Iowa Monument** along the southern base of Missionary Ridge.

Having seen Missionary Ridge, continue south to the mountain's terminus in **Rossville**, Georgia (pop. 3,601). You'll come out on Chickamauga Avenue (U.S. 27), where you should head north (right). After traveling 500 yards, turn south (left) onto Spring Street, which leads to the **John Ross House**, a cabin-like structure that served as Maj. Gen. Gordon Granger's headquarters during the battle of Chickamauga. The house has been rebuilt (with nearly all original material) and relocated, and was made famous by several wartime photographs.

Now you may wish to return to Chattanooga on U.S. 27, which becomes Rossville

Boulevard and then the William Howard Taft Highway. Turning north on Central Avenue brings you after one-half mile to **Chattanooga National Cemetery**, a fitting place to end the tour of the Chattanooga battlefields. One of the earliest Civil War National cemeteries, this facility held casualties from the nearby battles beginning in November 1863. About 12,000 Federal soldiers are buried on these grounds. One of the most striking plots contains the remains of eight Andrews Raiders, Union soldiers captured and executed by Confederates following their raid on the famous locomotive the *General*. They are James J. Andrews (a civilian), William H. Campbell, Samuel Robertson, Marion A. Ross, John M. Scott, Charles P. Shadrack, Samuel Slavens, and George D. Wilson, and were among the first to win the Medal of Honor. Two general officers lie within the cemetery, Brig.

THE EXECUTED ANDREWS RAIDERS, eight Federal soldiers captured after a daring locomotive raid in Georgia, lie buried in Chattanooga National Cemetery. The burying ground contains the remains of about 12,000 Union soldiers.

Gen. William P. Sanders, who was killed at Knoxville, and Bvt. Brig. Gen. Timothy R. Stanley. Exploring the grounds shows that many other Union officers are buried here and provides an excellent view of both Lookout Mountain and Missionary Ridge. This area shows the topography of Chattanooga nicely, something that general officers on both sides thought about constantly for a few months in 1863.

Chickamauga and Chattanooga National Military Park

Mailing address: P.O. Box 2128,
Fort Oglethorpe, Georgia 30742
Telephone: (706) 866-9241
Park established:
August 19,1890
Area: 9,059 acres

Chattanooga National Cemetery

Established: November 1863
Area: 126 acres
Civil War interments: about 12,000

Confederate Cemetery

(within Citizens Cemetery)
Established: 1866
Area: less than 1 acre
Civil War interments: about 1,000

Chattanooga accommodations

Finding accommodations in Chattanooga is relatively easy because the city contains twenty-one major hotels and motels with more than 3,000 rooms. The outlying area offers many more places to stay. You should not have a problem finding a place convenient to the area of town you are sightseeing.

Chapter 4

✪   ✪   ✪

Chickamauga

The deep Confederate lines suddenly appeared.
The woods in our front seemed alive.
On they came like an angry flood. . .pouring through
the opening made by Wood's withdrawal,
they struck his last brigade as it was leaving the line.
It was slammed back like a door, and shattered.

—Maj. Gates Phillips Thruston
describing Longstreet's frontal attack of September 20, 1863,
at the battle of Chickamauga.

Chickamauga is a spooky place to visit. The battlefield is located in the tangle of countryside south of Chattanooga near the town of Fort Oglethorpe, Georgia. The fields and woods scattered over the battleground are practically as wild as they were during the savage fight that rolled over the landscape here. The body of water etched through the field, Chickamauga Creek, derived its name from upcountry Cherokee dialect. When Cherokee villages lined the banks of the river, many of the inhabitants contracted smallpox. The stream came to be called Chickamauga, the river of death. The thick woods and lush fields spread over the battlefield today are filled with monuments, markers, cannon, and a generous helping of creatures such as spiders and snakes.

The greatest Confederate victory in the west, the battle of Chickamauga was fought on September 19 and 20, 1863, and stunned the Union high command. The action caused a major reorganization to prevent a Federal crisis in what was arguably the most strategically important theater of war.

Following the battle of Stones River in January 1863, Gen. Braxton Bragg withdrew the Confederate Army of Tennessee south to Tullahoma. His mission then was to prevent the Union capture of the vital rail center of Chattanooga. Union Maj. Gen. William Starke Rosecrans, commanding the Army of the Cumberland, fully expected to push on and occupy Chattanooga. The situation was uneventful until the end of June when Rosecrans moved forward and edged Bragg south of the Tennessee River.

During August, Bragg prepared for the coming test. He stationed his troops in a line south of the Tennessee with Lt. Gen. Leonidas Polk's Corps centered in Chattanooga. As the Federals crossed the Tennessee on September 9 and 10, Bragg evacuated the city and pulled together his forces at Lafayette, Georgia. Meanwhile, Rosecrans's army was dangerously separated in a line from Chattanooga and Bridgeport, Tennessee, to Alpine, Georgia. Deluded that the Confederates were in full flight, Rosecrans was about to march into a trap.

A full week of repositioning and minor skirmishing ensued. Bragg's plan called for crossing Chickamauga Creek and hitting the Federal army from the east. On the morning of September 19, the Confederate strategy went into motion as 66,326 soldiers moved toward the Union lines. Rosecrans's defenders numbered 58,222. The battle raged all day with repeated frontal attacks that made little progress. Early in the struggle the Federal Maj. Gen. George H. Thomas bore the brunt of several Confederate attacks.

The next morning was peaceful, briefly. Bragg's attack began at 9:30 A.M. and went well except that Union artillery opened up from Kelly Field and stopped a portion of the movement. Bragg now ordered his entire line to attack. By 11:30 A.M. Lt. Gen. James Longstreet punched a gaping hole in the Union line at the Brotherton Cabin.

This movement was greatly assisted by confusion in the Union line, the result of misunderstanding and miscommunication on Rosecrans's part. Rosecrans ordered the division under Brig. Gen. Thomas J. Wood to maneuver to assist Maj. Gen. Joseph J. Reynolds's division. The move created a one-fourth-mile-wide gap in the Union center into which Longstreet sent six divisions screaming the rebel yell. This Confederate breakthrough constituted one of the great frontal attacks of the war, and Longstreet's men swept the Federals back in disarray.

The Federal retreat gained momentum shortly after noon on the twentieth, and by default Thomas assumed command on the field—Rosecrans had left. The Confederate tidal wave pushed the Yankees onto Snodgrass Hill, where Thomas held fast, prevented a rout, and earned the sobriquet "Rock of Chickamauga." The battle had been a numbing loss for the Union, but fell short of a complete dis-

aster. The combined losses over the two days were 3,969 dead, 24,430 wounded, and 6,225 missing.

Chickamauga Tour

The Chickamauga battlefield is one component of the **Chickamauga and Chattanooga National Military Park**, and it lies twenty miles southeast of Chattanooga, immediately south of **Fort Oglethorpe** (pop. 5,880). Chickamauga envokes a special feeling not only because it was such a ferocious and strategically interesting battle, but also because it was the first national military park. Due largely to the efforts of Bvt. Brig. Gen. Henry Van Ness Boynton and Brig. Gen. Ferdinand Van Derveer, Congress enacted legislation in 1890 to memorialize the struggle that so haunted the Army of the Cumberland. Four more parks came along in the 1890s—Antietam, Shiloh, Gettysburg, and Vicksburg—and the government enterprise of preserving Civil War battlegrounds was under way.

The Chickamauga **Visitor Center** is located in the northern part of the park on Lafayette Road (U.S. 27). The superb museum inside contains Chickamauga relics and displays and the **Claude E. and Zenada O. Fuller Collection of American Military Arms**. The 355-piece display offers examples of some of the finest and rarest Civil War longarms. At the time of the battle, the **John McDonald House**, a prominent landmark during the fighting, stood near the present day visitor center.

To start the park tour, head south on Lafayette Road past the **Florida Monument** and turn east (left) onto Alexander Bridge Road. This route will take you along the Confederate lines during the first part of the tour and the Union lines during the final loop. At the intersection of Alexander Bridge Road and Lafayette Road, on the southeast corner, you'll see the **Kentucky Monument**. After crossing the stream, you may wish to park near the intersection of Alexander Bridge Road and Battle

44

Line Road and explore the monuments to the east where you'll find a striking line of Georgia regimentals. A footpath heading east from this area leads to the **Peyton H. Colquitt Death Monument**, where the colonel of the 46th Georgia Infantry was shot dead. The trail then leads to the **Benjamin Hardin Helm Mortal Wounding Monument**, marking the position where the Confederate brigadier general, and brother-in-law of Mary Todd Lincoln, was fatally wounded in his side. He died the following day.

Walking on a path extending north from this point will, after 250 yards, bring you to the **Army of Tennessee, Reserve Corps Headquarters Monument**, where Maj. Gen. William H. T. Walker commanded. Continuing on the eastward path 350 yards leads to two Confederate command positions, the **Army of Tennessee, D. H. Hill's Corps Headquarters Monument** and the **Army of Tennessee, Right Wing Headquarters Monument** where Lieutenant General Polk was in command.

Returning to the intersection, you may wish to head southeast on Alexander Bridge Road to follow the Confederate positions. After just over one-half mile, you'll see a short trail south of the road. This leads to the **John Ingraham Grave**, the burial site of a local Confederate soldier who was killed during the battle. Continue 500 yards to see the **32nd Indiana Infantry Monument** and the **49th Ohio Infantry Monument** at the intersection of Alexander Bridge Road and Brotherton Road. Turning northeast (left) onto Brotherton Road and traveling 350 yards brings you to a trail north of the road. Follow this path 370 feet to the **Philemon P. Baldwin Death Monument** where the Union colonel was killed instantly while leading a charge.

Continue on Brotherton Road 500 yards beyond a small creek. South of the road stands the **Army of Tennessee, First Headquarters Monument** where the overall Confederate commander, Gen. Braxton Bragg, planned the

A SIMPLE HEADSTONE stands over the grave of John Ingraham, a private soldier in the 1st Georgia Battalion who was killed at Chickamauga. Before the war, Ingraham had lived on the battlefield.

initial assault. At the intersection of Brotherton Road and Jay's Mill Road is the **Jay's Mill Site**, northwest of the crossroads. The ground surrounding the old mill served as a Confederate staging area during the battle. Confederate forces attacking from this area opened the battle on September 19. A short distance north of the mill site, at the intersection of Jay's Mill Road and Reed's Bridge Road, you'll find the **7th Pennsylvania Cavalry Monument** and the **4th U.S. Cavalry Monument**.

Head south on Jay's Mill Road and then northwest (right) on Alexander Bridge Road to return to the main Confederate line. After traveling just over one-half mile, you'll come to the **Winfrey House Site** south of the road. Heavy fighting erupted north and west of the house that stood here during the battle. Continue 250 yards to a path south of the road. This leads to the **Preston Smith Mortal Wounding Monument** where the Confederate brigadier general was shot after riding into a detachment of Federal infantry. Smith died about an hour after being wounded. Nearby you'll see the **13th Indiana Infantry Monument**, the **79th Illinois Infantry Monument**, the **89th Illinois**

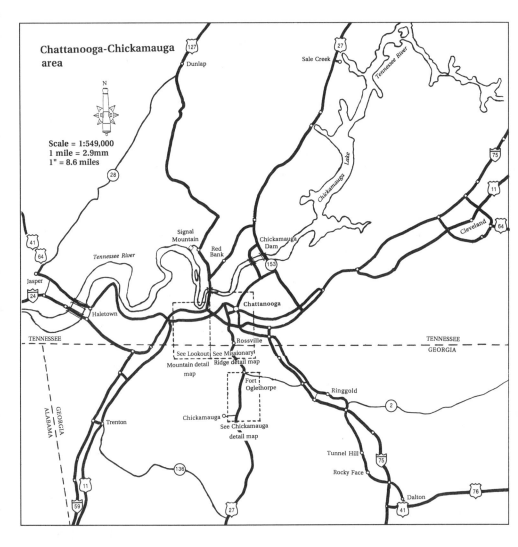

Chattanooga-Chickamauga area

Scale = 1:549,000
1 mile = 2.9mm
1" = 8.6 miles

Infantry Monument, and the **77th Pennsylvania Infantry Monument**.

Now turn southwest (left) onto Brotherton Road and you'll soon pass through the **Brock Field**, scene of heavy and repeated fighting. Longstreet's massive frontal attack that broke the Union line originated in this area. Immediately after crossing a small creek, you'll see a group of regimentals south of the road. These include the **1st Ohio Artillery Monument**, the **41st Ohio Infantry Monument**, the **124th Ohio Infantry Monument**, the **13th and 154th Tennessee Infantry Monument**, the **19th Tennessee Infantry Monument**, the **31st Tennessee Infantry Monument**, and the **33rd Tennessee Infantry Monument**. The **John Brock House Site** is located 200 yards south of the road. Continuing west takes you past the **31st Indiana Infantry Monument**, the **4th Georgia**

Sharpshooters Monument, the **24th Ohio Infantry Monument**, the **105th Ohio Infantry Monument**, and the **Bushrod Rust Johnson Division Monument**.

When you reach Lafayette Road, you may want to turn north (right) to see the rest of the Confederate line. Near the intersection you'll see the **Army of Tennessee, Simon B. Buckner's Corps Headquarters Monument**. This position also marks the site of the **Army of Tennessee, Left Wing, First Headquarters Site** of James Longstreet's command. You'll come back to the cabin across the road later. Head north to the intersection of Poe Road and look east (right) to see the **Georgia Monument**, one of the finest memorials on the field. Continue more than one-half mile to find the rebuilt **Elijah Kelly House** and **Kelly Field**, which spreads north and east of the cabin. In the field north of the cabin, you'll find the **4th U.S. Artillery Monument**, the **47th Georgia Infantry Monument**, the **87th Indiana Infantry Monument**, the **60th North Carolina Infantry Monument**, the **1st Ohio Artillery Monument**, the **20th Ohio Independent Artillery Monument**, and the **15th Ohio Infantry Monument**. Continue along Lafayette Road and turn east (right) onto Alexander Bridge Road.

Now head south on Battle Line Road at the intersection. This takes you past the scene of heavy fighting late in the battle when Confederate troops pushed the Federals west. You may wish to walk the path west of the intersection to see the **30th** and the **35th Indiana Infantry Monuments**. You can see many more regimentals along this route, including the **15th U.S. Infantry Monument**, the **16th**

A VIEW FROM THE WOODS into Kelly Field shows the Edward Augustin King Monument (foreground), where the Union colonel was killed by gunfire, and the rebuilt Kelly House (background).

THE 16th UNITED STATES INFANTRY MONUMENT on Battle Line Road memorializes a Federal sharpshooter taking aim at an onrushing Confederate attack.

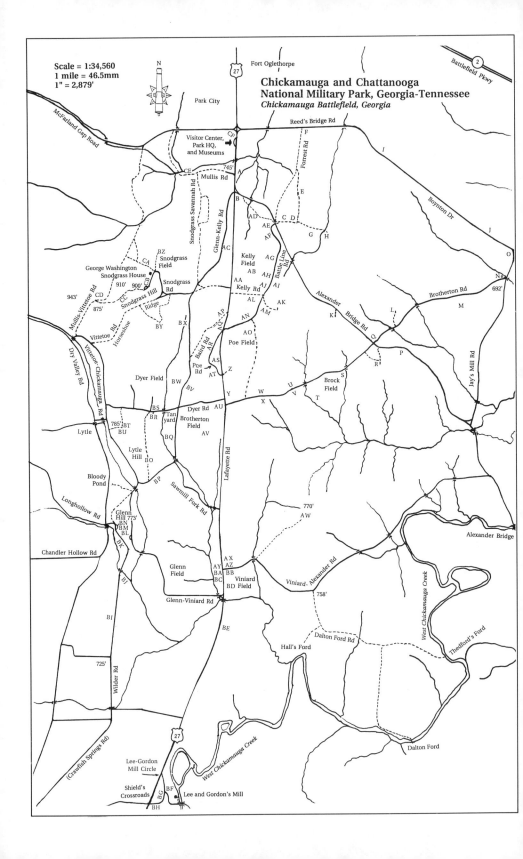

Key to Features on Chickamauga Map

A Florida Monument
B Kentucky Monument
C Peyton H. Colquitt Death Monument
D Benjamin H. Helm Mortal Wounding Monument
E Army of Tennessee, Reserve Corps HQ Monument (William H. T. Walker)
F Tennessee Artillery (U.S.V.) Monument
G Army of Tennessee, D. H. Hill's Corps HQ Monument
H Army of Tennessee, Right Wing HQ Monument (Leonidas Polk)
I 2nd Minnesota Infantry Monument
J 2nd Illinois Artillery Monument
    85th Illinois Infantry Monument
    86th Illinois Infantry Monument
    125th Illinois Infantry Monument
    52nd Ohio Infantry Monument
    69th Ohio Infantry Monument
K John Ingraham Grave
L Philemon P. Baldwin Death Monument
    4th Michigan Cavalry Monument
    1st Ohio Infantry Monument
    93rd Ohio Infantry Monument
    78th Indiana Infantry Monument
M Army of Tennessee, First HQ Monument (Braxton Bragg)
N Jay's Mill Site
    Army of Tennessee, Cavalry Corps HQ Monument (Nathan B. Forrest)
O 7th Pennsylvania Cavalry Monument
    4th U.S. Cavalry Monument
P Winfrey House Site
Q 32nd Indiana Infantry Monument
    49th Ohio Infantry Monument
R Preston Smith Mortal Wounding Monument
    13th Indiana Infantry Monument
    79th Illinois Infantry Monument
    89th Illinois Infantry Monument
    77th Pennsylvania Infantry Monument
S 1st Ohio Artillery Monument
    41st Ohio Infantry Monument
    124th Ohio Infantry Monument
    13th and 154th Tennessee Infantry Monument
    19th Tennessee Infantry Monument
    31st Tennessee Infantry Monument
    33rd Tennessee Infantry Monument

T John Brock House Site
U 31st Indiana Infantry Monument
    4th Georgia Sharpshooters Monument
V 24th Ohio Infantry Monument
W 105th Ohio Infantry Monument
X Bushrod Johnson Division Monument
Y Army of Tennessee, Left Wing, First HQ Site (James Longstreet)
    Army of Tennessee, Simon B. Buckner's Corps HQ Monument
Z Georgia Monument
AA Elijah Kelly House (rebuilt)
AB 4th U.S. Artillery Monument
    47th Georgia Infantry Monument
    87th Indiana Infantry Monument
    60th North Carolina Infantry Monument
    1st Ohio Artillery Monument
    20th Ohio Independent Artillery Monument
    15th Ohio Infantry Monument
AC 2nd Minnesota Infantry Monument
AD 30th Indiana Infantry Monument
    35th Indiana Infantry Monument
AE 15th U.S. Infantry Monument
    16th U.S. Infantry Monument
    18th U.S. Infantry Monument
    19th U.S. Infantry Monument
    2nd Ohio Infantry Monument
    33rd Ohio Infantry Monument
    10th Wisconsin Infantry Monument
AF 4th Indiana Artillery Monument
    38th Indiana Infantry Monument
    94th Ohio Infantry Monument
AG 24th Illinois Infantry Monument
    79th Pennsylvania Infantry Monument
    1st Wisconsin Infantry Monument
    21st Wisconsin Infantry Monument
AH 5th Indiana Artillery Monument
    6th Indiana Infantry Monument
    32nd Indiana Infantry Monument
    5th Kentucky Infantry Monument
AI 31st Indiana Infantry Monument
    1st Kentucky Infantry Monument
    2nd Kentucky Infantry Monument
    1st Ohio Artillery Monument
    90th Ohio Infantry Monument
AJ 9th Indiana Infantry Monument
    10th Indiana Infantry Monument
    36th Indiana Infantry Monument
    74th Indiana Infantry Monument
    6th Kentucky Infantry Monument
    23rd Kentucky Infantry Monument
    1st Ohio Artillery Monument
    6th Ohio Infantry Monument
    11th Ohio Infantry Monument

    24th Ohio Infantry Monument
    41st Ohio Infantry Monument
AK James Deshler Death Monument
AL Edward A. King Death Monument
AM Texas Monument
AN 21st Indiana Artillery Monument
    36th Ohio Infantry Monument
    92nd Ohio Infantry Monument
AO Alabama Monument
AP 68th Indiana Infantry Monument
AQ Army of the Cumberland, 14th Corps First HQ Monument (George H. Thomas)
AR 4th U.S. Artillery Monument
    10th Indiana Infantry Monument
    74th Indiana Infantry Monument
    75th Indiana Infantry Monument
    19th Indiana Infantry Monument
    1st Ohio Artillery Monument
    14th Ohio Infantry Monument
    31st Ohio Infantry Monument
    105th Ohio Infantry Monument
    101st Indiana Infantry Monument
AS Larkin H. Poe House Site
AT 2nd Georgia Infantry Monument
    15th Georgia Infantry Monument
    17th Georgia Infantry Monument
    20th Georgia Infantry Monument
    Havis' Georgia Battery Monument
    Georgia Massenburg Battery Monument
    1st Michigan Artillery Monument
    17th Ohio Infantry Monument
    32nd Tennessee Infantry Monument
AU George Brotherton House (rebuilt)
AV 25th Illinois Infantry Monument
    92nd Illinois Infantry Monument
    7th Indiana Artillery Monument
    18th Indiana Artillery Monument
    19th Indiana Artillery Monument
    9th Indiana Infantry Monument
    37th Indiana Infantry Monument
    44th Indiana Infantry Monument
    86th Indiana Infantry Monument
    8th Kansas Infantry Monument
    11th Michigan Infantry Monument
    41st Ohio Infantry Monument
    74th Ohio Infantry Monument
    26th Pennsylvania Independent Battery Monument
    15th Wisconsin Infantry Monument
    Bledsoe's Missouri (C.S.A.) Battery Monument
AW Army of Tennessee, Second HQ Monument (Braxton Bragg)
AX Log School House Site
AY Hans C. Heg Death Monument

(Continued)

(Continued from previous page)

AZ 15th Georgia Infantry Monument
  17th Georgia Infantry Monument
  20th Georgia Infantry Monument
  25th Illinois Infantry Monument
  35th Illinois Infantry Monument
  8th Kansas Infantry Monument
  26th Ohio Infantry Monument
  15th Wisconsin Infantry Monument
BA 1st Illinois Artillery Monument
BB 21st Illinois Infantry Monument
  22nd Illinois Infantry Monument
  27th Illinois Infantry Monument
  38th Illinois Infantry Monument
  42nd Illinois Infantry Monument
  51st Illinois Infantry Monument
  100th Illinois Infantry Monument
  8th Indiana Artillery Monument
  58th Indiana Infantry Monument
  81st Indiana Infantry Monument
  2nd Minnesota Artillery Monument
  101st Ohio Infantry Monument
  13th Michigan Infantry Monument
BC Viniard House Site
BD Army of the Cumberland, 20th Corps HQ Monument (Alexander M. McCook)
BE 35th Indiana Infantry Monument
  51st Ohio Infantry Monument
  99th Ohio Infantry Monument
  3rd Wisconsin Artillery Monument
BF 4th Georgia Cavalry Monument
BG Army of the Cumberland, 21st Corps HQ Monument (Thomas L. Crittenden)
BH 3rd Georgia Infantry Monument
  2nd Georgia Cavalry Monument
  3rd Georgia Cavalry Monument
  36th Illinois Infantry Monument
BI 59th Illinois Infantry Monument
  74th Illinois Infantry Monument
  75th Illinois Infantry Monument
  5th Wisconsin Artillery Monument
BJ Cave Spring
BK Chicago Board of Trade Battery Monument
  98th Illinois Infantry Monument
  123rd Illinois Infantry Monument
  17th Indiana Mounted Infantry Monument

22nd Indiana Infantry Monument
18th Indiana Infantry Monument
4th Indiana Cavalry Monument
2nd Indiana Cavalry Monument
39th Indiana Mounted Infantry Monument
72nd Indiana Mounted Infantry Monument
2nd Kentucky Infantry (C.S.A.) Monument
3rd Kentucky Infantry (C.S.A.) Monument
2nd, 4th, 5th, and 6th Kentucky Cavalry Monument
2nd Michigan Cavalry Monument
21st Michigan Infantry Monument
1st Ohio Cavalry Monument
3rd Ohio Cavalry Monument
4th Ohio Cavalry Monument
10th Ohio Infantry Monument
Ohio Sharpshooters Monument
9th Pennsylvania Cavalry Monument
1st and 3rd Tennessee Cavalry (U.S.V.) Monument
8th Wisconsin Artillery Monument
1st Wisconsin Cavalry Monument
BL John T. Wilder's Brigade Observation Tower
BM Widow Eliza Glenn House Site
BN Army of the Cumberland, First HQ Site (William S. Rosecrans)
BO William H. Lytle Mortal Wounding Monument
BP 36th Illinois Infantry Monument
  88th Illinois Infantry Monument
  11th Indiana Artillery Monument
  21st Michigan Infantry Monument
  24th Wisconsin Infantry Monument
BQ 44th Illinois Infantry Monument
  73rd Illinois Infantry Monument
  104th Illinois Infantry Monument
  42nd Indiana Infantry Monument
  88th Indiana Infantry Monument
  1st Ohio Artillery Monument
BR Army of Tennessee, Left Wing, Second HQ Monument (James Longstreet)
BS Robert Dyer House and Cemetery Sites
BT 15th Pennsylvania Cavalry Monument

BU Army of the Cumberland, Second HQ Monument (William S. Rosecrans)
BV Army of Tennessee, John B. Hood's Corps HQ Monument
BW John B. Hood Wounding Site
BX Blacksmith Shop Site
BY South Carolina Monument
  1st Michigan Artillery Monument
  1st Ohio Artillery Monument
  65th Ohio Infantry Monument
BZ 4th U.S. Artillery Monument
  37th Indiana Infantry Monument
  44th Indiana Infantry Monument
  86th Indiana Infantry Monument
  90th Indiana Infantry Monument
  3rd Kentucky Infantry Monument
  18th Ohio Artillery Monument
  41st Ohio Infantry Monument
  64th Ohio Infantry Monument
  65th Ohio Infantry Monument
  124th Ohio Infantry Monument
  125th Ohio Infantry Monument
CA Army of the Cumberland Final HQ and 14th Corps HQ Monument (George H. Thomas)
CB 19th Illinois Infantry Monument
  58th Indiana Infantry Monument
  74th Indiana Infantry Monument
  82nd Indiana Infantry Monument
  87th Indiana Infantry Monument
  4th Kentucky Infantry Monument
  9th Kentucky Infantry Monument
  10th Kentucky Infantry Monument
  17th Kentucky Infantry Monument
  11th Michigan Infantry Monument
  2nd Minnesota Infantry Monument
  9th Ohio Infantry Monument
  17th Ohio Infantry Monument
  18th Ohio Infantry Monument
  19th Ohio Infantry Monument
  31st Ohio Infantry Monument
CC Army of the Cumberland, Reserve Corps HQ Monument (Gordon Granger)
CD Tennessee Infantry (U.S.V.) Monument
CE Savannah Church Site
CF 88th Indiana Infantry Monument

U.S. Infantry Monument, the 18th U.S. Infantry Monument, the 19th U.S. Infantry Monument, the 2nd Ohio Infantry Monument, the 33rd Ohio Infantry Monument, and the 10th Wisconsin Infantry Monument.

As the road curves southeast and then south, you'll see the 4th Indiana Artillery Monument, the 38th Indiana Infantry Monument, and the 94th Ohio Infantry Monument. More than two dozen regimental monuments follow, including the 1st Wisconsin Infantry Monument, the 21st Wisconsin Infantry Monument, and the 79th Pennsylvania Infantry Monument.

When you reach the intersection with Kelly Road (now a trail), you'll find the Texas Monument. Near this spot a path leads east into the woods. Follow it 555 feet to the James Deshler Death Monument where the Confederate acting brigadier general was killed instantly by a shell. About 320 feet west of the intersection of Battle Line Road and Kelly Road is the Edward Augustin King Death Monument where the Union colonel was killed. Continue south on Battle Line Road 300 yards to a trail south of the road. This leads after a short distance to the Alabama Monument.

Crossing Lafayette Road and stopping at the intersection with Poe Road brings you to the Army of the Cumberland, First 14th Corps Headquarters Monument (north of the intersection) where early in the battle Maj. Gen. George H. Thomas held the Federal line. Continue along Poe Road to see many regimentals including the 14th Ohio Infantry Monument, the 31st Ohio Infantry Monument, the 4th U.S. Artillery Monument, the 1st Michigan Artillery Monument, Havis's Georgia Battery Monument, and the 1st Ohio Artillery Monument. Shortly thereafter you'll pass the Larkin H. Poe House Site, where a prominent battlefield landmark stood. You're now in the area where the mixup in the Union command occurred on September 20. Erroneously believing a gap existed in the Fed-

AT THE BROTHERTON CABIN at Chickamauga Confederates under Lt. Gen. James Longstreet broke through and sent the Yankees reeling. The cannon marks the position of Capt. James F. Culpeper's South Carolina Battery.

eral battle line, Rosecrans shifted troops and created a real gap and an opportunity for the Confederate breakthrough that followed. Extremely vigorous fighting raged through Poe Field, east of Lafayette Road.

Head south on Lafayette Road 250 yards to the rebuilt George Brotherton House, once the center of the great Confederate breakthrough. Many regimentals stand southwest of the Brotherton House in Brotherton Field, including Bledsoe's Missouri (C.S.A.) Battery Monument, the 11th Michigan Infantry Monument, the 8th Kansas Infantry Monument, the 25th Illinois Infantry Monument, and the 74th Ohio Infantry Monument.

Heading south on Lafayette Road takes you to the scene of vicious fighting along the Union right flank. Travel just under one mile to Viniard Field where Union regimentals can be found. Near the intersection of Lafayette Road and Viniard-Alexander Road, you'll pass the Log School House Site, the 15th Wisconsin Infantry Monument, the 15th Georgia Infantry Monument, the 17th Georgia Infantry Monument, the 20th Georgia

Infantry Monument, and the **8th Kansas Infantry Monument.**

Two hundred feet west of the road, in front of a tree line, stands the **Hans Christian Heg Mortal Wounding Monument.** This Union colonel was shot down on September 20. Regimentals in Viniard Field include the **13th Michigan Infantry Monument,** the **101st Ohio Infantry Monument,** the **2nd Minnesota Artillery Monument,** and the **Army of the Cumberland, 20th Corps Headquarters Monument,** a unit commanded by Maj. Gen. Alexander M. McCook. Across Lafayette Road is the site of the **Viniard House,** another wartime structure that no longer exists. Some 500 yards south of the field on Lafayette Road, you'll find the **51st Ohio Infantry Mon-**ument and the **3rd Wisconsin Artillery Monument.**

Continuing south nearly a mile and heading east on Lee-Gordon Mill Circle carries you toward the rebuilt **Lee and Gordon's Mill,** a structure photographed in the wake of the battle. The mill stands on the west fork of **Chickamauga Creek** and marks the southernmost position of the fighting. You'll also see several monuments on Lee-Gordon Mill Circle, including the **Army of the Cumberland, 21st Corps Headquarters Monument** marking the position of Union Maj. Gen. Thomas L. Crittenden, the **4th Georgia Cavalry Monument,** the **3rd Georgia Infantry Monument,** the **2nd Georgia Cavalry Monument,** and the **3rd Georgia Cavalry Monument.**

LEE AND GORDON'S MILL on Chickamauga Creek marks the site of the Federal right on September 19, 1863. Longstreet's attack drove the Union line from this part of the field.

A short trip to the town of Chickamauga will bring you to the **Gordon-Lee House** at 217 Cove Road, the only surviving battlefield structure. Built in 1847, the house served as Rosecrans's headquarters before the battle and a Union hospital afterward. To reach it from Lafayette Road, turn west (right) on Lee-Gordon Road and travel three-fourths mile. Turn south (left) on Crittenden Avenue, then west (right) on West 10th Street. When you reach Georgia 341, turn south (left), and you'll see the house on the west side of the road. Across the street from the Gordon-Lee House, you may see the **4th Georgia Cavalry Monument**, the **3rd Georgia Confederate Monument**, the **2nd Georgia Cavalry Monument**, and the **3rd Georgia Cavalry Monument**.

You may now wish to tour the Union battle lines that played a key role in the outcome at Chickamauga. Head north on Lafayette Road to Glenn-Viniard Road and turn west (left). As the road jogs north, you'll pass south of **Glenn Field**, part of the ground where the Confederate breakthrough pushed the Union army into retreat. As you reach **Glenn Hill**, you'll see **John T. Wilder's Brigade Observation Tower**, an eighty-five-foot-tall memorial to Colonel Wilder's Union "lightning brigade." Equipped with seven-shot Spencer repeating carbines, Wilder's brigade briefly checked part of Longstreet's breakthrough but soon abandoned the position. The tower is built on the site of the **Widow Eliza Glenn House**, which served as Rosecrans's headquarters from the start of the battle until Longstreet's attack. More than two dozen regimentals are in the area, including the **Chicago Board of Trade Battery Monument**, the **Ohio Sharpshooters Monument**, the **72nd Indiana Mounted Infantry Monument**, the **9th Pennsylvania Cavalry Monument**, the **1st Wisconsin Cavalry Monument**, the **3rd Ohio Cavalry Monument**, and the **1st and 3rd Tennessee Cavalry (U.S.V.) Monument**.

As you continue north, note where you cross a small stream. About 800 feet west of this

THE WILDER BRIGADE TOWER commemorates Col. John T. Wilder's brigade of Illinois and Indiana men who held this ground during much of Longstreet's attack. It was built on the site of the Widow Glenn House, Rosecrans's headquarters during part of the battle.

spot is the site of **Bloody Pond**, a wartime watering hole. Wounded soldiers crawled to Bloody Pond and stained the water red. The pond is now virtually dry. The site can also be reached on Dry Valley Road.

Stay on Glenn-Kelly Road as you cross Vittetoe-Chickamauga Road. Shortly after crossing, you'll see a trail heading north into the woods toward **Lytle Hill**. The 600-foot path leads to the **William Haines Lytle Mortal Wounding Monument**, where the Union brigadier general fell on September 20 while leading a counterattack. Shot in the head, Lytle died several hours later. Across the road and slightly north of the trail, you'll find a group of regimentals including the **24th Wisconsin**

GLENN FIELD and its many regimental monuments stand out in this view from the top of the Wilder Brigade Tower. Woods cover much of the southern portion of the battlefield.

Infantry Monument and the **88th Illinois Infantry Monument.** Continuing north brings you to another set of regimentals that includes the **44th Illinois Infantry Monument** and the **88th Indiana Infantry Monument.**

When you reach Dyer Road, turn west (left) to see a group of important sites. After his crushing attack, Longstreet established the **Army of Tennessee, Second Left Wing Headquarters,** marked by a monument. North of this marker is the site of the **Robert Dyer House,** around which the battle raged as the Confederates turned the Yankees northward. A short distance west of this position is the **Dyer Family Cemetery.** About 175 yards west of this spot, you'll see a trail leading south from the road. The path leads to the **Army of the Cum-**

berland, Second Headquarters Monument** where Rosecrans briefly established a base before retreating northward. Beside Rosecrans's headquarters stands the **15th Pennsylvania Cavalry Monument.**

Returning to Glenn-Kelly Road and heading north takes you to the **Army of Tennessee, John Bell Hood's Corps Headquarters Monument,** east of the road. Across the road is a path through the woods to the **John Bell Hood Wounding Site,** where the Confederate major general was shot in the right leg, the bone splintering, as the Rebels pressed the attack. Soon after surgeons amputated the general's leg. The area of heavy fighting west of the Hood Wounding Site is known as **Dyer Field.** As you continue north you'll pass the **Black-**

54

smith **Shop Site** (nothing remains) and Snodgrass Road, where you should turn west (left).

Although Longstreet's penetrating attack defined the battle of Chickamauga as a Confederate victory, it might have crushed the Army of the Cumberland. Largely due to the efforts of Maj. Gen. George H. Thomas, it didn't. You're now approaching **Snodgrass Hill** where Thomas's Corps held off the onrushing Confederates and allowed most of the Union army to retreat in good order, earning Thomas the sobriquet "Rock of Chickamauga."

As the road bends west you'll see the **George Washington Snodgrass House,** a rebuilt cabin marking the position of the wartime structure. **Snodgrass Field** contains many regimentals and the **Army of the Cumberland Final Headquarters and 14th Corps Headquarters Monument.** On the hill where Federals made their desperate stand, you'll see regimental monuments that include the **9th Ohio Infantry Monument** and the **11th Michigan Infantry Monument.** A trail from this position leads west to the **Army of the Cumberland Reserve Corps Headquarters Monument,** honoring Maj. Gen. Gordon Granger's command, and the **Tennessee Infantry Monument,** also reachable from Mullis-Vittetoe Road. A small connecting trail branches off of Vittetoe Road, south of Snodgrass Hill, and leads to the **South Carolina Monument.** The area of desperate fighting from the Snodgrass House to the Vittetoe-Chickamauga Road is known as **Horseshoe Ridge.**

From Snodgrass Hill the Union defenders eventually broke and fled north, leading to the large-scale fighting that erupted around Chattanooga later in 1863.

THE SNODGRASS CABIN on Snodgrass Hill witnessed the final clash of Chickamauga, where Federal Maj. Gen. George Henry Thomas held the attacking Confederates at bay until the Union army could escape in a semi-organized fashion. Here Thomas earned the sobriquet "Rock of Chickamauga."

Chickamauga and Chattanooga National Military Park

Mailing address: P.O. Box 2128, Fort Oglethorpe, Georgia 30742
Telephone: (706) 866-9241
Park established: August 19, 1890
Area: 9,059 acres

Chickamauga accommodations

The most convenient place to stay when visiting the Chickamauga battlefield is in nearby Chattanooga, Tennessee. This fine city contains twenty-one major hotels and motels with more than 3,000 rooms. The surrounding area offers more places to stay. You can also find accommodations in Dalton, Georgia, about twenty miles south of the park.

Chapter 5

✪　　✪　　✪

Fredericksburg, Chancellorsville, the Wilderness, and Spotsylvania

Except the few sentries along the front, the men had fallen asleep—
the living with the dead. At last, outwearied and depressed
with the desolate scene, my own strength sunk,
and I moved two dead men a little and lay down between them,
making a pillow of the breast of a third. The skirt of his overcoat drawn
over my face helped also to shield me from the bleak winds.
There was some comfort even in this companionship.

—Lt. Col. Joshua Lawrence Chamberlain, 20th Maine Volunteer Infantry,
describing a frigid night on the Fredericksburg battlefield,
December 13, 1862.

Strategically located midway between Washington and Richmond, Fredericksburg, Virginia, inevitably became the focus of battle during the Civil War. Three Civil War campaigns and four major battles raged through Fredericksburg and in the quiet fields west and south of the town. Heavy fighting surged through the town during two battles, making Fredericksburg a significant urban battle site. On a hot summer day in 1988, we drove south on Interstate 95 from Washington, bound for the Fredericksburg battlefields.

Having passed south of the beltway, we made good time through the small towns of Northern Virginia and after a forty-eight-mile drive arrived in **Fredericksburg** (pop. 19,027), a beautiful town on the west bank of the Rappahannock River with many well-preserved historic buildings. Fort A. P. Hill lies to the southeast, the Potomac River to the northeast, Quantico Marine Base to the north, and the Shenandoah Valley region to the north-

west. War touched Fredericksburg first on December 13, 1862, in one of the most poorly executed battles of the Civil War, the battle of Fredericksburg. After Gen. Robert E. Lee's defeat at Antietam, the Confederate commander had moved his army into the Shenandoah Valley where food was abundant.

By November 1862 Lee had 85,000 men facing Maj. Gen. George B. McClellan's 120,000. McClellan stalled and lost command of the Army of the Potomac to Maj. Gen. Ambrose E. Burnside, who by his own assessment was "unfit for high command" despite his successful expedition in North Carolina. Burnside chose Fredericksburg as a jumping off point for a move on Richmond. Slow movements delayed action until the end of November, giving Lee ample time to gather his forces in Fredericksburg and on the hills west of the city. The situation now required a massive attack across the Rappahannock River, through the town, and up several hills and ridges to overtake heavily fortified Confederate positions. It was a ridiculous plan, but one that Burnside pushed for and commenced on December 10 when Federal troops began crossing three pontoon bridges spanning the river.

In the snow, cold, and under a heavy fog, Union troops infiltrated the town by December 12 and initiated frontal attacks westward into the Confederate lines. Confederate artillery and small arms fire cut the Union ranks into pieces, forcing Burnside to retreat to the eastern side of the river and call off his plan. After the bloody battle the casualties amounted to 17,962 dead, wounded, or missing.

The following spring war passed close to Fredericksburg. By now Maj. Gen. Joseph Hooker had replaced Burnside as commander of the Army of the Potomac, and Lee and his chief subordinate, Lt. Gen. Thomas J. "Stonewall" Jackson, were leading their weary troops through a great series of bold victories. Hooker reorganized the Federal army and sent three of his corps to cross the Rapidan River at three fords while his other two corps crossed south of Fredericksburg.

Now potentially surrounded, Lee moved west and the battle of Chancellorsville, named for a tavern at a crossroads, began on May 1, 1863. At first dangerous for Lee, the four-day battle transformed into the best engagement Lee ever fought. The general split his forces and sent Jackson on a daring flank march around the Union army that stunned and crushed the Union center and even wounded the perplexed Federal commander. The great Confederate victory sent the Federals on the retreat but came with a heavy price when Jackson was mortally wounded by friendly fire on May 3 while reconnoitering his lines. As the battle raged at Chancellorsville, a second Union attack charged through Fredericksburg, and this time the Federals captured the town. Midway between Fredericksburg and Chancellorsville, a stiff skirmish erupted at Old Salem Church on the Orange Turnpike.

The densely wooded area around Chancellorsville was again the site of heavy fighting the following spring. On May 3, 1864, the Army of the Potomac crossed the Rapidan River northwest of Chancellorsville and faced Lee's army in a thickly overgrown region known as the Wilderness. The greatest movement of the war had now begun, the May or Overland campaign. The new Union commander was a decisive man from the west, Lt. Gen. Ulysses S. Grant, who commanded all Federal armies. (The commander of the Army of the Potomac was Maj. Gen. George G. Meade, victor of Gettysburg.)

Grant's 118,700 men now constituted the largest force in military history. Lee faced Grant with about 61,025 Confederates, many in entrenched positions. A ghastly series of battles now took place, the first of which was the battle of the Wilderness on May 5 to 7. The landscape was so thickly wooded that effective command by officers was impossible. The confusion was heightened when a region of brush caught fire, killing many wounded soldiers who were unable to crawl to safety. The casualties amounted to 25,416 dead, wounded, or missing.

Although Grant's army sustained severe losses in this action, Grant did not retreat as former Union commanders had. Instead, he repeatedly marched southeast and turned Lee's right flank, forcing the Confederate commander south toward Richmond. The armies raced to possess Spotsylvania Court House, an important junction, where the Confederates eventually entrenched and awaited the Yankees. The fighting at Spotsylvania erupted on May 9 and continued for eleven days before the Confederates broke and fled south. The casualties at Spotsylvania totaled nearly 30,000. Locked in a bulldog grip, the struggling armies continued a nearly constant series of battles south toward Richmond. The major ones that followed Spotsylvania are described along with Richmond in chapter 8.

Fredericksburg Tour

When you reach Fredericksburg, the best place to start is the **Fredericksburg and Spotsylvania National Military Park**, whose **Visitor Center** can be found on Lafayette Boulevard west of Willis Street. Throughout the first part of the Fredericksburg tour see the downtown Fredericksburg map (p. 62). The visitor center contains a fine museum with relics from the surrounding battlefields. Immediately west of the visitor center, you'll see the **Stone Wall** that extends 500 yards to the north. During the battle it served as a natural breastwork. Confederate soldiers posted here on December 13, 1862, hid in a **Sunken Road** behind the wall and fired on waves of Union attackers. The rise you see west of Sunken Road is **Marye's Heights**, the objective of the Union frontal attack during the first battle. Here Confederate artillery posted on the ridge smashed the Union ranks relentlessly.

If you walk north along Sunken Road, you'll come to the **Thomas Reade Rootes Cobb Monument**, marking the spot where the Confederate colonel, commander of "Cobb's Legion," was mortally wounded on December 13, 1862. West of the monument, up on Marye's Heights, is the **Willis House**, a postwar structure that replaces the earlier house. East of Sunken Road you'll find the **Martha Stevens House Ruin and Cemetery**. After he was hit by a minié bullet, Cobb died in the Stevens house. The wartime owner, who helped wounded Confederates during the battle, died in 1888 and is buried beside the foundation of her house. Immediately north of the Stevens House, you'll find the **Innis House**, a structure hit by small arms fire during the first battle. The house shows extensive bullet damage. From here you may wish to walk two blocks east on Mercer Street to the **Stratton House** on the northwest corner of Mercer and Littlepage Streets, a landmark reached by many Union troops attempting to charge the stone

THE STONE WALL along the base of Marye's Heights served as a breastwork that allowed Confederates to fight off repeated frontal assaults from the Yankees during the battle of Fredericksburg.

THE INNIS HOUSE at the base of Marye's Heights lay directly in the Federal line of fire. Many bullet holes in the structure's clapboards are still visible.

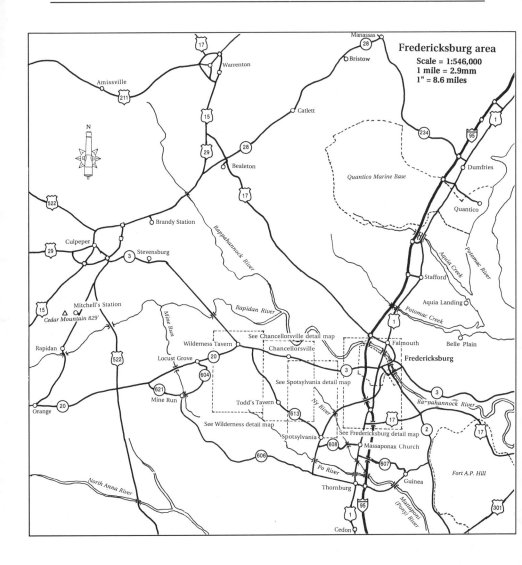

wall. The house served as shelter for sharpshooters attempting to pick off Confederates behind the wall. Three blocks northeast, at the northwest corner of Hanover and Lee streets, you'll find the **Rowe House**, another wartime structure that served as a barricade for attacking Union troops.

If you walk back to the Sunken Road, you can see the **Richard Rowland Kirkland Monument** honoring a Confederate sergeant—called the "Angel of Marye's Heights"—who aided wounded troops during the first battle. The impressive estate across the Sunken Road from the Kirkland Monument is the **John Lawrence Marye House**, "Brompton," a commanding brick mansion that now serves as housing for the president of Mary Washington College. The structure was a center of activity during all of the Fredericksburg campaigns, and a haunting series of photographs made on the grounds recorded wounded soldiers from the Wilderness around a large tree still visible southeast of the house.

Having explored the Sunken Road area, you may wish to return to your car to survey the town. Traveling east on Lafayette Boulevard, turning north (left) on Prince Edward Street, and heading west (left) on Amelia Street will bring you to the **Confederate Cemetery**, located within the old **City Cemetery**. Many distinguished Confederate officers are buried in the City Cemetery, including Brig. Gen. Seth M. Barton, Maj. J. Horace Lacy (owner of two famous Fredericksburg area houses), Maj. Gen. Dabney H. Maury, Brig. Gen. Abner M. Perrin, Brig. Gen. Daniel Ruggles, Brig. Gen. Henry Hopkins Sibley, and Maj. Gen. Carter L. Stevenson.

Heading east on William Street takes you past the **Old Slave Auction Block** at the corner of William and Charles Streets. Turning south (right) onto Princess Anne Street will take you past the towering spire of **St. George's Episcopal Church** and, just south of it, the **Stafford County Court House**, both artillery

marks for Union guns during the first battle. St. George's served as a hospital in the wake of each of the area battles. Artillery damage from the first battle of Fredericksburg is visible in the church's front pillar.

If you head east one block on Charlotte Street, you'll come to the **Fredericksburg Visitor Center** where you can collect literature relating to local sites of interest. From there, you may wish to travel north on Caroline Street until you reach William Street, where you should turn east (right). This will carry you over the **Rappahannock River**, past Scott's Island, and on to **Chatham Heights** on the east bank of the river in **Falmouth** (pop. 970). Here you may wish to turn left onto a road where you see the Park Service sign for Chatham Mansion. This will bring you to the **J. Horace Lacy Estate**, "Chatham," a prominent landmark during the Fredericksburg battles. Chatham is now a museum and headquarters for the Park Service, but during the war the house served as headquarters for five Union generals: Ambrose E. Burnside, John Gibbon, Rufus King, Irvin McDowell, and Edwin V. Sumner. During the two Fredericksburg battles, the grounds

TWO SEPARATE BATTLES raged through downtown Fredericksburg and its Princess Anne Street, on which you can see the towers of the Stafford County Courthouse and St. George's Episcopal Church.

THE J. HORACE LACY ESTATE, "Chatham," stands at Falmouth across the Rappahannock River from Fredericksburg. The house served as headquarters for five Union generals during the war, and the ridge on which it sits was a commanding artillery position.

Fredericksburg, Virginia
Downtown
Scale = 1:28,173
1 mile = 56.6mm
1" = 2,348'

Key to Features on Downtown Fredericksburg map

A J. Horace Lacy Estate, "Chatham"
B Old Stone Warehouse/Museum
C Center for Creative Arts (Silversmith House)
D Rocky Lane and City Dock
E Hugh Mercer Apothecary Shop
F Fredericksburg Visitor Center
G Rising Sun Tavern
H Town Hall
I St. George's Episcopal Church and Cemetery
J Stafford County Court House
K Baptist Church
L George Washington Masonic Lodge no. 4 and Museum
M St. James House
N Mary Washington House
O Old Slave Auction Block
P James Monroe Law Office
Q Masonic Cemetery
R Presbyterian Church
S Fielding Lewis House, "Kenmore"
T Thomas Jefferson Religious Freedom Monument
U Mary Washington Grave and Monument
V Hugh Mercer Monument
W City and Confederate Cemeteries
X Rowe House
Y Stratton House
Z Richard Rowland Kirkland Monument
AA Innis House
AB Martha Stevens House Ruin and Cemetery
AC National Park Service Visitor Center
AD John Lawrence Marye House, "Brompton"
AE Willis House
AF Thomas R. R. Cobb Monument
AG Willis Cemetery
AH Fredericksburg National Cemetery
AI Andrew A. Humphreys Monument
AJ 127th Pennsylvania Infantry Monument
AK 5th Army Corps Monument

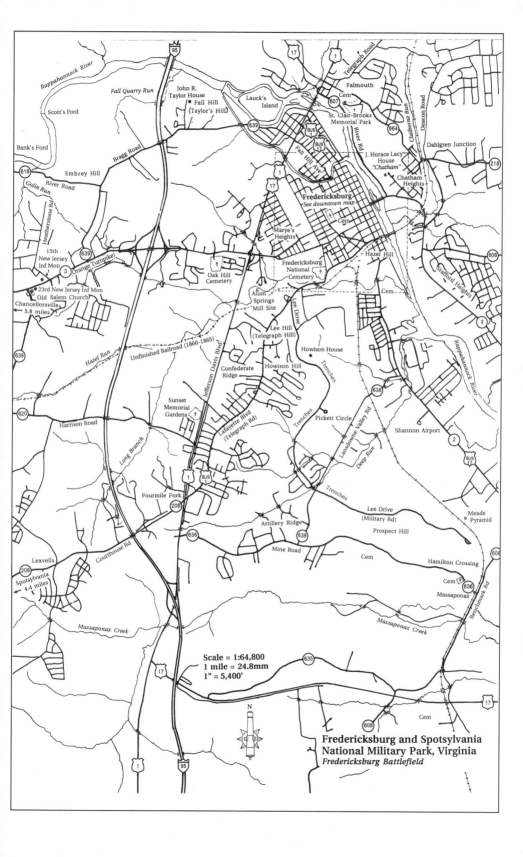

Fredericksburg and Spotsylvania National Military Park, Virginia
Fredericksburg Battlefield

Scale = 1:64,800
1 mile = 24.8mm
1" = 5,400'

supported Union artillery that bombarded the town. In the wake of the battles, Chatham was a hospital in which Clara Barton, Mary E. Walker, and Walt Whitman nursed wounded soldiers. Abraham Lincoln visited the house and reviewed troops on the field just northeast of it. In the Chatham museum you can see many relics including graffiti scrawled on the walls by Union soldiers.

You might now want to see the other preserved parts of the Fredericksburg battlefield. You can do this by leaving Chatham, recrossing the Rappahannock, and turning south (left) on Sophia Street. Just south of the intersection of Sophia and Frederick Streets is **Hazel Hill**, **Rocky Lane**, and the **City Dock**. The **Middle Pontoon Site**, where Burnside's troops made their most prominent crossing during the first battle, spanned the river just east of this area. The troops that crossed the river here marched up Rocky Lane on their way to Marye's Heights.

Next, proceed west on Lafayette Boulevard past the visitor center and turn south (left) onto Lee Drive. You'll now want to switch to the Fredericksburg detail map (p. 63). You will see extensive remains of trenches built along Lee Drive by the defending Confederates. About 650 yards after the turn, you may wish to stop at a woodland trail that leads to the summit of **Lee Hill** where an artillery piece marks the spot on which General Lee watched the Fredericksburg attack. Here the general allegedly said, "It is good that war is so terrible, lest we grow too fond of it." You can further explore the trenches along Lee Drive as it winds past **Howison Hill**, Pickett Circle (a mural marking the location of the mortal wounding of Confederate Brig. Gen. Maxcy Gregg) and the cannon along **Prospect Hill**. When you reach the Confederate artillery lines near the loop and the railroad line, you can see a peculiar monument, the **Meade Pyramid**, east of the railroad. Confederate veterans built the monument to mark the left flank of Meade's line, the point at which they stopped the Union general.

You've now seen most of the Fredericksburg park. Returning to the visitor center, you may wish to park and explore **Fredericksburg National Cemetery** on **Willis Hill** just west of the visitor center. Established in 1865, the cemetery holds the remains of 15,243 Federal soldiers killed in nearby battles. Among the important monuments in the cemetery is the **Andrew Atkinson Humphreys Monument**, honoring the Union major general who served as Meade's chief of staff. You'll also see the **5th Army Corps Monument** and the **127th Pennsylvania Infantry Monument**. Due north of the National Cemetery, over the wall, you might glimpse the **Willis Cemetery**, burial ground of the Willis family.

Chancellorsville Tour

Having seen Fredericksburg proper, your next objective is the Chancellorsville battlefield. To reach it, leave Fredericksburg to the north on Prince Edward Street, which becomes Fall Hill Avenue (Virginia 639). After traveling one and one-half miles, you'll cross an aqueduct. Shortly thereafter you'll see the Fall Hill Professional Park. About 175 yards after this point, turn right into a one-fourth-mile-long lane that leads to the **John R. Taylor House**, "Fall Hill." The privately owned home witnessed Confederate artillery, posted throughout the grounds, raking the Union troops during the first Fredericksburg battle.

Continue west on Virginia 639, also called Bragg Road, past Interstate 95 and for another one and three-fourths miles until the road joins the Orange Turnpike (Virginia 3). You can proceed west on the turnpike one-half mile to the **15th New Jersey Infantry Monument** on the north side of the road. After 300 more yards at a junction where the Old Salem Church Road (Virginia 639) turns south, turn and park at the **Old Salem Church**. During the first battle of Fredericksburg local citizens moved to the church and watched their town as it was shelled. During the Chancellorsville campaign, on May 3, 1863, an intense battle flared

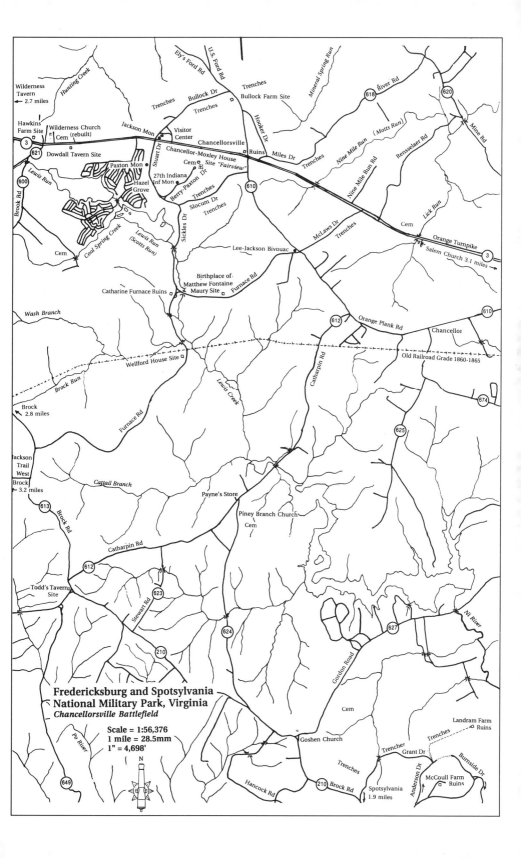

Fredericksburg and Spotsylvania National Military Park, Virginia
Chancellorsville Battlefield

Scale = 1:56,376
1 mile = 28.5mm
1" = 4,698'

BULLET-POCKED OLD SALEM CHURCH was the focus of a fierce battle fought concurrently with the much larger clash at Chancellorsville. Afterward the building served as a hospital.

around the church. The structure's brick walls show extensive damage from small arms fire. Confederate sharpshooters fired from the second story into Maj. Gen. John Sedgwick's oncoming Federals, who overtook the ground only to be driven back toward the town. After the battle, Salem Church became a hospital with dozens of wounded soldiers cramped inside, the blood so abundant it stood in puddles on the church floor. On the grounds of the church, you can see its little cemetery and the **23rd New Jersey Infantry Monument**. Now switch to the Chancellorsville detail map (p. 65). Traveling another two and one-half miles west on the Orange Turnpike brings you to the **Zoan Baptist Church** south of the road. The wartime church, site of a brief meeting between Lee and Jackson on May 1, 1863, was damaged during the war and the present structure built on its site.

Continuing four miles east on the turnpike brings you to the **Chancellorsville Visitor Center** where you can park and explore the museum. The collection inside includes minié bullets scorched in the Wilderness fire, personal belongings of General Lee, a gold coin reputedly given to a local girl by Maj. Gen. James E. B. "Jeb" Stuart, and the bullet supposedly removed from Stonewall Jackson's right hand following his fatal wounding. Between the visitor center and the turnpike, you can see the **Thomas Jonathan "Stonewall" Jackson Monument** marking the spot where Jackson was mistakenly hit by fire from his own troops. A few paces away stands the quartz boulder originally marking the site, placed there in 1888.

Having seen the museum, you may wish to travel north on Bullock Drive past extensive lines of trenches erected by Union troops during the battle. When you reach the intersection

FOUNDATION STONES are all that remain of Chancellorsville Tavern, which marks the center of the Chancellorsville battlefield. The tavern was hit by artillery throughout the battle, including one shell that wounded Maj. Gen. Joseph Hooker, the Federal commander. By battle's end the structure had burned to the ground.

A GRANITE OBELISK marks the spot where Lt. Gen. Thomas J. "Stonewall" Jackson was accidentally shot and mortally wounded by Confederate troops on May 2, 1863.

with Ely's Ford Road (Virginia 610), you'll be at the site of the **Apex of Hooker's Last Line**, visible across the road from the intersection. On the south corner of the intersection stood the **Oscar Bullock Farmhouse**, now completely gone but during the battle a prominent landmark.

Traveling one-half mile south on Ely's Ford Road brings you to the **Chancellorsville Tavern Ruins**, the centerpiece and namesake of the Chancellorsville battlefield. Federal commander Maj. Gen. Joseph Hooker established headquarters at this large brick stagecoach inn, occupied at the time of the battle by Frances Chancellor and a succession of boarders. On May 1, 1863, the large structure became a hospital housing wounded Union soldiers, even as the battle raged around it. Hooker and the Federal center occupied the area until the morning of May 3 when a furious Confederate attack hit the Union army from three sides, sending

it reeling. Hooker himself was a casualty: as he leaned on one of the tall columns supporting the porch, a shell hit the column, knocking him senseless. Rather than relinquishing command, the dazed general continued to fight a confused battle that turned into a Federal rout. The house was blown apart and burned during the battle, and in 1927 a second building on the site burned. Only the foundations of the original structure and the postwar burial site of two infant children remain.

If you cross the turnpike, you can turn west on Slocum Drive, which becomes Sickles Drive, to see extensive wartime trenches. After crossing **Lewis Run**, continue until you reach the **Catherine Furnace Ruins**. Once a great iron manufacturing operation, Catherine Furnace was one of the most prominent landmarks on the Chancellorsville field. On May 2 Jackson and 26,000 Confederate soldiers passed the furnace on their flank march around the Union army. Here they met light resistance, but not enough to disrupt their surprise attack of the following morning. (Hooker somehow believed

CATHERINE FURNACE was a prominent landmark during Stonewall Jackson's flank march around the Union army at the battle of Chancellorsville. The buildings comprising this furnace burned in 1864; only the ruin of the stone stack remains.

Jackson was retreating.) Only the stone stack of Catherine Furnace remains. Traveling south just over one-half mile on the Jackson Trail East brings you to the **Charles C. Wellford House Site** west of the road, another prominent battlefield landmark passed by Jackson on the flank march. A stone foundation marks the site of the Wellford House. The Jackson Trail heads south from the Wellford House, briefly jogs south on Brock Road, then continues west and north parallel to Brock Road. The trail marks the route along which Jackson's men made their famous flank march.

Returning to Catherine Furnace, bear east (right) on Furnace Road and continue about 600 yards to the **Birthplace of Matthew Fontaine Maury Site** marked by a stone monument. The house in which the great Confed-

erate naval officer, the "Pathfinder of the Seas," was born no longer stands. Traveling on just under a mile will bring you to a junction where you can see the **Lee-Jackson Bivouac Monument**. In what would be their final meeting, the two generals conferred at this crossroad on May 2, the night before Jackson's fatal wounding. Lee and Jackson planned strategy for the final part of Chancellorsville, Jackson allegedly sitting on an old cracker box. Continuing on McLaws Drive will bring you to the turnpike, where you should turn west (left).

Should you travel slightly more than two miles west on the turnpike, you'll pass Chancellorsville Tavern and again come to the visitor center. This time you may want to turn south (left) on Stuart Drive. After 400 yards you'll see on the west side of the road the

Elisha Franklin "Bull" Paxton Monument, marking the approximate location where this Confederate brigadier general was killed on May 3, 1863. A journey of another 400 yards brings you to **Hazel Grove**, a clearing where you'll see artillery lined up on a small ridge. Early on May 3 Hooker foolishly abandoned Hazel Grove and retreated toward the turnpike, but not before Jackson's men captured Union artillery here and opened fire on the Federals across the clearing. Turning north (left) on Berry-Paxton Drive leads to the **27th Indiana Infantry Monument** and then to the **Chancellor-Moxley House Site**, "Fairview," the site of a house where the slave overseer employed by Frances Chancellor lived. Federal artillery placed at Fairview on May 3 fired back at Confederate guns at Hazel Grove. This artillery duel persisted for some time. After the battle the house became a hospital. **Fairview Cemetery**, southeast of the house site, contains the graves of many Chancellors and was fought around during the battle of Chancellorsville.

Returning to the Orange Turnpike, head west just under a mile to the **Dowdall Tavern Site**, most of which lies under the eastbound lane of the turnpike. The wooden structure that stood here was another home and tavern in the Chancellor family and was another prominent landmark along Jackson's flank march. Before the battle Federal Maj. Gen. Oliver O. Howard established headquarters at the house. After its capture by Jackson, the structure became a Confederate hospital. Dowdall's Tavern survived the battle only to burn in 1869. Some 300 yards west of the Dowdall Tavern Site, you'll find the rebuilt **Wilderness Baptist Church** north of the turnpike. A prominent landmark on the Chancellorsville battlefield, the church was substantially damaged during the war. The present structure was erected in 1899. Just over one mile west of the church on the turnpike marks the position where, after the sixteen-mile flank march, Stonewall first opened up on the dazed Union army.

Wilderness Tour

You're now approaching the Wilderness battlefield, the campaign now shifting from the spring of 1863 to the spring of 1864. The fortunes of war had changed by this time, and Grant's army had begun its grinding movement toward Richmond. Jackson was dead, and the Confederacy badly outnumbered. Lee's single advantage was an ability to fight a defensive battle while Grant was constantly on the attack.

Now you'll want to consult the Wilderness detail map (p. 71). To start your tour of the Wilderness battlefield, you may wish to continue northwest on Virginia 3 (the Orange Turnpike), which becomes Germanna Plank Road. The split occurs at the stoplight where the Orange Turnpike turns southwest and becomes Virginia 20. This is the wartime road Federals used marching southeast to battle and to the Wilderness field. About four miles northwest of the split, you'll reach a spot where Germanna Plank Road crosses the **Rapidan River**. This is **Germanna Ford**, site of the beginning of Grant's May campaign that led to

GRANT CROSSED THE RAPIDAN at Germanna Ford, where Germanna Plank Road now crosses the river, and began the Overland campaign toward Richmond. The ruins of bridge supports are postwar structures; the Army of the Potomac crossed on pontoon bridges.

the Wilderness, Spotsylvania, and battles around Richmond and Petersburg. At this ford the Army of the Potomac's 5th and 6th Corps crossed pontoon bridges and marched south into the Wilderness on May 4, 1864. Turn around and head southeast on Germanna Plank Road and you'll now be following the route of these Federal soldiers.

Continuing southeast until just after the intersection with the Orange Turnpike will bring you to a pulloff at the **Wilderness Tavern**, a battlefield landmark that now consists of a small brick ruin. Elements of the Federal 5th Corps camped around this abandoned stage tavern after their crossing. Stonewall Jackson's arm was amputated near this site during the battle of Chancellorsville. The several buildings here survived the war but burned in the twentieth century. The preserved stone ruin is that of an outbuilding. The ruins of the tavern lie scattered beneath the highway median.

If you turn around and head southwest on the Orange Turnpike, you can see the area where the battle of the Wilderness began. Travel just over one-half mile and turn left into a small, unmarked road with a gate. From here you can walk along the lane a distance

THE RUINS OF WILDERNESS TAVERN stand near the intersection of Germanna Plank Road and Orange Plank Road. The structure and its outbuildings survived the battle only to burn in the twentieth century.

of about 600 yards to the **Maj. J. Horace Lacy Farm**, "Ellwood," an important wartime building owned by the same Confederate officer who possessed the Chatham mansion in Falmouth. Ellwood served as 5th Corps commander Maj. Gen. Gouverneur K. Warren's headquarters during the Wilderness battle, and here Lt. Gen. U. S. Grant and Maj. Gen. George G. Meade spent time during the fighting. Nearby in the **Lacy Cemetery**, you can see the stone marking the burial spot of Stonewall Jackson's left arm.

Continuing southwest on the Orange Turnpike just over one mile brings you to the **Wilderness Exhibit Shelter** on the north (right) side of the road. The field north and east of the shelter is **Saunders Field**, the area where the Wilderness battle began. The **140th New York Infantry Monument** stands in Saunders Field and pays tribute to the regiment that led the opening attack of the battle, commanded by Col. George Ryan, who was killed in action three days later.

You may wish to continue southwest on the Orange Turnpike until you reach Hill-Ewell Drive, which heads south from the pike. Along this road you'll see trenches constructed by both sides as their lines faced each other early in the battle. About 400 yards after crossing **North Wilderness Run**, you'll pass the **Higgerson Farm Site**, southwest of the road. Nothing remains of this wartime structure. One-half mile after crossing **South Wilderness Run**, as the road curves to the left, you'll pass the **Chewning Farm Site**, located some 400 yards south of the road. This farmhouse stood in the path of the Federal movement early in the battle. When you cross the next little creek, the **Widow Tapp Spring Drain**, you'll be 700 yards north of the **Widow Tapp Farm Site**, another wartime structure that is no more. Passing more trenches along the way, you'll shortly come to an intersection with the Orange Plank Road (Virginia 621).

Turning southwest (right) onto the Orange Plank Road will bring you, after one-half mile,

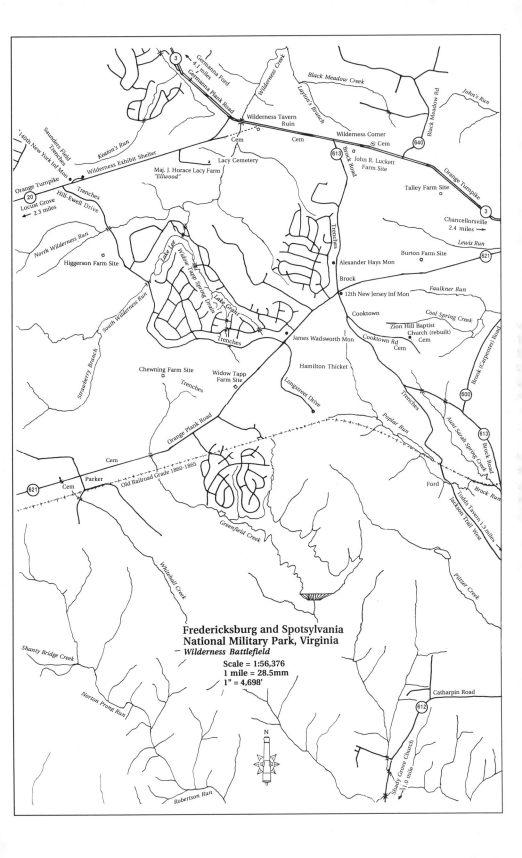

Fredericksburg and Spotsylvania
National Military Park, Virginia
— *Wilderness Battlefield*

Scale = 1:56,376
1 mile = 28.5mm
1" = 4,698'

THE MAJ. J. HORACE LACY FARM, "Ellwood," served as headquarters for the Federal 5th Corps under Maj. Gen. Gouverneur Kemble Warren during the Wilderness battle. A relic from an earlier encounter, Stonewall Jackson's left arm, lies buried in the Lacy Family Cemetery near the house (above).

to the Tapp Farm Site just north (right) of the road. Continuing another two miles brings you to **Parker**, a crossroads with a small tavern, called **Parker's Store** during the war. Along this thick part of the Wilderness, Federal troops formed a line during the first hours of the battle. Reversing direction on the Orange Plank Road, you can turn south (right) onto Longstreet Drive after again passing the Tapp Farm Site. On this road you'll see remnants of trenches erected during the battle. Returning to the Orange Plank Road, continue northeast and you'll see the **James Samuel Wadsworth Monument** marking the position where this Union brigadier general was mortally wounded, hit by a minié bullet in the back of the head on May 6, 1864. He died in a Confederate field hospital two days later. The region immediately south of you is the **Hamilton Thicket**, an area between the main battle lines of May 5 and 6. Travel northeast on the Orange Plank Road until you reach the intersection with Brock Road (Virginia 613) where you should head north (left).

At the junction you'll see the **12th New Jersey Infantry Monument**, and after traveling 600 yards north, you'll come to the **Alexander Hays Monument** on the west side of the road. This Federal brigadier gen-

eral was killed instantly while reconnoitering his troops on the morning of May 5, 1864. Continuing north on Brock Road just over one mile brings you to the **John R. Luckett Farm Site**, just south of the intersection with the Orange Turnpike. The farmhouse, destroyed before 1935, was a jumping off point for a Confederate attack during Chancellorsville and a year later served as a Union 5th Corps hospital.

Now you can reverse direction and head south on Brock Road. After you pass the Orange Plank Road intersection, you may wish to bear left on Cooktown Road, which after one-half mile takes you to the rebuilt **Zion Hill Baptist Church**. The wartime structure that stood here served as a hospital in the wake of each of the battles that surrounded it. Now switch to the Spotsylvania detail map (p. 74). Returning to the Brock Road and heading south will take you past more trenches and, after about three miles, to the site of **Todd's Tavern** located at the intersection of Brock Road and Catharpin Road (Virginia 612). Union Maj. Gen. Winfield Scott Hancock concentrated his 2nd Corps around this site before marching north and joining the Wilderness battle on May 5, 1864. After the battle, the Federal army passed Todd's Tavern on their race southward, and Lieutenant General

Grant, after mistakenly riding near the Confederate lines, slept on the ground at this site on May 7. Meade arrived at the site just after midnight on the eighth and, after conferring with Grant, ordered the cavalry southward. Distant shots rang out, and the battle of Spotsylvania, at a crossroads four miles south, began.

Spotsylvania Tour

Traveling northeast two miles on the Catharpin Road will bring you to the site of **Payne's Store** at the intersection of Piney Branch Road (Virginia 624). Heading south (right) on Piney Branch Road will bring you to the relocated and rebuilt **Piney Branch Church**. Skirmishes between units and major movements of troops occurred at each of these sites between the Wilderness and Spotsylvania. The Federal 9th Corps under Maj. Gen. Ambrose E. Burnside concentrated around the Piney Branch Church after the Wilderness. Continuing south one and three-fourths miles brings you back to Brock Road, which after one-half mile leads to the rebuilt **Goshen Baptist Church** at the intersection with Gordon Road. The wartime structure here witnessed thousands of soldiers marching into the Spotsylvania fight. Continue south 300 yards to the **Alsop Farm Site** where a wartime farmhouse stood east (left) of the road.

Travel on Brock Road another three-fourths mile and you can turn northeast (left) onto Grant Drive. Immediately afterward you'll see the **John Sedgwick Monument** on the west side of the road. One of the most

JOHN SEDGWICK, the Union 6th Corps commander at Spotsylvania, proclaimed the Confederates "couldn't hit an elephant at this distance." Moments later he was killed, struck in the head by a minié bullet. The John Sedgwick Monument honors the major general.

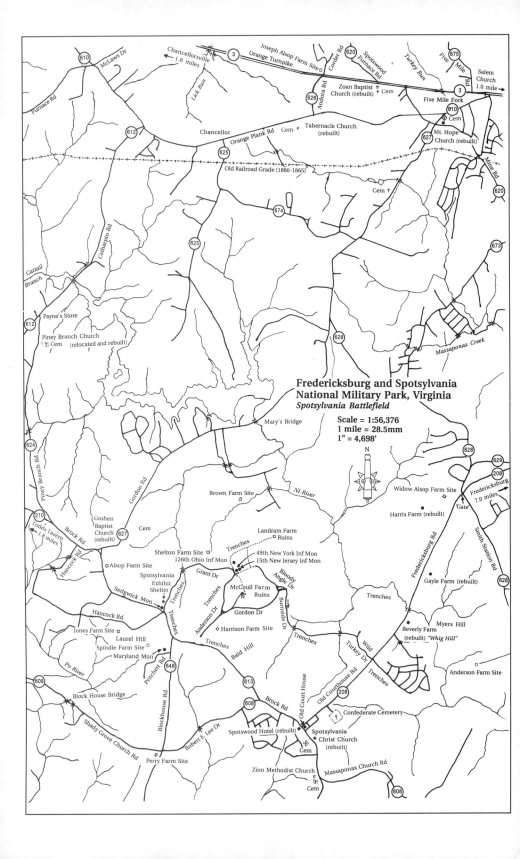

Fredericksburg and Spotsylvania National Military Park, Virginia
Spotsylvania Battlefield

Scale = 1:56,376
1 mile = 28.5mm
1" = 4,698'

beloved officers in the Army of the Potomac, Major General Sedgwick, commanding the 6th Corps, stood near this spot on May 9, 1864, as the battle of Spotsylvania flared about him. Cautioned by his staff, Sedgwick replied, "They couldn't hit an elephant at this distance." Seconds later a minié bullet struck him below the left eye, killing him instantly. Continuing along the road brings you to the **Spotsylvania Exhibit Shelter** and, after curving north and east, to the central and climactic field at Spotsylvania.

You may wish to park and explore the **Bloody Angle** where heavily entrenched Confederates, who won the race to this vital crossroads, blocked the Union push to the south. Instead of a relatively brief battle like that at the Wilderness, the fight at Spotsylvania would be a micro-siege lasting from May 8 through May 21, 1864. Union attackers faced the well-preserved Confederate trenches in this region, which were formed in a giant C-shape and nicknamed the Mule Shoe. Numerous assaults plunged toward the Confederate cen-

ter and were repelled with heavy losses. The musket fire in this area was among the heaviest of the war. Only after repeated attempts would the Yankees eventually break the Rebel lines and force the Confederates south toward Richmond.

In the field north of the Bloody Angle stand three monuments to Union regiments that spearheaded attacks. They are the **15th New Jersey Infantry Monument**, the **49th New York Infantry Monument**, and the **126th Ohio Infantry Monument**. A footpath that parallels a wood line north of the field leads to the **Landram Farm Ruins** where a stone foundation marks the position of the Landram House. Facing the massive Confederate Mule Shoe, the Landram House served as a launching point for the decisive attack by Maj. Gen. Winfield Scott Hancock that broke the Confederate ranks. Walking back to the Bloody Angle will let you discover a plaque marking the site of a twenty-two-inch oak tree felled by small arms fire in this ferocious battle. The oak

SO HEAVY WAS THE COMBAT in the Mule Shoe at Spotsylvania that a twenty-two-inch oak tree was cut down by small arms fire. The stump, recovered in 1865 by Federal Maj. Gen. Nelson A. Miles, can be seen in the National Museum of American History in Washington (above and at right).

stump, recovered in 1865 by Maj. Gen. Nelson A. Miles, is on display at the National Museum of American History in Washington.

Continue along Anderson Drive, a dead-end road that will take you past trenches along the Confederate lines. As you return northward, you'll pass the **Harrison Farm Site**, which lies south of the road, after 300 yards. This area marks the western end of the Confederate Mule Shoe salient. During the battles the house served as headquarters for Rebel Lt. Gen. Richard S. Ewell. Gen. Robert E. Lee conferred with various officers in and around this house during the Spotsylvania encounter. The general also observed an attack on May 10 from this house, when the young Union Col. Emory Upton briefly broke into the Confederate salient. Traveling east on Gordon Drive allows you to bear left on a small road leading to the **McCoull Farm Ruins**, the principal structure that stood within the Mule Shoe. Now marked by a stone foundation, the McCoull House served as headquarters for Confederate Maj. Gen. Edward Johnson, who was captured during the battle.

You may wish to head east on Gordon Drive again, which will take you past extensive trenches along the eastern side of the Mule Shoe. Continue along Bloody Angle Drive to view the Landram House area as the Confederate defenders saw it. Now heading south will take you to Burnside Drive, across two branches of the **Ni River**, and along Wild Turkey Drive to an intersection with Fredericksburg Road (Virginia 208). Turn north (left) and proceed one-half mile to pass the rebuilt **Beverly Farm**, "Whig Hill," southeast of the road. Union Maj. Gen. Gouverneur K. Warren, commanding the 5th Corps, used the wartime Beverly house as headquarters. The rebuilt **Gayle Farm**, located east of the road one-third mile north of Whig Hill, witnessed an encampment of Maj. Gen. Ambrose Burnside's 9th Corps on May 9, 1864.

Some one-half mile farther north on Fredericksburg Road is the rebuilt **Harris Farm**, which stands west of the road. Here on May

THE LANDRAM HOUSE at Spotsylvania, now marked by foundation ruins, served as Maj. Gen. Winfield Scott Hancock's headquarters, the point from which he launched the decisive attack on the Mule Shoe.

19 Confederate Lt. Gen. Richard S. Ewell encountered Federal resistance that resulted in numerous casualties. About 400 yards northeast of the Harris Farm is the **Widow Alsop Farm Site**, west of the road. Although the house here no longer stands, a famous set of photographs of the dead, made after Ewell's engagement, recorded the scene. A peculiar landmark stood at the intersection of the Fredericksburg Road and the Smith Station Road at the time of the battle. A wooden enclosure called the **Gate** blocked the road here, and at this point Major General Burnside was ordered to establish his command. Instead Burnside marched south to the Gayle Farm, and confusion resulted when the Federals attacked.

You may now wish to return south on Fredericksburg Road, which will become Old Courthouse Road before you reach **Spotsylvania Court House**. Slightly more than one-half mile after crossing Wild Turkey Drive, turn southeast (left) into the **Confederate Cemetery**, a burying ground established in 1866 after local farmers found large numbers of Confederate dead buried across the landscape. Some 600 rebel soldiers lie here. Shortly after the cemetery, you'll come to the town of Spotsylvania Court House, with its rebuilt **Spotswood**

Hotel. In this building Union Major General Miles recovered the famous oak tree stump after the war ended. You'll see nearby the **Old Court House,** after which the town is named.

Heading south on Brock Road takes you to **Spotsylvania Christ Church,** which is partly rebuilt but still marked by damage from small arms fire. Continuing on brings you to **Zion Methodist Church,** a wartime structure that served as a Confederate hospital following the battle. The church's balcony contains the original bloodstained floorboards.

After seeing the Zion Church, you may wish to travel northwest on Brock Road to see the scene of heavy fighting west of the Mule Shoe. After passing through town, travel one mile and you'll see **Bald Hill** east of the road. This area, south of the Harrison Farm Site, witnessed extensive fighting as the Confederates retreated southward. After another one-half mile you'll come to Pritchet Road, where you may wish to turn southwest (left) to see the **Maryland Monument,** which honors the 7th Maryland Infantry's deepest point of attack during the battle's first day. Continuing north on Brock Road, you can turn west (left) onto Hancock Road to see more trenches. But beware: the road is poorly maintained and sometimes difficult to travel. Near the point where the road bends northwest is **Laurel Hill,** scene of heavy fighting throughout the battle. Laurel Hill contains the **Spindle Farm Site** and the **Jones Farm Site,** both overgrown former structures that stood throughout the fight.

For the remainder of the tour see the Fredericksburg area map (p. 60). You can continue by returning to Spotsylvania Court House and heading east on the Massaponax Church Road (Virginia 608). Travel along this road for nearly five miles, following the route of the ambulance that carried Stonewall Jackson after his mortal wounding, to reach **Massaponax Church.** Following the successful Federal attack at Spotsylvania, Grant again turned Lee's right and pushed him south toward Richmond. As the Union armies moved south, the commander held a war council in the front yard of this church, his staff having removed pews so officers could sit. A spectacular sequence of three photographs captured the scene between Grant and his generals, the pews placed around the massive tree in front of the church.

From the church, you may wish to head south on U.S. 1 about two-thirds mile and then turn southeast (left) on Virginia 607. This road continues the route over which Jackson's ambulance passed on May 4, 1863, carrying the wounded commander toward a railroad station that would take him on to Richmond. A journey of nearly five miles brings you to **Guinea's Station** on the Richmond, Fredericksburg, and Petersburg Railroad. Follow the National Park Service signs to the **Thomas C. Chandler Farm,** "Fairfield," where on May 10 Jackson died. Although the main house no longer stands, the **Farm Office Building** contains the room in which the general expired, his last words being "let us pass over the river and rest under the shade of the trees."

Having spent some time in the Jackson room, which contains the clock present when Jackson died, my father and I concluded our tour of the busiest area of battlefields in the eastern theater and headed north for Fredericksburg

STONEWALL JACKSON DIED on May 10, 1863, in the farm office building at the Thomas C. Chandler Farm, "Fairfield," at Guinea's Station.

on Interstate 95. The battlefields in and around Fredericksburg offer one of the greatest tours of Civil War history, and it was a fitting end to see the Jackson shrine at the little station by the railroad.

Fredericksburg and Spotsylvania National Military Park

Mailing address: 120 Chatham Lane, Fredericksburg, Virginia 22405-2508
Telephone: (540) 373-6122
Park established: February 14, 1927
Area: 8,352 acres

Fredericksburg National Cemetery

Established: July 15, 1865
Area: 12 acres
Civil War interments: 15,243

Confederate Cemetery

(Fredericksburg, within City Cemetery)
Established: October 1867
Area: about 2 acres
Civil War interments: 3,353

Confederate Cemetery

(Spotsylvania)
Established: 1866
Area: 5 acres
Civil War interments: about 600

Fredericksburg accommodations

Motels convenient to all of the battlefields surrounding Fredericksburg can be found in town or close to it. Fredericksburg has ten hotels, motels, and inns, and provides more than one thousand rooms.

Chapter 6

✪   ✪   ✪

Gettysburg

We opened on these troops and batteries
with the best we had in the shop,
and appeared to do them considerable damage,
but meanwhile Pickett's division just seemed to
melt away in the blue musketry smoke which now covered the hill.
Nothing but stragglers came back.

—Col. Edward Porter Alexander, Chief of Artillery, Longstreet's Corps,
describing Pickett's Charge at Gettysburg
on the afternoon of July 3, 1863.

Gettysburg, Pennsylvania (pop. 7,025), is the king of Civil War sites. Although in recent years the town has been commercialized, the thousands of acres within Gettysburg and in the fields north and south of town comprise the largest and most well-marked Civil War site you can visit. The business of memorializing the battle of Gettysburg began a few months after the event when Abraham Lincoln traveled to sleepy, shell-shocked Gettysburg and delivered his great address. Like Chickamauga and Vicksburg, the serious effort to memorialize what occurred in the park developed in the 1890s. Many significant structures stand on the Gettysburg battlefield, both in and out of the park boundaries, and more than 2,000 monuments, tablets, and markers highlight important actions during the momentous three-day struggle.

As my father and I drove east on U.S. 30 from Chambersburg, the anticipation of again seeing Gettysburg was exhilarating. Though we had been to the battlefield many times, the size and scope of this hallowed ground always allowed something new to crop up. We traveled through Cashtown and approached the battlefield, retracing the route of thousands of Confederate soldiers who marched toward the town. Gettysburg can be reached not only from Chambersburg, but also from Harrisburg, Pennsylvania, to the north; York, Pennsylvania, to the east; Frederick, Maryland, to the south; and Hagerstown, Maryland, to the southwest.

Gettysburg is universally recognized as the great and decisive battle of the Civil War. Yet it occurred, as did the siege and fall of Vicksburg, midway through the war. Gettysburg was the high point of the Confederacy, which would slide into oblivion over the next twenty-two months, and the beginning of an eventual Union military victory. The three-day battle of Gettysburg took place on July 1, 2, and 3, 1863, the result of Gen. Robert E. Lee's second invasion of the North.

Lee's movement, really a gigantic raid, followed the battle of Chancellorsville in May

1863. This decisive Confederate victory emboldened Lee to strike north to gain the initiative from the Yankees, to draw the war away from Virginia, to perhaps gain recognition from Britain or France, and certainly to draw Grant away from his stranglehold on Vicksburg in the west. Lee moved north on June 9 and by the end of the month the Federals, under Maj. Gen. George Gordon Meade, pursued. By happenstance, the armies converged on the railroad center of Gettysburg where Confederate troops, searching for shoes in the town, ran into Union cavalry.

The battle of Gettysburg, originally an accident, spun rapidly out of control as more and more units were pushed in from each side. Lee engaged some 75,000 men versus Meade's 88,289. The battle was really three battles, the first day's fight north and west of the town, and through the town; the decisive second day's fight south of town; and the dramatic third day's fight that sealed the fate of Lee's best, remaining men. After three days of fighting, the greatest battle in the Western Hemisphere produced 7,058 men dead on the fields and another 44,054 wounded or missing. Meade lost one-quarter of his army; Lee nearly forty percent.

Should you travel to Gettysburg on the Confederate route via Chambersburg and Cashtown, you can briefly see the town (Chambersburg) burned by Confederate Maj. Gen. Jubal Early on July 30, 1864, as retaliation for the Federal campaign in the Shenandoah Valley. In tiny Cashtown, seven miles west of Gettysburg on U.S. 30, you may see the **Cashtown Inn**, an historic structure that served as a headquarters for Confederate Lt. Gen. A. P. Hill on July 1, 1863.

Gettysburg Tour

Once you reach Gettysburg, you may want to start at the **Gettysburg National Military Park Visitor Center**, which contains a superb museum of Civil War artifacts. From the center of town, travel south on Baltimore Street, turn right on Steinwehr Avenue, and turn left on Taneytown Road. In the museum you'll see relics such as chairs from the Gettysburg Address speaker's platform, the saddle Lincoln rode to the ceremony, the table on which Stonewall Jackson's arm was amputated, a field desk used by Robert E. Lee, Brig. Gen. John W. Geary's saddle, and uniforms belonging to Brig. Gens. Samuel W. Crawford, James J. Pettigrew, and Samuel K. Zook. An "electric map" uses lights to show how the battle unfolded. In the nearby **Cyclorama Center**, located just to the south, you can see the famous **Gettysburg Cyclorama**, a 356 foot by 26 foot circular painting depicting the battle, completed in 1884 by Paul Philippoteaux. Although the schedule for exhibition changes periodically, the Cyclorama Center frequently displays one of the five known copies of the **Gettysburg Address**, on loan from the Library of Congress. The museum will give you a great warm-up for the park itself.

Gettysburg offers so much to see that the best way to tour the park uses three loops, one covering the first day's field, Culp's Hill, and Cemetery Hill; the second covering the second day's field, the Round Tops, Devil's Den, the Wheatfield, the Angle, and the Confederate lines; and the final loop covering the town and National Cemetery.

Loop One

Consult the Gettysburg detail, North Sector map (p. 82). Take Baltimore Street north from the visitor center until you reach Middle Street, where you should head west. After crossing **Pitzer's Run**, a tiny creek fought along on the first and second days, turn right (north) on Reynolds Avenue, which leads to **McPherson's Ridge**. Along this road you'll find many regimental monuments and, after crossing Meredith Avenue, you'll see on the left a small obelisk back in the woods. This is the **John Fulton Reynolds Death Monument**, marking the spot where the Federal 1st Corps commander, a major general, was killed by a minié bullet just after the battle began.

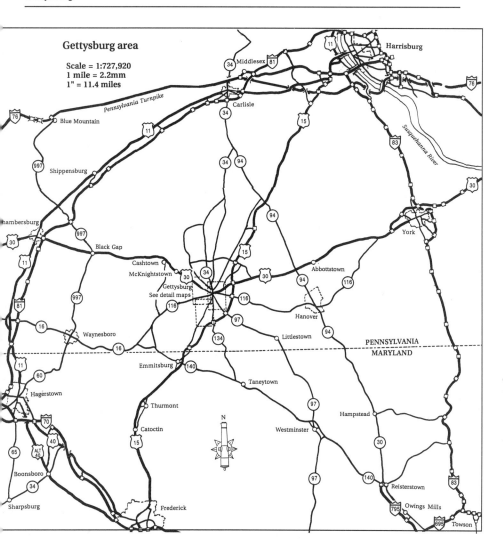

Gettysburg area

Scale = 1:727,920
1 mile = 2.2mm
1" = 11.4 miles

Before reaching the Chambersburg Pike (U.S. 30), you'll see the **Abner Doubleday Monument** and the **Abner Doubleday Headquarters Monument** on the right side of the road. Federal Major General Doubleday took command of the 1st Corps when Reynolds died. Turn left on the Chambersburg Pike and you'll immediately pass the **Edward McPherson Farm**, site of early action in the battle. The barn served as a hospital following the battle. You may wish to travel 250 yards and pull off on the right side of the road. Here you'll see the **John Buford Monument**, recognizing the Union brigadier general whose cavalry started the battle, and the **John Fulton Reynolds Monument**, an equestrian statue honoring the fallen corps commander. The Buford monument contains the cannon tube that fired the first artillery shot of the conflict.

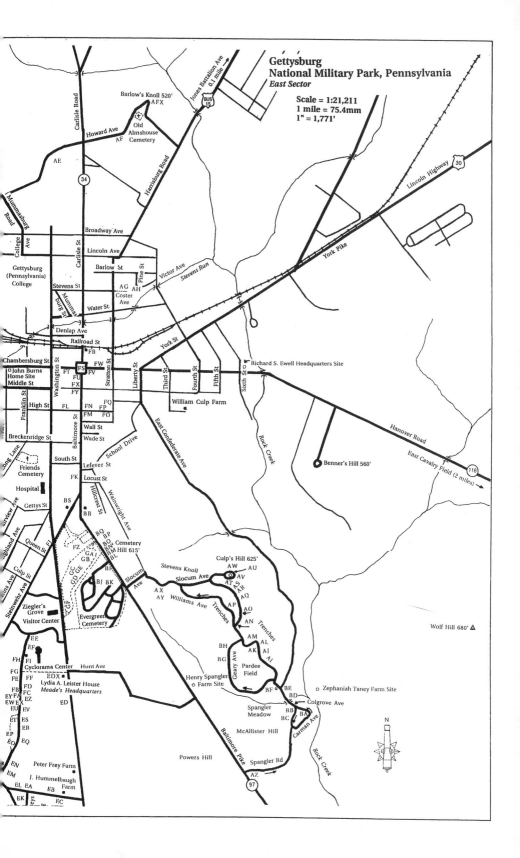

Gettysburg
National Military Park, Pennsylvania
East Sector

Scale = 1:21,211
1 mile = 75.4mm
1" = 1,771'

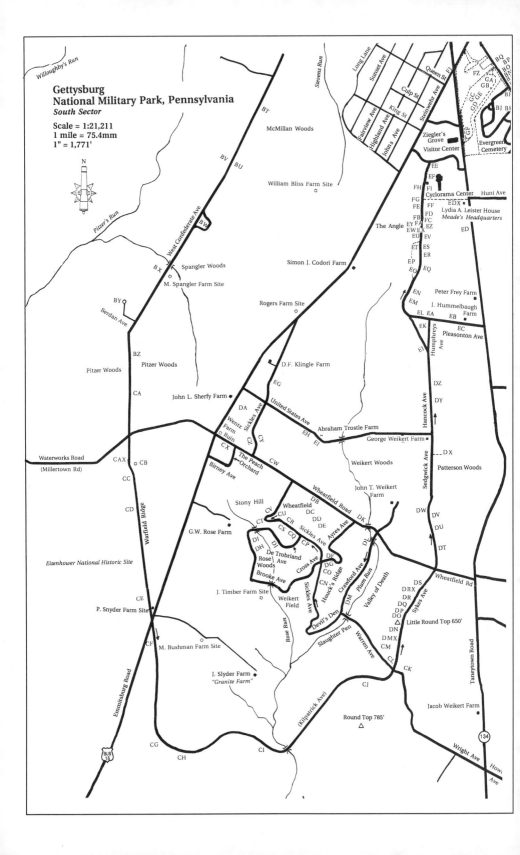

Key to Features on Gettysburg Maps

A 121st Pennsylvania Infantry Monument
B 149th Pennsylvania Infantry Monument
C John Fulton Reynolds Monument
D John Buford Monument
E Mathew B. Brady Pond
F John Burns Monument
G 7th Wisconsin Infantry Monument
H 6th Wisconsin Infantry Monument
I 26th North Carolina Infantry Monument
J 24th Michigan Infantry Monument
K 151st Pennsylvania Infantry Monument
L Abner Doubleday Monument
M John Fulton Reynolds Death Monument
N Abner Doubleday HQ Monument
O 8th Illinois Cavalry Monument
P 143rd Pennsylvania Infantry Monument
Q 84th New York (14th Brooklyn) Infantry Monument
R 6th Wisconsin Infantry Monument
S James Samuel Wadsworth Monument
T 56th Pennsylvania Infantry Monument
U 6th New York Cavalry Monument
V 17th Pennsylvania Cavalry Monument
W 90th Pennsylvania Infantry Monument
X Oak Ridge Observation Tower
Y 12th Massachusetts Infantry Monument
Z 88th Pennsylvania Infantry Monument
AA 83rd New York Infantry Monument
AB 11th Pennsylvania Infantry Monument
AC John Cleveland Robinson Monument
AD 13th Massachusetts Infantry Monument
AE 1st Ohio Battery Monument
AF 26th Wisconsin Infantry Monument
AFX Francis Channing Barlow Monument
AG 154th New York Infantry Monument
AH John Kuhn Brickyard Site
AI 20th Connecticut Infantry Monument
AJ 123rd New York Infantry Monument

AK 29th Pennsylvania Infantry Monument
AL 2nd Maryland Infantry Monument
AM 111th Pennsylvania Infantry Monument
AN John White Geary Monument
AO 23rd Pennsylvania Infantry Monument
AP 67th New York Infantry Monument
AQ 149th New York Infantry Monument
AR 78th and 102nd New York Infantry Monument
AS 150th New York Infantry Monument
AT 1st Maryland Infantry Monument
AU Culp's Hill Observation Tower
AV George Sears Greene Monument
AW 66th Ohio Infantry Monument
AX 5th Maine Battery Monument
AY Henry Warner Slocum Monument
AZ 21st Pennsylvania Cavalry Monument
BA 13th New Jersey Infantry Monument
BB 2nd Massachusetts Infantry Monument
BC 3rd Wisconsin Infantry Monument
BD 27th Indiana Infantry Monument
BE Indiana Monument
BF Spangler's Spring
BG 147th Pennsylvania Infantry Monument
BH 5th Ohio Infantry Monument
BI Evergreen Cemetery Gatehouse
BJ Mary Virginia "Jennie" Wade Grave
BK John Burns Grave
BL 4th Ohio Infantry Monument
BM Winfield Scott Hancock Monument
BN 1st Pennsylvania Artillery Monument
BO 7th West Virginia Infantry Monument
BP Oliver Otis Howard Monument Oliver Otis Howard HQ Monument
BQ 73rd Pennsylvania Infantry Monument
BR McClellan House (Jennie Wade House)
BS Dobbin House Tavern
BSX General HQ, Army of Northern Virginia (Robert E. Lee)
BSY Samuel Simon Schmucker Hall, Lutheran Theological Seminary
BT North Carolina Monument
BU Tennessee Monument
BV Ambrose Powell Hill HQ Monument

BW Robert Edward Lee Virginia Monument
BX Florida Monument
BY First U.S. Sharpshooters Monument
BZ Louisiana Monument
CA Mississippi Monument
CAX James Longstreet HQ Monument
CB Warfield Ridge Observation Tower
CC Georgia Monument
CD South Carolina Monument
CE Arkansas Monument
CF Texas Monument
CG Alabama Monument
CH Confederate Soldiers and Sailors Monument
CI William Wells Monument
CJ 10th Pennsylvania Reserves (38th Pennsylvania Infantry) Monument
CK 20th Maine Infantry Monument
CL 9th Pennsylvania Reserves (38th Pennsylvania Infantry) Monument
CM 83rd Pennsylvania Infantry (Strong Vincent) Monument
CN 4th New York Battery Monument
CO 124th New York Infantry (Augustus VanHorn Ellis) Monument
CP 4th Michigan Infantry Monument
CQ Irish Brigade Monument
CR 66th New York Infantry Monument
CS 32nd Massachusetts Infantry Monument
CT 2nd Massachusetts Sharpshooters Monument
CU 28th Massachusetts Infantry Monument
CV 116th Pennsylvania Infantry Monument
CW 9th Massachusetts Battery (First Position) Monument
CX Pennsylvania Artillery Monument
CY 7th New Jersey Infantry Monument
CZ Excelsior Brigade Monument
DA 73rd New York Infantry Monument
DB Samuel Kosciuszko Zook Monument
DC 1st New York Artillery Monument
DD 27th Connecticut Infantry Monument
DE 81st Pennsylvania Infantry Monument
DF 13th Pennsylvania Reserves (42nd Pennsylvania Infantry) Monument
DG 5th New Hampshire Infantry Monument

(Continued)

(Continued from previous page)

DH 53rd Pennsylvania Infantry Monument
DI 27th Connecticut Infantry Monument
DJ 17th Maine Infantry Monument
DK 96th Pennsylvania Infantry Monument
DL Samuel Wylie Crawford Monument
DM 40th New York Infantry Monument
DMX Strong Vincent Mortal Wounding Monument
DN 44th and 12th New York Infantry Monument
DO 140th New York Infantry (Patrick Henry O'Rorke) Monument
DP 91st Pennsylvania Infantry Monument
DQ Gouverneur Kemble Warren Monument
DR 155th Pennsylvania Infantry Monument
DRX Stephen Hinsdale Weed Monument
DS 121st New York (Emory Upton) Monument
DT 2nd Rhode Island Infantry Monument
DU John Sedgwick Monument
DV George Sykes HQ Monument
DW John Sedgwick HQ Monument
DX New Jersey Brigade Monument
DY William Corby Monument
DZ New York Auxiliary Monument
EA 8th Pennsylvania Cavalry Monument
EB 15th and 50th New York Engineers Monument
EC John Newton HQ Monument
ED Henry Jackson Hunt HQ Monument

EDX General HQ, Army of the Potomac (George Gordon Meade) Monument
EE Alexander Hays Monument
EF Grand Army of the Republic (Albert Woolson) Monument
EG 120th New York Infantry Monument
EH Daniel Edgar Sickles HQ Monument
EI 9th Massachusetts Battery (Final Position) Monument
EJ 1st Minnesota Infantry Monument
EK Pennsylvania Monument
EL Winfield Scott Hancock HQ Monument
EM Vermont (Lewis Addison Grant) Monument
EN 13th Vermont Infantry (George Jerrison Stannard) Monument
EO U.S. Regulars Monument
EP 20th Massachusetts Infantry Monument
EQ John Gibbon Monument
ER 42nd New York Infantry Monument
ES 1st Rhode Island Battery Monument
ET High Water Mark Monument and Copse of Trees
EU 106th Pennsylvania Infantry Monument
EV 1st Pennsylvania Cavalry Monument
EW 72nd Pennsylvania Infantry Monument
EX Lewis Addison Armistead Monument
EY Alonzo Hereford Cushing Monument
EZ Alexander Stewart Webb Monument
FA 71st Pennsylvania Infantry Monument

FB Andrews's Massachusetts Sharpshooters Monument
FC 1st New York Artillery Monument
FD 39th New York Infantry Monument
FE 1st Delaware Infantry Monument
FF George Gordon Meade Monument
FG 12th New Jersey Infantry Monument
FH 111th New York Infantry Monument
FI Abram Bryan Farm
FJ Wagon Hotel Site
FK Farnsworth House Inn
FL Francis Xavier Catholic Church
FM Gettysburg Presbyterian Church
FN Gettysburg Public Library
FO City Offices (former Adams County Prison)
FP Former Gettysburg Public School
FQ Trinity United Church of Christ (former German Reformed Church)
FR Gettysburg Visitor Center (former railroad station)
FS Lincoln Square (the "Diamond" or Gettysburg Square)
FT Christ Lutheran Church (Chambersburg Street)
FU House of Bender Building
FV David Wills Building
FW Brafferton Inn
FX Samuel Fahnestock Clothing Store
FY Adams County Court House
FZ Gettysburg National Cemetery
GA John Fulton Reynolds Monument
GB New York Monument
GC Charles Henry Tuckey Collis Grave
GD Kentucky Monument
GE Soldier's National Monument
GF Lincoln Gettysburg Address Memorial

To visit **McPherson's Woods**, cross the Chambersburg Pike and enter Stone Avenue. Here you'll find many regimentals, scattered along the McPherson property, and a small pond called the **Mathew B. Brady Pond**. At this spot Brady took a famous photograph of himself after the battle. Nearby is the **John Burns Monument**, a statue commemorating the local farmer who, in his seventies, took up arms and fought with the 7th Wisconsin Infantry against the Confederates. If you look across the road from the monument, toward the northwest, you'll see the fields that lead down to **Willoughby's Run**, a small creek where the first small arms shots of the battle rang out. Confederate troops marched across these fields toward Gettysburg and pushed the Union troops, which lacked reinforcements, back into town. Continue on Meredith Avenue, turn left on Reynolds Avenue, then continue straight across the Chambersburg Pike. This will lead you to the northern part of the first day's field.

Along Reynolds Avenue you'll see regimentals including the **84th New York (14th Brooklyn) Infantry Monument**, and you'll pass over a railroad that was in 1863 the **Unfinished Railroad Cut** through which Union troops in the Iron Brigade made a stand against the onrushing Confederates. On the right of the road, you'll see the **James Samuel Wadsworth Monument** honoring the Union brigadier general who gallantly led a division at Gettysburg. Continuing west and north on Buford Avenue will carry you past more regimentals and the **John Forney Farm Site**, across Mummasburg Road, and on to the **Eternal Light Peace Memorial** on **Oak Ridge**. During the first day Confederate artillery positioned here battered the retreating Union army, still waiting for reinforcements, and raised the

possibility of a major Confederate victory. Seventy-five years later, during the final large scale reunion of Civil War veterans, Gettysburg soldiers heard President Franklin D. Roosevelt dedicate the Peace Memorial to symbolize the reunited nation.

Continuing on Buford Avenue and recrossing Mummasburg Road will bring you to the **Oak Ridge Observation Tower**, which affords a good view of the first day's field and the town of Gettysburg. More regimentals stand along Doubleday Avenue. You may wish to continue along Robinson Avenue, a looping section of road that contains the **John Cleveland Robinson Monument**, a tribute to the Union brigadier general who held the Confederates at bay for four hours on Oak Ridge. You'll now want to switch to the Gettysburg detail, East Sector map (p. 83). To continue with the first day's field, turn right on Mummasburg Road, travel 500 yards, and turn left on Howard Avenue. Here you'll see the **1st Ohio Battery Monument**. Cross Carlisle Road (S.R. 34) to reach the **Old Almshouse Cemetery**, a local burying ground. Just beyond this stands **Barlow's Knoll** and the **Francis Channing Barlow Monument** where the young brigadier general was severely wounded and left on the field for dead.

After seeing Barlow's Knoll, you may wish to turn south (right) on the Harrisburg Road (Business U.S. 15) and return to town, or you may turn north and proceed 200 yards to Jones Battalion Avenue, which contains a few monuments. Back in town, follow the Harrisburg Road until it reaches Lincoln Avenue and turn right. Then you may want to turn left on Stratton Street and stop when you reach Coster Avenue, a walking path on which you can see the **154th New York Infantry Monument** and the **Jacob Kuhn Brickyard Site**. Here Union infantry held Confederate attacks from the north that eventually pushed the Yankees south through the town.

During most of the Gettysburg battle, Robert E. Lee lacked his cavalry under Maj.

THE ETERNAL LIGHT PEACE MEMORIAL on Oak Ridge, dedicated by Franklin D. Roosevelt at Gettysburg's seventy-fifth anniversary ceremonies, celebrates the nation reunited in tranquility.

Gen. James E. B. "Jeb" Stuart, a force that rode around the Union army and captured trains and supplies. When Stuart did arrive on July 3, Union cavalry under Maj. Gen. Alfred Pleasonton intercepted him and fought a cavalry battle east of the main battlefield. To see the cavalry site, you should travel east on the Hanover Road (S.R. 116). From Coster Avenue, head south on Stratton Street and turn left on the Hanover Road. Along the way you can see the **Richard Stoddert Ewell Headquarters Monument** on the left side of the road at Sixth Street (Confederate headquarters of Ewell's Corps) and, on your right a mile from Stratton Street, **Benner's Hill**, a Confederate artillery perch during the final two-thirds of the battle. Continue slightly more than two miles beyond Benner's Hill and you can turn north (left) into East Cavalry Avenue. Continue north on Low Dutch Road, turn west (left) on Gregg Avenue, continue north on Confederate Cavalry Avenue, and you'll find yourself in the middle of the **East Cavalry Battlefield Site** where you'll see several regimental monuments. To return to the main battlefield tour, continue northwest on Cavalry Field Road and turn west (left) on York Pike, which will bring you back into town.

Continue on York Street until you reach Liberty Street, where you should turn south (left). Continue along as this becomes East Confederate Avenue. You're now approaching **Culp's Hill**, a major area of battle on July 2 when Confederate troops unsuccessfully attacked the Union regiments holding its crest. Savage fighting ensued around the base of this hill throughout the second and third days, producing large numbers of casualties. When you reach Slocum Avenue, you may wish to turn north (right). This will carry you past many regimental monuments and up to the summit of Culp's Hill. On the way you'll see the **John White Geary Monument**, which honors the Federal brigadier general who helped hold the hill. At the summit you'll find the **Culp's Hill Observation Tower**, which provides a superb view of the battlefield and the

countryside surrounding it. Nearby stands the **George Sears Greene Monument** honoring the brigadier general whose troops held the highest ground on the hill. Continue west on Slocum Avenue and you'll find the **Henry Warner Slocum Monument**, an equestrian statue immortalizing the Union 12th Corps commander. You've now finished the first circuit through Culp's Hill.

You may wish to turn south on the Baltimore Pike (S.R. 97) to see the rest of Culp's Hill. To do so, head south on the Baltimore Pike three-fourths of a mile and turn east (left) on Spangler Road. (Halfway to the turn you'll pass the **Henry Spangler Farm Site** on the left side of the road.) On Spangler Road you'll see several regimentals. When you reach a loop, bear east (right) on Carman Avenue. You'll see the **13th New Jersey Infantry Monument**. Turn south (left) on Spangler Road and you'll see the **2nd Massachusetts Infantry Monument** and the **3rd Wisconsin Infantry Monument**. Turn east (left) on Carman Avenue and you'll cover the loop again, a necessity due to the one-way roads. This time, however, continue north on Colgrove Avenue. This leads you to a significant battle area, **Spangler's Meadow**, where you'll see the **Indiana Monument**. Although they were turned back at Culp's Hill, Confederate troops seized this area on July 2 and held it until the next morning. Across from the meadow you'll see **Spangler's Spring**, a place where thirsty, wounded troops from both sides shared precious water. Continuing along and turning west (left) on Geary Avenue will bring you to **Pardee Field**, where Lt. Col. Ario Pardee Jr. led his 147th Pennsylvania Infantry in an attack that defied orders but captured a stone wall that served as an effective fortification. The wall is still visible along the tree line on the northern edge of Pardee Field. Continuing north on Williams Avenue, which becomes Slocum Avenue, will again bring you to the Baltimore Pike, where this time you may wish to turn north.

You're now on **Cemetery Hill**, one of the most crucial spots on the Gettysburg battlefield. Here on the afternoon and evening of the first day, Union troops held the high ground and prevented the Confederates from pushing them south of town. On the crest of Cemetery Hill, you'll see a large group of monuments including the **Winfield Scott Hancock Monument** and the **Oliver Otis Howard Monument**, both equestrian statues, and the **Oliver Otis Howard Headquarters Monument**. Major General Hancock arrived on the field late in the first day and assumed the overall command assigned to him by Meade (who was traveling toward Gettysburg but still away from the field). Major General Howard, commanding the 11th Corps, ranked Hancock and did not appreciate serving under his subordinate. After arguing on the hill where you're standing, the two agreed that Hancock should assume command. The artillery batteries on the crest, now marked by monuments, staved off vicious Confederate attacks from the town and points east.

Across the pike stands the **Evergreen Cemetery Gatehouse**, a prominent landmark that was substantially damaged during the battle. Ironically, a sign within the local cemetery had proclaimed that anyone using firearms within the cemetery grounds would be prosecuted to the full extent of the law. Within **Evergreen Cemetery**, you can see the graves of many local residents whose names are associated with Gettysburg landmarks, including the town's founder James Gettys. You'll also find

THE EVERGREEN CEMETERY GATEHOUSE marks the position where Union troops made their initial stand on the first day at Gettysburg. The structure was extensively damaged by small arms fire during the battle.

the **Mary Virginia "Jennie" Wade Grave**, the burial spot of the twenty-year old, the only civilian casualty of the battle, and the **John Burns Grave**, the resting place of the spirited resident who fought with the 7th Wisconsin. You can also find the grave of Bvt. Lt. Col. Emmor B. Cope, who after the war contributed much to the mapping and planning of the Gettysburg park. When you're finished in Evergreen, you may wish to travel north on Baltimore Street, turn south on Steinwehr Avenue, and proceed south on Taneytown Road to return to the visitor center. You've now completed the first of the three Gettysburg battlefield loops.

Loop Two

The second loop begins at the visitor center and takes you north on Taneytown Road, which becomes Washington Street, to Chambersburg Street, where you should turn west (left). Now you should switch to the Gettysburg detail, North Sector map (p. 82). At the corner of Chambersburg and West Streets, you'll pass the **John Burns Home Site**. Continuing west takes you past the **Shead House** and to the **Mary Thompson House** on the Chambersburg Pike. Preserved in superb condition, the Thompson House is now a museum filled with Gettysburg relics. Across the pike from this house, you'll see the **General Headquarters, Army of Northern Virginia Monument**, where General Lee and his staff set up tents and directed the Confederate part of the battle. From the Thompson House, you may wish to travel south on Confederate Avenue (Seminary Avenue) to see the **Lutheran Theological Seminary**, a prosperous academy during Civil War days. The central building in the campus is **Samuel Simon Schmucker Hall**. As the

LEE'S HEADQUARTERS were established on the Chambersburg Pike opposite the Mary Thompson House, a well-preserved stone dwelling that now contains a museum.

battle erupted Maj. Gen. John F. Reynolds and Brig. Gen. John Buford climbed into the cupola of this building and watched the approaching Confederates through field glasses. Continuing south on Confederate Avenue, you'll cross the Hagerstown Road and see on the southeast corner of the intersection the **Shultz House**, another wartime structure.

By traveling south on West Confederate Avenue, you'll be tracing **Seminary Ridge**, the position of the Confederate battle lines, particularly as they formed for the massive attack known as Pickett's Charge that occurred on the third day. After one-half mile you'll see the **McMillan Farm** on the left side of the road. You're now entering the **McMillan Woods**. Now consult the Gettysburg detail, South Sector map (p. 84). Another 400 yards will bring you to the **North Carolina Monument**, which marks the northern position from which Pickett's Charge commenced. Some 350 yards south of this position you'll find the **Tennessee Monument**, left of the road, and the **Ambrose Powell Hill Headquarters Monument** on the right side. Continuing another 400 yards will bring you to the **Robert Edward**

Lee Virginia Monument, which marks the center of the Confederate lines and the position from which Lee planned Pickett's Charge. The superb equestrian statue is one of the best of Lee in existence. South of the Lee monument, you'll move into the **Spangler Woods**, cross Pitzer's Run, and see the **Florida Monument** on the right of the road. Across the road from this monument is the **M. Spangler Farm Site**. Nearly 400 yards south of this spot, where the road bends due south, you may wish to turn west (right) onto Berdan Avenue, where you'll see the **First United States Sharpshooters Monument**. In this area Col. Hiram Berdan led his elite regiment into a skirmish with Confederates on the second day.

Continuing south on West Confederate Avenue will carry you into the **Pitzer Woods**

THE NORTH CAROLINA MONUMENT on West Confederate Avenue stands along the lines where troops in Brig. Gen. James J. Pettigrew's division began Pickett's Charge. The Copse of Trees on the horizon marks the center of the Union line.

ROBERT EDWARD LEE sits on horseback in the Virginia Monument on West Confederate Avenue. Near this spot Lee directed the disastrous final assault on the Union center and afterward told his men, "It's all my fault."

and along the spine of **Warfield Ridge**. You'll see the **Louisiana Monument**, the **Mississippi Monument**, and cross Waterworks Road (Millertown Road). After crossing the road, you can climb the **Warfield Ridge Observation Tower** to get a fine view of the southern part of the field. Across the road from this tower stands the **James Longstreet Headquarters Monument** where this Confederate lieutenant general concentrated his forces. To the south, just before crossing Emmitsburg Road, you'll find the **Georgia Monument**, the **South Carolina Monument**, and the **Arkansas Monument**. North of this intersection is the **P. Snyder Farm Site**. Continuing on South Confederate Avenue brings you to the **Texas Monument**, the **Alabama Monument**, and the **Confederate Soldiers and Sailors Monument**. From this position you can see to the northeast the **J. Slyder Farm**, or "Granite Farm." Beyond this structure you can see the strategically important hills that held the key to success at Gettysburg.

As South Confederate Avenue winds east and becomes Kilpatrick Avenue and then Sykes Avenue, you'll encounter the **William Wells Monument** honoring the Union major who led the 1st Vermont Cavalry on a charge against the Confederate line. When you cross **Rose Run**, you're at the base of the largest hill in the area, **Round Top**. Union and Confederate troops scrambled up Round Top on the second day only to find it useless for military purposes because the summit was too heavily wooded for artillery. The strategic focus, then, fell on **Little Round Top**, a smaller hill north of Round Top, with a ragged, rocky ridge along its summit that would command the battlefield when equipped with big guns. On July 2 during the crucial moments of the battle, Union regiments seized control of Little Round Top and fought back repeated assaults from Confederate attackers.

You may want to continue until you reach Wright Avenue and turn east (right), which after 50 yards brings you to the **20th Maine Infantry Monument** in the hollow between Round Top and Little Round Top. The stone wall running north from this monument marks the site where the 20th Maine, led by its Col. Joshua Lawrence Chamberlain, held the critical ground here. After running out of ammunition, the regiment fixed bayonets and charged, an action for which Chamberlain was awarded the Medal of Honor. Reversing direction on Wright Avenue, you'll cross Sykes Avenue and travel northwest on Warren Avenue for an excellent view of Little Round Top to the north. In the woods after crossing Sykes Avenue, you can see the **83rd Pennsylvania Infantry Monument**, a statue of Brig. Gen. Strong Vincent, mortally wounded here on July 2.

As you reach the base of Little Round Top, you'll cross **Plum Run** and then turn south into the **Devil's Den**. Here Confederate sharpshooters hid in the rocks and fired at Union troops on Little Round Top. A brisk battle between troops at Devil's Den and Little Round Top flared throughout the second and third days of the engagement, making the valley between the features an enormous shooting gallery. The tremendous casualties that piled up in this

A LONE CANNON overlooks the J. Slyder Farm, known as the Granite Farm, and Little Round Top beyond. Confederate troops moved over this ground and fought for the hill but were unable to hold it.

OUTCROPS OF GRANITE dot the landscape in the Devil's Den where Confederate sharpshooters hid in makeshift rifle pits and harassed Federal troops on Little Round Top.

THE 4th NEW YORK INDEPENDENT BATTERY, immortalized by a monument near Devil's Den, helped stem the tide of a Confederate attack from the west. Little Round Top is visible in the background.

region gave it the name the **Valley of Death**. An area of particularly savage fighting at the base of Devil's Den, now an overgrown pool through which Plum Run trickles, is the **Slaughter Pen**. Numerous images of dead were produced several days after the battle in and around the Devil's Den, the Slaughter Pen, and the Valley of Death. The most famous of these shows a dead Confederate sharpshooter at a rock formation still visible on the western side of Devil's Den. The photograph, made by Alexander Gardner, was contrived, the body moved from its original site.

As you travel north on what becomes Sickles Avenue, you'll pass **Houck's Ridge**, see several regimental monuments, and come out of the woods at another savagely bloody field of battle, the **Wheatfield**. This area witnessed numerous attacks by both sides on the second day when Union and Confederate regiments took, lost, and retook the field time and time again. In the end nothing came of the Wheatfield fight excepting hundreds of casualties. In the center of the field, you can now see several regimental monuments. When the road loops west and then north, the ground to the west is **Stony Hill**. After traveling 200 yards, you'll reach Wheatfield Road, where you should turn west (left). After 600 yards you'll reach an enclosed square grove of trees on the left side of the road. This is the **Peach Orchard**, a part of the **John L. Sherfy Farm**, which lies across Emmitsburg Road. On the second day Federal Maj. Gen. Daniel E. Sickles marched his 3rd Corps out from the base of Little Round Top, across the Wheatfield and up to the Peach Orchard, exposing his corps to enfilading fire from the Confederate lines and a massive attack from Longstreet's corps. He did so against orders and nearly created a Union disaster in the process. Sickles was hit grievously in the leg (and subsequently lost it), but shouted orders and chewed a cigar as he was carried off the field. Across Wheatfield Road from the Orchard, at the junction with Emmitsburg Road, is the **Wentz Farm Ruin**.

THE WHEATFIELD witnessed repeated attacks on the second day as Confederate charges smashed into Federal regiments. The day's action here was inconclusive but created monstrous numbers of casualties. Wheat now grows about a monument honoring the 1st New York Light Artillery.

THE PEACH ORCHARD, part of the John L. Sherfy Farm, witnessed bloody carnage on July 2 as Union Maj. Gen. Daniel E. Sickles, against orders, marched his Third Corps into the area, creating an exposed salient. Sickles lost his leg and risked losing the battle.

You can loop around the Peach Orchard by turning south (left) on the Emmitsburg Road, turning east (left) on Birney Avenue, turning east (right) on the Wheatfield Road, and proceeding north (left) on Sickles Avenue. This will take you past several regimental monuments, including the **Excelsior Brigade Monument.** By turning west (left) on United States Avenue and then heading south (left) on Emmitsburg Road, you can get a close look at the Sherfy Farm. Next, you may wish to head east (left) on Wheatfield Road and pass the northern edge of the Wheatfield. On this side you'll see the **Samuel Kosciuszko Zook Monument** where this Union brigadier general was mortally wounded on July 2, dying shortly after midnight the next day. Continuing on, head south (right) on Ayres Avenue and you'll see several regimentals relating to the Wheatfield fight. The road becomes Cross Avenue which in turn becomes Brooke Avenue when you cross Rose Run and pass the **J. Timber Farm Site**, left of the road. Now you're entering the **Rose Woods** where numerous Confederate casualties piled up on the second day. As the road again crosses Rose Run, the **G. W. Rose Farm** lies 100 yards west of you. The road now becomes de Trobriand Avenue and contains many regimental monuments. Continue along Sickles Avenue until you reach the Wheatfield Road, where you should head east (right).

You can now drive through the center of the Valley of Death by turning south (right) on Crawford Avenue. Just before that turn, after crossing Plum Run, note the **John T. Weikert Farm** to the left. On Crawford Avenue you'll find the **Samuel Wylie Crawford Monument** (the plaque misspells his name), which honors the Union brigadier general who commanded the Pennsylvania Reserve Corps, part of the 5th Corps which fought through the Valley of Death. As you reach the base of Little Round Top, head east (left) on Warren Avenue and then turn north (left) on Sykes Avenue. This leads you to the summit of Little Round Top, the crucial strategic position of the battle.

At the time of the battle, the craggy face of Little Round Top had recently been cleared of timber. Here you can see several important monuments marking the Union's hold on Little Round Top. The most prominent is the **Gouverneur Kemble Warren Monument**, a bronze statue of Meade's chief engineer. Major General Warren recognized the importance of taking and holding Little Round Top, and his special efforts to ensure the position made him a hero of Gettysburg. Near the Warren monument, you'll find the **155th Pennsylvania Infantry Monument**, the **91st Pennsylvania Infantry Monument**, the **140th New York Infantry (Patrick Henry O'Rorke) Monument**, and the **44th and 12th New York Infantry Monument**. North of these regimentals, slightly downhill from the crest, you'll find the **121st New York Infantry Monument**, a statue of Col. Emory Upton. Nearby stands the **Stephen Hinsdale Weed Monument** honoring the young artillerist who was mortally wounded and died on July 2.

If you travel north on Sykes Avenue, you'll cross Wheatfield Road and continue on Sedgwick Avenue, where you'll see the **John**

THE STRATEGIC KEY AT GETTYSBURG was Little Round Top, a 650-foot hill that served as a Federal artillery perch after a ferocious struggle for ownership on the battle's second day.

GOUVERNEUR KEMBLE WARREN, General Meade's chief engineer, peers over the Gettysburg battlefield from the crest of Little Round Top. A Gettysburg hero, Major General Warren helped seize control of the important position on July 2.

Sedgwick Monument, an equestrian statue memorializing the commander of the Federal 6th Corps. About 100 yards north of this you'll see the George Sykes Headquarters Monument marking the position of Sykes's headquarters of the Federal 5th Corps. Slightly farther north and across the road stands the John Sedgwick Headquarters Monument, site of the Union 6th Corps headquarters. Just north of this monument, you'll enter the wartime Patterson Woods, and after traveling 500, yards you'll see the George Weikert Farm at the junction with United States Avenue. As you continue north on Hancock Avenue, you'll encounter the William Corby Monument (Corby was Chaplain of the Irish Brigade) and the New York Auxiliary Monument on the right side of the road. Where the road forks, bear right on Humphreys Avenue. You may wish to turn east (right) on Pleasonton Avenue.

At the junction of Humphreys and Pleasonton stands the massive Pennsylvania Monument, the largest and most elaborate structure on the field. The tablets fastened to the monument's marble walls record the names of the more than 30,000 soldiers from Pennsylvania who fought at Gettysburg. Across Pleasonton Avenue you'll see the Winfield Scott Hancock Headquarters Monument marking the location of the 2nd Corps headquarters. Hancock, who seized control of the battle early on, was on the third day badly wounded near his headquarters. Following east on Pleasonton Avenue takes you past the J. Hummelbaugh Farm, the house in which Confederate Brig. Gen. Lewis A. Armistead died, having been mortally wounded in Pickett's Charge. Damage from small arms fire is still visible on the clapboards of this house. Across the road you'll see the John Newton Headquarters Monument marking the position of the Federal 1st Corps after Newton assumed command from Abner Doubleday.

To continue the tour, you may wish to turn north (left) on Taneytown Road. After traveling 150 yards, you'll pass the Peter Frey Farm on the left of the road. Another 400 yards takes you to the Henry Jackson Hunt Headquarters Monument, which marks the headquarters site of the commander of the Federal artillery for the Army of the Potomac. Hunt's artillery barrage on the third day wrecked any chance for the success of Pickett's Charge. Just beyond this monument, on the left side of the road, is an important wartime structure. (You may have to park on Hunt Avenue, across Taneytown Road, to explore it.) The Lydia A. Leister House served as Maj. Gen. George G. Meade's headquarters during the battle, and in this house Meade held a crucial council of war on the night of July 2 and decided to stay and fight on the third day. Next to the house you'll see the General Headquarters, Army of the Potomac Monument. Around this house the Union high command operated the battle that would signal the beginning of the end for the Confederacy.

You may wish to continue north on Taneytown Road and turn west (left) into Ziegler's Grove Drive, north of the visitor center. This will take you on the final, closing loop of the main park roads, to the scene of the final, cli-

MEADE ESTABLISHED HEADQUARTERS at the Lydia A. Leister House on Taneytown Road, and here, on the night of July 2 held a crucial council of war to determine Union strategy for the climactic third day.

mactic action at Gettysburg. As you enter **Ziegler's Grove**, you'll wind southward past the **Alexander Hays Monument** honoring the Union brigadier general whose division held the line in Ziegler's Grove against Pickett's Charge. Turning south (left) on Steinwehr Avenue will take you past the **Grand Army of the Republic Monument** paying tribute to the GAR and its last bonafide combat survivor, Albert Woolson, who died in 1956.

The stretch of Steinwehr Avenue you are now on, which becomes the Emmitsburg Road, will take you through the center of the Pickett's Charge field. The attack, planned by Generals Lee, Pickett, and Pettigrew, was a desperate attempt to send 15,000 Rebel troops punching through the Union center, thereby routing the Federal army and sending it retreating in confusion. Just after noon on the third day, Confederate artillery along West Confederate Avenue, some 170 guns, opened up on the Union lines on Hancock Avenue. Soon the 175 Union artillery pieces placed from Cemetery Hill in the north to Little Round Top in the south, but concentrated along Hancock Avenue, responded. The greatest artillery duel up to that time ensued. After ninety minutes the guns fell silent. Most of the Confederate shells had sailed high over their targets. The Union gunners had stopped in peculiar spurts, mimicking an exhaustion of ammunition. Lee took the bait and launched the famous charge. Many of the 15,000 men were cut to pieces by an explosive renewal of Federal gunnery that hit the oncoming Confederates from three sides.

From the GAR monument, travel south on Emmitsburg Road for 700 yards until you reach the **Simon J. Codori Farm** on the left side of the road. You're now near the center of the Pickett's Charge field. Continuing another 400 yards takes you to the **Rogers Farm Site**, where you should bear left onto Sickles Avenue, past the **D. F. Klingle Farm**. When you reach United States Avenue, you may wish to turn east (left) to see the **Daniel Edgar Sickles Headquarters Monument**, the site

where Sickles established the 3rd Corps position in his endangered salient. Just beyond that marker, on the north side of the road, stands the **Abraham Trostle Farm**, a prominent battlefield landmark. Artillery damage is visible in the brick portions of the Trostle barn west of the clapboard farmhouse. You may wish to proceed across Plum Run, continue to Hancock Avenue, and turn north (left). This will take you to the climactic ground at Gettysburg, the receiving end of Pickett's Charge.

Continue north on Hancock Avenue past the Pennsylvania Monument, beyond which stands the **Vermont Monument**, which incorporates a statue of Col. Lewis Addison Grant. The nearby **13th Vermont Infantry Monument** features Brig. Gen. George Jerrison Stannard. Numerous monuments are scattered between the Vermont markers and the visitor center, most of which indicate the positions of the Federal regiments that met Pickett's Charge. The **United States Regulars Monument**, a huge obelisk, stands 100 yards to the north. Across the road the **John Gibbon Monument** honors the Union brigadier general who assumed command of the 2nd Corps when Hancock was wounded.

THE TROSTLE BARN on United States Avenue lies adjacent to the headquarters site of Maj. Gen. Daniel E. Sickles. The reconstructed barn shows artillery damage from more than one cannonball.

The most significant symbolic monument at Gettysburg can be found 150 yards north of the Gibbon Monument. Placed in the **Copse of Trees**, a stand of oak trees that Lee used as his mark for the Union center, the **High Water Mark Monument** commemorates the commands that took part in Pickett's Charge on both sides of the fence. The monument's tablet and cannon symbolize the high water mark of the Confederate war effort. Just north of this monument, you'll find **the Angle**, the spot where the low stone wall running along this part of the line makes a ninety-degree bend. Here the relatively few Confederates who made it to the Union line engaged in hand-to-hand combat with the Union defenders. You'll also see in this area several important monuments. The **Lewis Addison Armistead Monument**

marks the position where the Confederate brigadier general fell mortally wounded. The **Alonzo Hereford Cushing Monument** memorializes the young Wisconsin artillerist who fell dead after firing one last shot from his battery. The **72nd Pennsylvania Infantry Monument** illustrates the brutal nature of Pickett's Charge. The **Alexander Stuart Webb Monument** honors the Union brigadier general who staunchly defended the center of the Union line. On the eastern side of Hancock Avenue, you'll see the **George Gordon Meade Monument**, a magnificent equestrian statue celebrating the Federal commander. Farther north, west of the Cyclorama Center, you'll see the **Abram Bryan Farm**, the reconstructed house of a free Black who lived on the grounds at the time of the battle. You've now

THE HIGH WATER MARK MONUMENT, located on Hancock Avenue at the Copse of Trees, commemorates the commands that took part in Pickett's Charge. Lee's army lost a third of its remaining men in the fiasco, which ended in hand-to-hand combat.

seen the major features of the park and may wish to return to the visitor center.

Loop Three

To see the third and final loop of Gettysburg landmarks, begin again at the visitor center. Consult the Gettysburg detail, East Sector map (p. 83). From there, you can head north on Taneytown Road, turn right on Steinwehr Avenue, and turn north (left) on Baltimore Street. On the southeast corner of Baltimore and High Streets, you'll see the **Gettysburg Presbyterian Church** where Abraham Lincoln attended services during his November trip to deliver the Gettysburg Address. Heading east on High Street, you'll come to the **Gettysburg City Offices Building**, a structure that was the Adams County Jail at the time of the battle. Across the street is the **Gettysburg Public School Building**, another wartime structure. Turning north (left) on Stratton Street carries you past the **Trinity United Church of Christ**, the German Reformed Church during Civil War days. Crossing the railroad tracks and turning west (left) on Water Street, then south (left) on Carlisle Street, leads you to the **Gettysburg Visitor Center**, the wartime railroad station where Lincoln first saw Gettysburg. Continue south on Carlisle Street and you'll come to **Lincoln Square**, the town center, where you may wish to see several buildings. The **David Wills Building** stands on the southeast corner of the square. Lincoln stayed with Wills on his Gettysburg journey and made a brief public appearance from the second floor. The building now houses a museum relating to Lincoln's stay and to Wills, a lawyer whose energy helped start the Soldier's National Cemetery. If you travel south on Baltimore Street a distance of one-half mile, you'll see on the left of the road the **McClellan House**, known as the Jennie Wade House. Here young Wade was fatally hit by gunfire while baking bread.

Continuing south on the Baltimore Pike 200 yards brings you to the **Gettysburg National Cemetery**, the final stop on your Gettysburg tour. Known originally as the Soldier's National Cemetery, the twenty-acre site contains 3,629 graves of Civil War dead. The prominent landmarks within the cemetery, established after Abraham Lincoln's dedicatory remarks on November 19, 1863, are worth exploring. The first is the **John Fulton Reynolds Monument**, a bronze statue honoring the fallen Federal 1st Corps commander. Farther inside the grounds you'll see the **New York Monument**, a tall obelisk, and the **Soldier's National Monument**, an elaborate obelisk built in 1869 to commemorate the Gettysburg Address. Although this shaft is supposed to mark the spot on which Lincoln delivered the great, brief speech, research shows that the actual location was probably across the iron fence inside Evergreen Cemetery, on or near the Brown family vault, which was erected in the 1950s. Inside the circular rows of recessed headstones, you'll see the **Charles Henry Tuckey Collis Grave**, burial site of a prominent brevet brigadier general and Gettysburg resident. Inside the grounds you'll also encounter the

THE SOLDIER'S NATIONAL MONUMENT, erected in 1869, is the primary memorial in Gettysburg National Cemetery. It does not mark the exact position from which Abraham Lincoln delivered the Gettysburg Address, however, as it was intended to do.

Kentucky Monument and the **Lincoln Gettysburg Address Memorial.**

Having seen the major features of the battlefield of Gettysburg, you are an experienced Civil War battlefield buff. The vast outlay of real estate involved in the Gettysburg battle and incredibly detailed and extensive memorialization here make it by far the greatest of the Civil War battlefields. The monuments here will ensure that the significance of Gettysburg lives on long after our living are gone, as it has over the past century and since the days of the war itself.

Gettysburg National Military Park

Mailing address: 97 Taneytown Road, Gettysburg, Pennsylvania 17325-2804
Telephone: (717) 334-1124
Park established: February 11, 1895
Area: 5,990 acres

Gettysburg National Cemetery

(Soldier's National Cemetery)
Established: November 19, 1863
Area: 20.6 acres
Civil War interments: 3,629

Gettysburg accommodations

Gettysburg, although a relatively small town in terms of population, has an incredible abundance of motels. At least nineteen motels and hotels, nine bed and breakfast inns, and seven campgrounds operate within Gettysburg. Only during extremely rare events—a major reenactment or motion picture in production—should you find yourself without accommodations in this town. Should you opt not to stay within town, however, you may also find motels in nearby Hanover and Waynesboro.

Chapter 7

✪　　✪　　✪

Petersburg, Five Forks, and Appomattox Court House

Suddenly the earth trembled under our feet.
An enormous mass sprang into the air.
A mass without form or shape, full of red flames,
and carried on a bed of lightning flashes, mounted towards heaven
with a detonation of thunder.
It spread out like a sheaf, like an immense mushroom
whose stem seemed to be of fire and its head of smoke.

—Brig. Gen. Philippe Régis Dénis de Keredern de Trobriand
describing the Petersburg Mine Explosion
of July 30, 1864.

The American Civil War witnessed many firsts. The dizzying number of innovations was not limited to the technology of new arms or the widespread use of photography. The war also revolutionized conflicts to come by introducing trench warfare.

The bloody Overland, or May, campaign initiated by Lt. Gen. U. S. Grant at Germanna Ford, Virginia, had a long shadow. As the spring of 1864 waned and Grant pushed Lee toward Richmond, a costly succession of battles occurred. The Wilderness, Spotsylvania, and Cold Harbor solved little but allowed Grant continually to turn Lee's right flank, inching both armies closer to the Confederate capital. Yet even as Grant told the nation he would "fight it out on this line if it takes all summer," he imaginatively abandoned a direct operation on Richmond and, with Meade's Army of the Potomac and Butler's Army of the James, moved south to concentrate on Petersburg. By moving his base to the south bank of the James River, Grant could release Butler, who was "bottled up" at Bermuda Hundred, and control the remaining rail lines into Richmond. Grant carried out the complex move perfectly, outwitting Lee.

Confederate defenses around Petersburg consisted of small forts and redans connected by miles of entrenchments with important approaches obstructed by trees and brush. In mid-June the Federal army's first series of attacks on Petersburg was unsuccessful in breaking through the Confederate defenses. Grant was perfectly willing to repeat the strategy successfully carried out at Vicksburg, however. The operations around Petersburg settled into a siege that would last ten months until the very end of the war.

Fighting erupted daily around the Petersburg lines between June 1864 and April 1865. The Union and Confederate works were so closely placed that Civil War soldiers at Petersburg invented prolonged trench warfare. Although the operations were continuous, some major battles occurred between the daily skirmishes.

The first assault came on June 9, 1864, even before the main armies arrived. Major General Butler attacked Petersburg's 2,500 defenders with two infantry brigades and three cavalry regiments. The assault did not succeed. The earliest large-scale attacks occurred from June 15 to 18. On the fifteenth Union Maj. Gen. William F. Smith halted his attack at nightfall. If he had pressed on, Smith would have captured the main road linking Richmond and Petersburg. His hesitation, one of the great blunders of the war, forestalled the capture of the town.

After Grant changed his base, numerous important actions took place both south and north of the James River. Those south of the James included operations on the Weldon Railroad (Jerusalem Plank Road, Williams's Farm, and Davis's Farm, June 22–23), the Petersburg Mine Assault (Battle of the Crater, July 30), Globe Tavern (Six-Mile House, Weldon Railroad, August 18–21), Reams's Station (August 25), Poplar Springs Church (Peeble's Farm, Pegram's Farm, September 30–October 2), Hatcher's Run (Boydton Plank Road, Vaughan Road, Burgess Farm, October 27), Dabney's Mills (Hatcher's Run, Boydton Plank Road, Armstrong's Mill, Rowanty Creek, Vaughan Road, February 5–7, 1865), and Fort Stedman (March 25, 1865). Those north of the James included Deep Bottom Run (Strawberry Plains, Malvern Hill, New Market Road, Darbytown, July 27–29 and August 13–20), New Market Heights (Chafin's Farm, Laurel Hill, Fort Harrison, Fort Gilmer, September 28–30), and Darbytown and New Market Roads (October 7). The latter group is covered in chapter 8, "Richmond and City Point."

The complex operations around Petersburg extended westward at the end of March 1865, after the Union punched through the Confederate lines. On April 1 the armies clashed at Five Forks, a junction twelve miles southwest of Petersburg. As Lee's Army of Northern Virginia abandoned the city and evacuated Richmond

following the Union attack on April 2, the Federals pursued. The last major battle of the eastern theater of war occurred at Sayler's Creek near Farmville on April 6, when Union forces captured nearly 8,000 Confederates including six general officers. Three days later at Appomattox Court House, Lee surrendered to Grant and the war was essentially over.

Petersburg (pop. 38,386) stands twenty-three miles south of Richmond near the confluence of the James and Appomattox Rivers. **Petersburg National Battlefield**, on the eastern side of town, contains a fraction of the fortifications used during the operations of 1864 and 1865. Fredericksburg and Washington lie to the north of Richmond and Petersburg, Charlottesville and the Shenandoah Valley to the northwest, Lynchburg and Roanoke to the west, and Hampton, Newport News, Norfolk, and Portsmouth to the east. Petersburg is easily reachable on good roads from practically any point in Virginia.

Petersburg Tour

When we first pulled into the city to track the extensive remains of the Petersburg siege, my father and I headed to the **National Park Service Visitor Center** east of the city, off of East Washington Street (Virginia 36). The museum within the center holds a superb collection of artifacts from the Petersburg campaign including relics recovered from the mine and the crater.

So many earthworks and sites of forts and homes exist in and around Petersburg that this chapter will describe only the most important examples. The Petersburg environs map shows the locations of many sites not described in the text.

Outside the visitor center, you'll see an exceptional collection of gun tubes representing the cannon used during the Petersburg siege. Continue walking northward on the path and you'll come to **Battery 5**, one of many dozens of forts and gun emplacements used during the siege. Battery 5 was one of the emplacements in the original Confederate defenses called the Dimmock Line after the Virginia engineer Col. Charles Dimmock. A Union assault on June 15, 1864, captured this position. Continue along the path and you'll see **the Dictator**, a thirteen-inch seacoast mortar used by the Union army to shell the town. The mortar now in position is a replacement; the original Dictator, made famous in wartime photographs, is believed to be the piece now on the grounds of the State House in Hartford, Connecticut. Battery G of the First Connecticut Artillery used the gun during the siege.

As you stand at the Dictator, you're close to the site of the old **City Point Railroad**, which carried supplies back and forth from the Union lines at Petersburg to Grant's base at City Point. For a short time the Dictator was used while mounted on a flatcar. West of the visitor cen-

ter are the sites of three wartime houses, the **Josiah Jordan House Ruin**, "Clermont"; the **Charles Friend House Site**, "Whitehall"; and the **Gibbon Farm Site**. After its capture, the Jordan House hosted the Union 6th Army Corps. The Friend House was Maj. Gen. Orlando B. Willcox's headquarters in the spring of 1865.

You can trace the Dimmock Line south by following the park road, crossing East Washington Street, and arriving at **Fort Friend** (Battery 8). To do so consult the Petersburg Environs map (p. 108). Confederate Battery 8 was captured by Union troops and renamed for the nearby Friend House. Nearby stands **Battery 9**, captured by Black Union troops on the first day of the battle. This area served as winter quarters in 1864 and 1865 for the Union 9th Army Corps. A footpath leads southeast through the woods to the site of **Meade**

CANNON TUBES line the ground near the visitor center at Petersburg National Battlefield. The selection of field and siege guns represents the artillery used during the long Petersburg campaign.

HEAVY UNION MORTARS such as the Dictator, a railroad-mounted siege gun, battered the city of Petersburg from the Union lines. The original Dictator is thought to be the mortar on the grounds of the Connecticut State Capitol in Hartford.

Station, an important depot on the wartime U.S. Military Railroad. During the summer months Park Service historians operate a living history encampment at this site that includes a reconstructed earthern fort, sutler's store, and officer's hut. The **James Dunn House Site** lies to the southwest.

Continuing along the park road, you'll turn westward, away from the Dimmock Line and into the initial Union siege line. After crossing **Harrison Creek,** you'll pass the **Gibbon House Site** south of the road. After being driven from their original positions, Confederate troops fell back to this area and dug in along

the creek. After two days the Confederates fell back again to an inner defense line closer to the city and near the Union siege line. These lines were maintained throughout many battles until the fall of the city. After crossing the creek, you'll arrive at **Fort Stedman,** the principal Union fort in this area. On March 25, 1865, General Lee attempted a Confederate breakout through Fort Stedman and at first captured the fort. After several hours, however, Union troops under Brig. Gen. John F. Hartranft recaptured the position. The **Otway P. Hare Farm Site** lies east of the fort. A trail that begins at the fort leads to **Colquitt's Salient,** where the Con-

A CONFEDERATE BREAKOUT at Fort Stedman on March 25, 1865, failed when Union regiments recaptured the fort four hours later. The failure meant the eventual fall of Petersburg.

federate assault began, and to the **1st Maine Infantry Monument** commemorating the regiment with the greatest losses at Petersburg.

After the park road bends south, you'll come to **Fort Haskell**, the position where the Confederate attack of March 25, 1865, was stopped. Continuing south, note where the road curves west. Here you'll find the **William Byrd Taylor Farm Ruin**, "Spring Garden," a once prominent group of buildings that was demolished at the start of the siege. The outbuilding chimney that still stands was used by Union artillery as a mark for spotting. During the battle of the Crater on July 30, 1864, Union artillery, nearly 200 guns strong, lined this ridge and pelted the Confederate lines with balls and shells. South of the Taylor Farm is the site of **Fort Morton**.

THE TAYLOR FARM now consists solely of a chimney, one that served as an artillery mark during the siege. The Taylor farm buildings are completely gone and the chimney is thought to be from an outbuilding rather than the main house.

The park road now loops north to the most infamous spot in Petersburg, **the Crater.** This circular depression marks the site of one of the most dramatic and disastrous events of the war. During the siege the incredible closeness of the Union and Confederate lines offered the opportunity for a creative attack. Lt. Col. Henry Pleasants and his 48th Pennsylvania Infantry, a regiment consisting largely of coal miners, concocted an idea to utilize their talent. Pleasants convinced Maj. Gen. Ambrose Burnside and eventually Grant himself to permit the miners to tunnel beneath the Confederate lines, pack the mine with explosives, and blow up a section of the Confederate defenses. Union infantry could then easily break through the breach and take the city.

The tunneling began on June 25, 1864, and continued until July 30 when Pleasants exploded the mine. (The Confederates, meanwhile, were aware of the mine construction and dug a countermine to determine what was going on.) Nine companies of the 19th and 22nd South Carolina Infantry were blown into the air, killing several hundred Confederates. The crater, 170 feet long, sixty to eighty feet wide,

AN OVERGROWN SINKHOLE marks the position of the Crater, where on July 30, 1864, Union troops exploded four tons of black powder in a mine under the Confederate lines, creating a confused, disastrous melee. The debacle accomplished nothing but produced over 5,000 casualties.

and thirty feet deep, filled with onrushing Union attackers. Instead of capturing the Confederate position, however, hundreds of Union soldiers, without adequate leadership, bogged down and were captured or shot. The attack was a disaster, and Union Brig. Gens. Edward Ferrero and James H. Ledlie cowered near the mine drinking rather than leading their troops, many of whom were Blacks. Ferrero's and Ledlie's careers were finished. Confederate Brig. Gen. William Mahone gallantly led a counterattack which successfully pushed the Federals back to their old position. Nothing had been gained. The **William Mahone Monument,** an obelisk adjacent to the Crater, honors the general.

At the end of the park road, turn north (right) on Crater Road and proceed one-third mile to **Blandford Church and Cemetery,** one of the oldest and most historic burying grounds in Virginia. Established in 1702 (the church was built in 1735), the 114-acre site holds the largest number of Confederate soldiers of any cemetery, some 30,000. Many are buried in a Confederate section that surrounds the **William Mahone Tomb,** a mausoleum containing the Confederate commander mentioned above. Memorial Day may have had its origin at Blandford when Mary Logan, wife of Union Maj. Gen. John A. Logan, watched Petersburg girls placing flowers on the graves of Confederate soldiers. Logan later enacted legislation for Decoration Day, which became our more modern Memorial Day.

You may now wish to visit more extensive parts of the Union siege line and Confederate defense line south of town. Many of the sites lie outside of the park. Head south on Crater Road and note when you cross Interstate 95. About one-third mile south of here, west of the road, are the **McKenzie** and the **Winfree Farm Sites.** About 400 yards farther, east of the road, is the **Rives Farm Site.** You're now back on a section of the Dimmock Line. At the intersection of Crater Road and South Boulevard, you'll see the **George Gowan Monument**

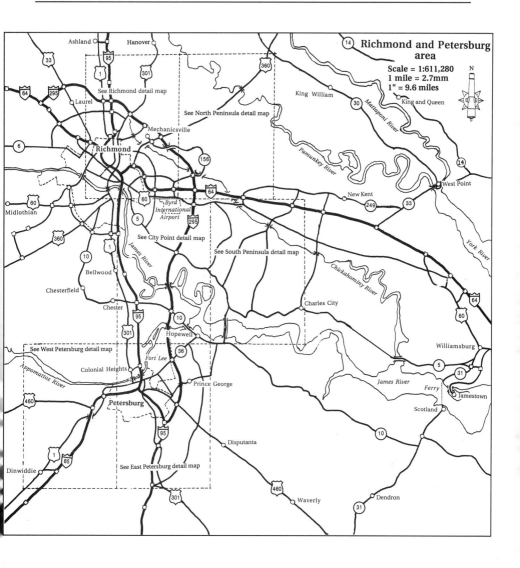

Richmond and Petersburg area

Scale = 1:611,280
1 mile = 2.7mm
1" = 9.6 miles

honoring the colonel of the 48th Pennsylvania Infantry who was killed on April 2, 1865, during one of the final attacks. About one-fourth mile south of the monument, on the southeast corner of Crater Road and Morton Avenue, is the site of **Fort Sedgwick**. The principal Federal fort south of the defense line, Sedgwick was nicknamed "Fort Hell" because of relentless Confederate fire.

Continue south just over one-half mile on Crater Road (which becomes the Jerusalem Plank Road, U.S. 301), and you'll reach the site of **Fort Davis**, west of the road. East of this position is the **J. Chieves Farm Site**. You're now following the extended Union siege works that formed a great arc south of the city. Turn west (right) onto Flank Road to reach, after nearly a mile, the site of **Fort Alexander Hays**, 300

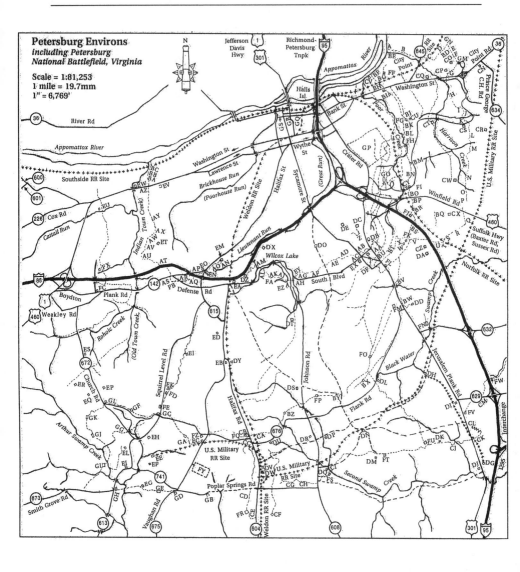

Petersburg Environs
including Petersburg
National Battlefield, Virginia

Scale = 1:81,253
1 mile = 19.7mm
1" = 6,769'

yards west of the road. Another important wartime site, **Hancock Station** on the U.S. Military Railroad, lies one-half mile east of the road. Proceed 500 yards to the **Strong Farm Site** just south of Black Water Creek. Another mile brings you close to the site of **Fort Howard**, which lies 500 yards north of the road, and the site of **Parke Station** on the U.S. Military Railroad, one-half mile southeast of the road.

You may wish to continue until you reach Halifax Road where you should turn south (left). You're now driving through the area of vicious fighting that erupted during June and August 1864 along the Weldon Railroad, which paralleled Halifax Road on the latter's east side. One-third mile south of the turn, east of the road, is the site of **Globe Tavern**, also called Yellow Tavern and Six Mile House. The building

Key to Features on Petersburg Environs Map

A-BC The Confederate Dimmock defense line with 371 guns. (The principal redoubts, redans, lunettes, and entrenched batteries were originally numbered 1–55, respectively.)

BD-BV The initial Union siege line consisting of nineteen positions with 128 guns, originally numbered IV–XXII, respectively.

BW-CM The extended Union siege works with positions originally numbered XXIII–XXXIX, respectively.

CN Peebles House Site
CO Josiah Jordan House Ruin, "Clermont"
CP Charles Friend House Site, "Whitehall"
CQ Gibbon Farm Site
CR Meade Station Site, USMRR
CS James Dunn House Site
CT Gibbon House Site
CU Otway P. Hare Farm Site
CV Hare Jr. House Site
CW Shands Farm Site
CX Col. John Avery Farm Site
CY William Byrd Taylor Farm Ruin, "Spring Garden"
CZ At Sallys Farm Site
DA Tatum Farm Site
DB Rives Farm Site
DC McKenzie Farm Site
DD J. Chieves Farm Site
DE Winfree Farm Site
DF Gregory Farm Site
DG Crawford Station Site, USMRR
DH Hancock Station Site, USMRR
DI Finn Farm Site
DJ Temple Farm Site
DK Williams Farm Site
DL Strong Farm Site
DM Browder Farm Site
DN Parke Station Site, USMRR
DO Wilcox Farm Site
DP Aiken Farm Site

DQ Dr. Gurley Farm Site
DR Lanier Farm Site
DS H. Risdon Farm Site
DT G. Bailey Farm Site
DU Dunlop Farm Site
DV Globe Tavern Site (Yellow Tavern, Six Mile House)
DW Warren Station Site, USMRR
DX Captain Banks Farm Site
DY P. Davis Farm Site
DZ Fisher Farm Site
EA Vaughan Farm Site
EB Ragland Farm Site
EC Flowers Farm Site
ED W. Johnson Farm Site
EE Patrick Station Site, USMRR
EF Poplar Springs Church Site
EG Widow Smith Farm Site
EH Job Talmage Farm Site
EI Clements Farm Site
EJ W. W. Davis Farm Site
EK Robert Chappell Farm Site
EL William Peebles Farm Site
EM C.S.A. Lead Works Site
EN Boydton Plank Road Tavern Site
EO Boydton Plank Road Toll Gate Site
EP J. D. Boswell Farm Site
EQ Oscar Pegram Farm Site
ER Dr. Alfred Boisseau Farm Site
ES Robert Jones Farm Site
ET R. O. McIlwaine Farm Site
EU Turnbull Farm Site (last C.S.A. HQ in Petersburg)
EV Model Farm Site
EW C.S.A. Powder Mill Site

EX-FE Confederate Forts:

EX Fort Mahone, "Fort Damnation"
EY Fort New Orleans
EZ Fort Walker
FA Fort Pegram
FB Fort Lee
FC Fort Gregg
FD Fort Cherry
FE Fort Bratton

FF-GL Union Forts (The first eighteen had letters as well as names.)

FF A Fort McGilvery

FG B Fort Stedman
FH C Fort Haskell
FI D Fort Morton
FJ E Fort Meikle
FK F Fort Rice
FL G Fort Sedgwick, "Fort Hell"
FM H Fort Davis
FN I Fort Prescott
FO K Fort Alexander Hays
FP L Fort Howard
FQ M Fort Wadsworth
FR N Fort Dushane
FS O Fort Davison
FT P Fort McMahon
FU Q Fort Stevenson
FV R Fort Blaisdell
FW S Fort Patrick Kelly
FX Fort Baldwin (former C.S.A. Fort Whitworth)
FY Poplar Grove National Cemetery and the site of the 50th New York Engineers rustic church and camp
FZ Fort Keene
GA Fort Tracy
GB Fort Clarke
GC Fort Urmston
GD Fort Siebert
GE Fort Emory
GF Fort Conahey
GG Fort Wheaton (former C.S.A. Fort Archer)
GH Fort Cummings
GI Fort Sampson
GJ Fort Gregg
GK Fort Welch
GL Fort Fisher
GM National Park Service Visitor Center
GN The Dictator, replacement, 13-inch seacoast mortar
GO The Crater
GP Blandford Church and Cemetery
GQ Centre Hill Mansion
GR Exchange Building, containing the Siege Museum
GS Petersburg Visitor Center and the Old Towne District

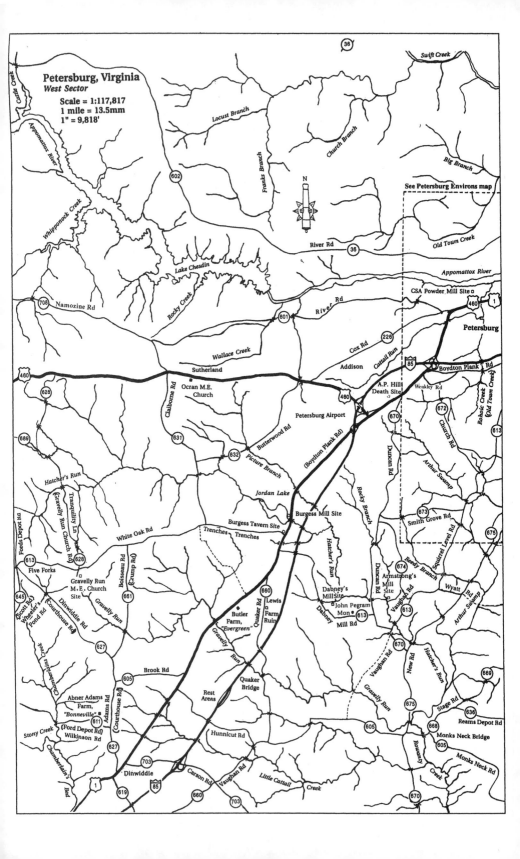

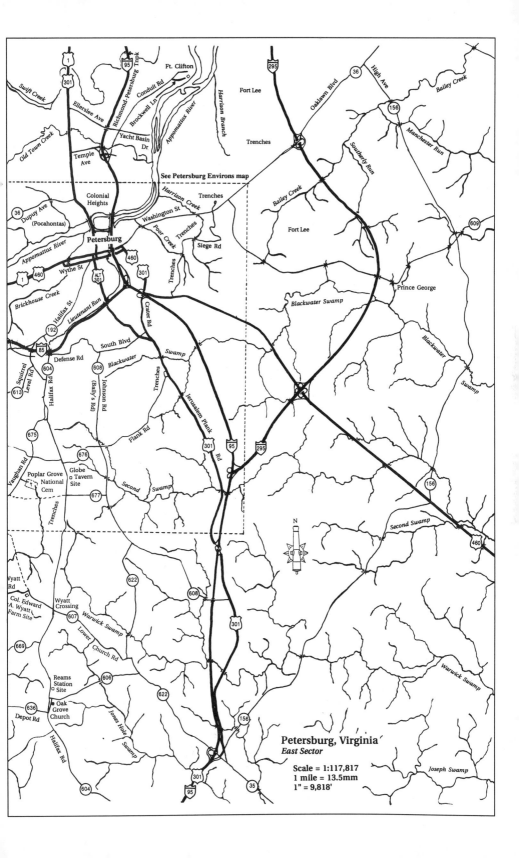

Petersburg, Virginia
East Sector

Scale = 1:117,817
1 mile = 13.5mm
1" = 9,818'

served as Maj. Gen. Gouverneur K. Warren's headquarters during part of the Petersburg campaign. About 150 yards south of the Globe Tavern stood **Warren Station** on the U.S. Military Railroad.

Two important sites can be found south of Petersburg. To find them see the Petersburg East Sector map (p. 111). To reach the site of **Reams Station** on the Weldon Railroad, head south on Halifax Road (Virginia 604) and note where you cross Virginia 607. Just over one and one-half miles south of Virginia 607, you'll arrive at the site of Reams Station, east of the road and about 300 yards north of the intersection with Virginia 606. On August 25, 1864, Union Maj. Gen. Winfield Scott Hancock clashed with Confederate Lt. Gen. A. P. Hill around this site. The battle resulted from Hancock's attempt to destroy the railroad. Hill captured some 2,000 Federals, nine cannon, and a large cache of small arms. The **Oak Grove Church**, southeast of the intersection of Halifax Road and Virginia 606, was a hospital following the battle.

You can continue your tour by heading north on Halifax Road, past the Globe Tavern site. Turn west (left) onto Flank Road. Again, you'll need the Petersburg Environs map (p. 108). Near the intersection you'll see **Fort Wadsworth**, which stands on the site of the battle of the Weldon Railroad that occurred August 18-21, 1864. Major General Warren's Federals struck out from this point to destroy Confederate communications and railroad track as far south as possible. The fighting was indecisive, with attacks and counterattacks taking and retaking the same ground. Near the fort you can see the **Hagood Brigade Monument**, which honors Confederate Brig. Gen. Johnson Hagood's soldiers.

Head west on Flank Road again to see **Fort Keene** and the **Flowers Farm Site** southwest of the junction with the Vaughan Road. Just over 400 yards west of Fort Keene is the site of **Fort Tracy**. Turn south (left) on the Vaughan Road and travel one-half mile to see the

Poplar Grove National Cemetery, burying ground for 6,178 Union soldiers. Returning to Flank Road, head west to the intersection with Squirrel Level Road. On the northwest corner is the site of **Fort Urmston**, constructed in October 1864 by the Federals after they captured the ground during the battle of Peebles Farm. About 200 yards north of Fort Urmston is the Confederate stronghold **Fort Bratton**. Continuing west on Flank Road just under one-half mile brings you to **Fort Conahey**, another Union fort built after Peebles Farm. Traveling an equal distance again takes you to **Fort Fisher**, the largest earthen fort in the campaign. Completed in March 1865, the fort was never active in the campaign.

You may now wish to turn southeast (left) on Church Road and proceed one-third mile to **Fort Wheaton**, the former Confederate Fort Archer. About 600 yards south of Fort Wheaton is the **William Peebles Farm Site** where brisk skirmishing occurred during the late stages of the campaign. Two more Union strongholds constructed late in the campaign, **Fort Gregg** and **Fort Welch**, stand west of Fort Wheaton, but are inaccessible by road.

Follow Church Road north to the next areas of interest. In the next mile you'll pass the **J. D. Boswell Farm Site**, the **Oscar Pegram Farm Site**, the **Dr. Alfred Boisseau Farm Site**, and the **Robert Jones Farm Site**, all wartime houses no longer extant. These structures stood in the midst of the action during the battle of Peebles Farm. Turn right on Weakley Road, then onto the Boydton Plank Road (Simpson Road), you'll see the site of **Fort Gregg**, part of the Confederate defense line. This spot served as the outpost guarding the western approach to Petersburg. Fort Gregg and **Fort Whitworth** (later Union Fort Baldwin), 500 yards north on Seventh Avenue, held Grant's attack on April 2, 1865, long enough so that Lee's army could escape westward.

Traveling east on the Boydton Plank Road will take you along the inner Confederate line. One mile east of Fort Gregg stand the remains of **Fort Lee**. At the junction take Defense Road east just under a mile to the **Vaughan Farm Site**, a position north of the road on the wartime Weldon Railroad. Four hundred yards northeast of the Vaughan site is the **Fisher Farm Site**, another wartime residence no longer standing. As the road curves north and arcs east again, you'll reach the position of **Fort Pegram**, sometimes called Battery Pegram, another Confederate stronghold in the defensive line. The fort is on the south side of the road. **Fort Walker** stands 400 yards southeast of Fort Pegram. North of the road, as it bends south and becomes South Boulevard, is the position of **Fort New Orleans**.

Traveling about three-fourths mile to the intersection of South Boulevard and Sycamore Street brings you to the position of the great Confederate stronghold **Fort Mahone**, called "Fort Damnation" by the soldiers. The position is marked by the **Pennsylvania Monument**, an obelisk honoring Union regiments that participated in the final attacks on April 2 and 3, 1865. You've now closed the loop of the outer and inner lines and, at this position, are less than 700 yards northwest of Fort Sedgwick, from which the final attack came. The heavy artillery and small arms fire between the two forts constituted some of the most intense fighting of the war, and many famous photographs made after the city's fall show dead soldiers in Forts Mahone and Sedgwick.

You may now wish to head north on Sycamore Street to view the sights of downtown Petersburg. At the **Petersburg Visitor Center** in the McIlwaine House in Market Square you can obtain general information about the historical sites in and around Petersburg, especially relating to the **Old Towne District**, which contains many nineteenth century structures. The **Siege Museum** in the Exchange Building at 15 West Bank Street contains a superb collection of Civil War artifacts relating to the Petersburg area. The **Petersburg Court House** on Sycamore Street was the city's principal landmark during the war

and housed many Confederate offices during the siege. The **Centre Hill Mansion** on the corner of North Adams Street and East Tabb Street served as Union headquarters following the city's fall.

From downtown you may take the Jefferson Davis Highway (U.S. 1, U.S. 301) north across the Appomattox River to **Colonial Heights** (pop. 16,064). See the Petersburg East Sector map (p. 111). About one mile north of Petersburg, you'll see the **Violet Bank Museum** east of the road. This structure served as Lee's headquarters during the early part of the siege, from June to October 1864. Another site of interest can be reached by taking Temple Avenue east to Conduit Road, traveling north

THE PETERSBURG COURTHOUSE dominated the city's skyline during the war. Continuously occupied by Confederate officers during the siege, the court house signaled the end of the siege when Union troops raised the U.S. flag over the building on April 3, 1865.

one mile, then heading east (right) on Brockwell Lane. This leads to the site of **Fort Clifton**, a Confederate gun emplacement guarding its overlook of the Appomattox River.

Several important sites from the Appomattox campaign are scattered west of Petersburg. Consult the Petersburg West Sector map (p. 110). On April 2 and 3, 1865, as Petersburg was evacuated, Lee's army fled westward in hopes of meeting supply trains and then breaking out to unite with Gen. Joseph E. Johnston's army to the south. The ragged condition of the Army of Northern Virginia, low in numbers and supplies, made the task impossible. As Petersburg fell all knew the war would soon be over. Grant's well-supplied army dashed westward in pursuit to harass and capture the remnants of the once mighty gray-clad foe.

Returning to Petersburg and heading south on Halifax Road, then west (right) on the Boydton Plank Road will take you to the scene of one of the final actions in the eastern theater. Cross Rohoic Creek, continue past Fort Gregg, and turn southwest where Boydton Plank Road joins U.S. 1. About one mile south of this intersection, look for a roadside historical marker north of the road. This sign marks the **Ambrose Powell Hill Death Site** where the Confederate lieutenant general was killed on April 2, 1865, while riding into a group of Federal pickets.

Traveling another three miles south brings you to the **Burgess Mill Site** on **Hatcher's Run**. One-third mile farther south is the **Burgess Tavern Site**. Grant ordered an assault here on October 27, 1864, in hopes of cutting Boydton Plank Road and the Southside Railroad. Some 43,000 Federals attacked 28,000 troops from the Army of Northern Virginia. The fighting was inconclusive and both armies withdrew to former positions. The field opposite the site of the Burgess Tavern, at the intersection of Boydton Plank Road and White Oak Road, also has the distinction of holding famous cattle. In September 1864 Confederate Maj. Gen. Wade Hampton, distressed at General Lee's lack of rations, captured 2,486 cat-tle near City Point and returned them to a pen in this field. The "beefsteak raid" greatly helped Lee's soldiers. About one and three-fourths miles west of this intersection (at the junction of White Oak Road and Claiborne Road) is the site of the battle of White Oak Road, which occurred on March 31, 1865.

Another bloody battle of Hatcher's Run occurred February 5-7, 1865, and you can see the battlefield by turning east (left) onto Dabney Mill Road (Virginia 613) and traveling two miles. The **John Pegram Monument** marks the position where the Confederate brigadier general was killed on February 6, 1865.

Returning to Boydton Plank Road, head south just over one-half mile and then turn south (left) onto Quaker Road (Virginia 660). A one-half-mile trip takes you to the **Lewis Farm Ruin** where the battle of the Quaker Road occurred on March 29, 1865. Grant again attempted to cut Lee's supply line, the Southside Railroad. Union Brig. Gen. Joshua L. Chamberlain attacked Confederate Maj. Gen. Bushrod R. Johnson here before falling back and entrenching. Four days later, after the battle of Five Forks, the Southside Railroad was finally broken. Head back to Boydton Plank Road and turn south. After nearly a mile you'll see the **Butler Farm**, "Evergreen," east of the road. This house served as Union Maj. Gen. Gouverneur K. Warren's headquarters after the battle of the Quaker Road.

Continue south across **Gravelly Run** nearly four miles to **Dinwiddie**, where you can see **Dinwiddie Court House**. The court house witnessed Union cavalry arriving on March 30, 1865, to prepare for what would become the battle of Five Forks. Union Maj. Gen. Philip H. Sheridan used the court house as headquarters during the Five Forks operation. You can retrace the route to Five Forks by heading north on Dinwiddie Road (Virginia 627). After one and one-third miles you'll see the **Abner Adams Farm**, "Bonneville," a prominent wartime structure, west of the road. Around this house on March 31, 1865, the armies clashed in the battle of Dinwiddie Court House, prelude to Five Forks.

114

Five Forks Tour

Travel four miles to reach **Five Forks**, an intersection of five roads that marks the location of a decisive battle on April 1, 1865. The **Five Forks Unit** of Petersburg National Battlefield was established in 1990. At this position 9,000 Union cavalry under Sheridan and 12,000 infantry under Maj. Gen. G. K. Warren clashed with Maj. Gen. George E. Pickett's 6,400 infantry and Maj. Gen. Fitzhugh Lee's 4,200 cavalry. Warren, miffed at being placed under Sheridan's command—Warren was the senior Corps commander of the two—arrived late in the afternoon. Regardless, the overwhelming Union attack interrupted operation of the Southside Railroad and necessitated evacuation of the city. The Confederates scurried westward in panic.

From Five Forks head three-fourths mile east on White Oak Road to the position of **the Angle** where Warren's infantry opened the battle by smashing into the Confederate lines, breaking them, and capturing numerous prisoners. Another three-fourths mile east and 250 yards south is the site of the **Gravelly Run Methodist Episcopal Church** where wounded Federals languished after the battle. Returning to Five Forks and continuing west on White Oak Road just under a mile brings you to the position of the Confederate escape route, a trail heading north through the fields. Just under one-half mile south of this position stands the **Gilliam House**, "Burnt Quarter," around which heavy cavalry fighting erupted. Six unidentified Confederate soldiers are buried on the house's grounds.

Heading north from Five Forks on Fords Depot Road (Virginia 627) brings you to **Boisseau's Field**, where Union Maj. Gen. Samuel W. Crawford attacked the rear of the Confederate line, and to the **Shad Bake Site** on

FIVE FORKS, a junction where five roads meet, marks the battlefield site of a decisive Union victory at the end of the Petersburg siege. The battle helped precipitate the Confederate withdrawal toward Appomattox.

Hatcher's Run. Near this spot, as the battle started, Pickett and Fitzhugh Lee were caught off guard while enjoying a shad bake hosted by Brig. Gen. Thomas L. Rosser. Their delinquency here may have contributed to the confused Confederate actions at Five Forks.

Appomattox Campaign Tour

Two major sites west of Petersburg commemorate the end of the Army of Northern Virginia. To reach them, continue north and then head west on U.S. 460. (These do not appear on the maps in this chapter but can be found straightforwardly with the directions provided here.) Your first destination is **Farmville** (pop. 6,046), fifty-three miles west of the U.S. 460 junction. Fleeing westward, Lee hoped to rally his troops and receive wagon trains of supplies at Amelia Court House, but Grant—aware of the two routes Lee could use as means of escape—had taken steps to intercept the Confederates along both roads. On April 4 Lee found no supplies at Amelia Court House—they had been captured by Sheridan's cavalry. On the fifth the Army of Northern Virginia headed south toward Farmville, hoping to be resupplied from Lynchburg.

After four long years, even the experienced, battle-hardened, most loyal Confederates were breaking. The long night march crushed morale. Starving men fell out of ranks. Union cavalry struck at the Confederate rear. The Federal army caught up with Lee at **Sayler's Creek** (variant but incorrect spellings are Saylor's Creek and Sailor's Creek), where the last major battle of the eastern theater occurred. From the village of Rice, turn west (right) onto Virginia 307 and then north onto Virginia 617, which leads to **Sayler's Creek Battlefield Historical State Park**. On April 6, 1865, Lee found himself blocked in front. While attempting to figure his next action, the Federals attacked the army's rear and overwhelmed the Confederates, capturing between 7,000 and 8,000 prisoners, including Lt. Gen. Richard S. Ewell,

Maj. Gens. Joseph B. Kershaw and George W. C. Lee, and Brig. Gens. Montgomery D. Corse, Dudley M. DuBose and Eppa Hunton. The **James Moses Hillsman House** at Sayler's Creek served as a Federal position during the early part of the battle and a hospital following. The structure's original floors are visibly bloodstained.

After the stunning defeat at Sayler's Creek Lee's army cut westward to **High Bridge**, an enormous wartime railroad span, then north of the Appomattox River to **Appomattox Court House**. The huge Federal army, sensing victory, was in hot pursuit. To reach **Appomattox Court House National Historical Park**, continue west on U.S. 460 a distance of thirty miles to **Appomattox** (pop. 1,707) and turn north (right) onto Virginia 131, a spur road connecting to Virginia 24. Traveling two miles brings you into the park.

Before walking the streets of the reconstructed village of Appomattox Court House, see the **Grant Headquarters Site** south of the road. Across the road from this position is **Custer's Roadblock** where on April 8, 1865, Union cavalry under Brig. Gen. George A. Custer blocked Lee's route of escape. The next morning Union infantry under Maj. Gen. Edward O. C. Ord emerged from the woods and the Confederates were surrounded. Later that day General Lee went to see General Grant, the former declaring he would "rather die a thousand deaths."

Continue east on Virginia 24 to the **North Carolina Monument**, south of the road. This memorial marks the position of the last shots fired by the Army of Northern Virginia. About one-fourth mile east of this spot is the **Raine Family Cemetery**, a local burying ground, and the **Appomattox Confederate Cemetery** on the north side of the road, located near the old Richmond-Lynchburg Stage Road that passes through the center of the village. A short distance from the Confederate Cemetery, you'll see the entrance to the park.

Journeying back to Appomattox always brings out the same strange feelings about this event that triggered the end of the Civil War. Explore the many historic structures in the town and you'll pick up that same momentous feeling. The **Visitor Center** is inside **Appomattox Court House** itself, which contains a museum of artifacts relating to the surrender. A footpath leads to the **Appomattox County Jail**, the ruins of the **Old Jail**, the **Isbell House**, the **Kelly House**, the **Mariah Wright House**, and the **Peers House**. At the **Surrender Triangle** on April 12, 1865, 26,765 Confederate soldiers, all that was left of Lee's army, stacked their arms for the last time. Walk back to the northwest side of the Court House and you can see the **Clover Hill Tavern**, the **Meeks General Store**, and the **Lafayette Meeks Grave**, resting place of a Confederate soldier and Appomattox resident.

The primary attraction at Appomattox is southwest of the Court House, the **Wilmer McLean House**, a reconstruction using mainly original materials. Grant and Lee met

THE WILMER McLEAN HOUSE at Appomattox Court House witnessed Lee's surrender to Grant on Palm Sunday, April 9, 1865. The event effectively ended the war. Wilmer McLean, who escaped Bull Run when Confederates commandeered his house, could say with jocularity, "The war began in my back yard and ended in my front parlor" (Above and at right).

in the front parlor of this building on Palm Sunday, April 9, 1865. The surrender meeting lasted a short time, and then Lee rode off to deliver his farewell General Order Number 9. Grant admonished the cheering Federal soldiers, telling them that the Rebels were their countrymen again. Confederate armies still existed in the field south and west of Virginia, but with the premier Rebel army surrendered, the war was effectively over. In one of the great ironies of the war, McLean had moved away from Manassas, Virginia, after the first battle of Bull Run. Confederate officers had inhabited his farmhouse and he wanted to relocate far away from the war. Wilmer McLean later told nostalgia seekers, "The war began in my back yard and ended in my front parlor."

Petersburg National Battlefield

Mailing address: 1539 Hickory Hill Road, Petersburg, Virginia 23803-4721
Telephone: (804) 732-3531
Park established: July 3, 1926
Area: 2,659 acres

Appomattox Court House National Historical Park

Mailing address: Highway 24, P.O. Box 218, Appomattox, Virginia 24522
Telephone: (434) 352-8987
Park established: August 3, 1935
Area: 1,774 acres

Blandford Cemetery

Established: 1702
Area: 11.4 acres
Civil War interments: about 30,000

Poplar Grove National Cemetery

Established: July 1866
Area: 8.7 acres
Civil War interments: 6,178

Petersburg accommodations

Petersburg itself contains four hotels and motels, and plentiful accommodations exist relatively nearby in the Richmond area. The most convenient place to stay when visiting Appomattox Court House is the Lynchburg area.

Chapter 8

✪　　✪　　✪

Richmond and City Point

Early the next morning the whole town was on the street.
Ambulances, litters, carts, every vehicle that the city could produce,
went and came with a ghastly burden;
those who could walk limped painfully home, in some cases
so black with gunpowder they passed unrecognized.

—Constance Cary Harrison
describing Richmond the morning after the battle of Seven Pines,
June 1, 1862.

The capital of the Confederacy and its sur-rounding area is a region steeped deeply in Civil War history. As the central focus of Con-federate memorialization, **Richmond**, Vir-ginia (pop. 203,056), contains fabulous museums and preserved houses relating to wartime Richmond and the Confederate strug-gle. As the central focus of two major military campaigns during the war, the city's outlying areas are pockmarked by pieces of battlefield that have survived the growth of the city around them. As is the case with nearby Peters-burg, the relatively recent establishment of the park and urban outgrowth in the area means that much of the historic ground fought over in 1862, 1864, and 1865 now holds commer-cial and residential buildings.

Although the Richmond battlefields are hardly preserved completely, you can tour what is left and get a great sense of the battles that flared around the young Confederacy's gov-ernmental homeland. The war struck close at Richmond twice, the first time during Union

Maj. Gen. George B. McClellan's Peninsular campaign in 1862, and the second as the result of Lt. Gen. Ulysses S. Grant's 1864 May cam-paign, also called the Overland campaign. The latter maneuver resulted in the siege of Peters-burg and eventually the end of the war.

As at Bull Run, the fields of conflict in Rich-mond in 1864 were sometimes the same places where battles occurred two years prior, or often fell very close to the old battlefields. Because of this, and because the fighting went on for periods of weeks at a time, touring the Rich-mond battlefields in a straightforward, chrono-logical order is difficult. As we approached Richmond for the fourth time, my father and I were just getting to the point where we under-stood the movements of the armies during the campaigns. Yet touring the Richmond battle-fields is relatively simple compared with fol-lowing the campaign at Petersburg.

Richmond sits on the James River in the cen-tral part of eastern Virginia, by Petersburg (close to the south); Hampton, Newport News, and

CHIMBORAZO VISITOR CENTER was built on the site of what was the Confederacy's largest hospital, a forty-acre spread where doctors treated 76,000 Confederate soldiers.

Norfolk (to the southeast); Fredericksburg and Washington (to the north); and Charlottesville (to the northwest). When we arrived in the city, we proceeded to the **Chimborazo Hospital Richmond National Battlefield Park Visitor Center**, which stands in the southeastern part of town at 3215 East Broad Street. The visitor center contains a museum of Richmond artifacts. A former weather station, this postwar building in Chimborazo Park marks the site of the largest hospital in the Confederacy, where forty acres held dozens of buildings and hundreds of tents in which doctors and nurses helped more than 76,000 wartime patients.

The Peninsular Campaign and Cold Harbor Tour

Throughout the first part of the Richmond tour use the Richmond, Virginia, map (p. 123). From Chimborazo, head southeast on Government Road a distance of one and one-fourth miles and turn east (left) onto Williamsburg Road. After 300 yards you'll see the **Richmond National Cemetery** south of the road. In this ten-acre site lie the remains of 6,670 Union soldiers who died in the battles and hospitals surrounding Richmond. Continuing along Williamsburg Road two and one-half miles and turning north (left) onto South Laburnum Avenue will take you toward the first of the Richmond battlefields. After five miles you'll reach the Mechanicsville Turnpike (U.S. 360), where you should turn northeast (right). This road is the same that carried Confederate defenders toward the Union attackers during the 1862 and 1864 campaigns. After traveling two-thirds mile, you'll see a park sign and road south of the turnpike. You can turn here into the **Chickahominy Bluffs**. To appreciate what transpired

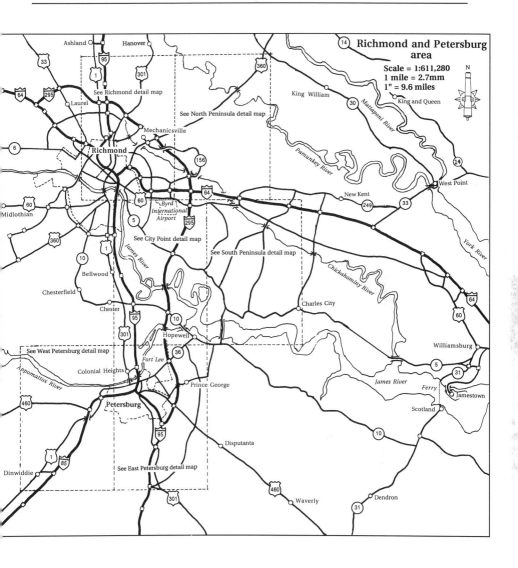

Richmond and Petersburg area

Scale = 1:611,280
1 mile = 2.7mm
1" = 9.6 miles

over these quiet fields, hills, and valleys requires a brief examination of McClellan's 1862 campaign.

In early summer of 1862, Major General McClellan hatched a plan to move his Army of the Potomac southward by ship and attack Richmond by means of the Virginia peninsula. By doing so, McClellan could avoid an overland movement like the failed Bull Run campaign of the previous summer. After arguing against such a plan, President Lincoln finally agreed to allow McClellan to put his Peninsular campaign into action. The Union army, however, lacked accurate maps and underestimated the difficulty of the swampy terrain between Fort Monroe at Hampton, where most of the troops landed, and the Confederate capital. After engagements at Yorktown and Williamsburg,

the Federals succeeded in pushing the Confederate defenders back toward Richmond, and a savage series of battles with a bewildering array of alternate names occurred from June 25 to July 1, 1862.

Collectively called the Seven Days, the battles were Oak Grove on June 25 (also called the Orchard, Henrico, French's Field, and King's School House), Mechanicsville on June 26 (Meadow Bridge, Ellison's Mills, Beaver Dam Creek), Gaines's Mill on June 27–28 (First Cold Harbor, Chickahominy Bluffs), Garnett's Farm on June 27–28 (Golding's Farm), Savage's Station on June 29 (Allen's Farm, the Peach Orchard), White Oak Swamp on June 30 (Glendale, Frayser's Farm, Nelson's Farm, Turkey Bridge, Charles City Crossroads, Newmarket Road), and Malvern Hill on July 1 (Harrison's Landing, Crew's Farm, Poindexter's Farm).

Despite the bloody effort by McClellan, whose army advanced to a position eight miles outside of the city, the Peninsular campaign failed. Before the Seven Days fighting erupted, battles had taken place at Drewry's Bluff (Fort Darling) on the James River, a heavily armed bastion that protected Richmond from hostile warships, and at Seven Pines (Fair Oaks) on the peninsula. These events transpired on May 15 and May 31, 1862. By early July, after the Seven Days, the Union army returned northward and abandoned the effort. During the Peninsular campaign McClellan had faced a new opponent, little known outside of Virginia. Gen. Robert E. Lee had assumed command of the Army of Northern Virginia after its former commander, Gen. Joseph E. Johnston, was wounded at Seven Pines.

The first of the Seven Days sites, Chickahominy Bluffs, contains remnants of entrenchments that constituted part of the outer Confederate line surrounding the city. The overlook provides an outstanding view of **Mechanicsville** (pop. 22,027). Near this spot General Lee watched the opening of the Seven Days battles. Continuing northeast on Mechanicsville Road will carry you across the Chickahominy River. At Mechanicsville turn south (right) onto Virginia 156, which after one mile leads you to another park site, south of the road, **Beaver Dam Creek**. This area, the site of **Ellison's Mill**, was part of the Union line attacked unsuccessfully by the Confederates on June 26. Continuing on Virginia 156 one and one-fourth miles brings you to the **Walnut Grove Baptist Church**, north of the road. Constructed in 1846, this building served as a meeting place for Lee and Stonewall Jackson as they plotted strategy on June 27, 1862.

Now switch to using the Virginia Peninsula (North Sector) map (p. 124). Head south on Virginia 156, now called Cold Harbor Road, and you'll soon reach the **Cold Harbor battlefield**, site of a very costly battle in Grant's 1864 campaign. Following Grant's prolonged and vicious fight at Spotsylvania Court House in May 1864, he maneuvered the Army of the Potomac southeastward toward Richmond. This forced Lee to block Grant by staying between the Union force and the capital city. The Confederate army constructed massive entrenchments along an extended line centered near Cold Harbor. On June 3 Grant launched a frontal attack that produced 7,000 Union casualties in less than half an hour. Cold Harbor cast the war in a new

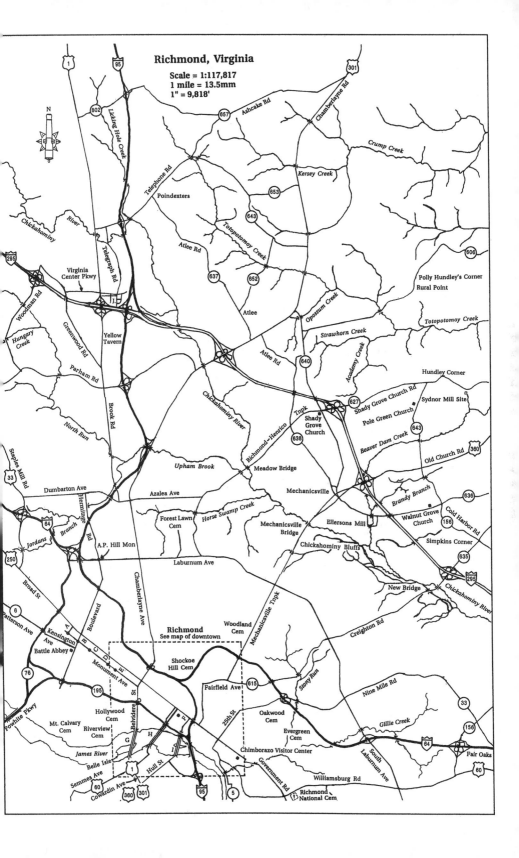

Richmond, Virginia

Scale = 1:117,817
1 mile = 13.5mm
1" = 9,818'

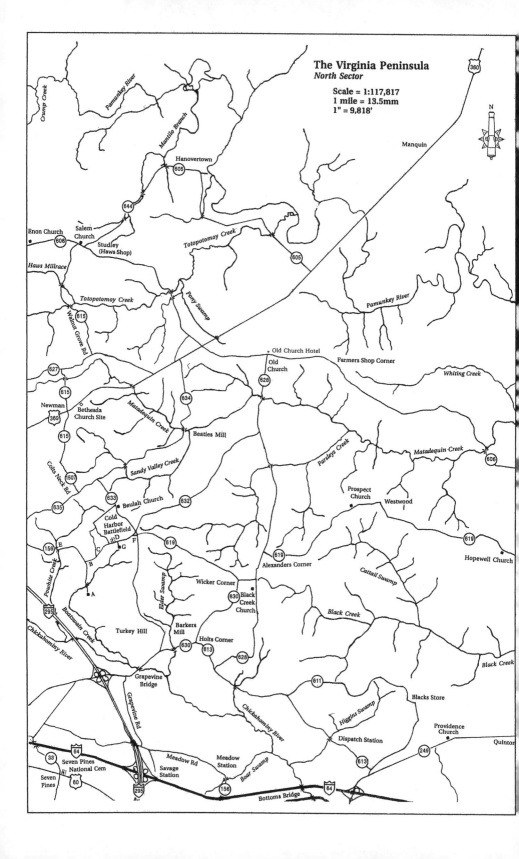

Key to Features on Virginia
Peninsula, North Sector Map

A Sarah Watt House
B New Cold Harbor
C Cold Harbor NPS Shelter
D Cold Harbor National Cemetery

E Gaines's Mill
F Old Cold Harbor
G Garthright House

light, one of siege operations rather than pitched battles. Heavy fighting shifted to the Confederate forts constructed southeast of the city. Meade's Army of the Potomac and the Federal Army of the James, commanded by Maj. Gen. Benjamin F. Butler, shifted away from Richmond and settled into a siege of nearby Petersburg, a vital rail and supply center that if captured would cause the abandonment of the Confederate capital.

As you approach Cold Harbor, note when you cross Powhite Creek. North of the road lies a small tablet marking the site of **Gaines's Mill**, after which the third of the Seven Days battles was named. Continue ahead to **New Cold Harbor**, and after crossing Boatswain's Creek, you'll arrive at the **Sarah Watt House**. The restored house served as Union Maj. Gen. Fitz John Porter's headquarters during the battle of Gaines's Mill. Confederate troops broke the

THE SARAH WATT HOUSE at Gaines's Mill served as headquarters for Union Maj. Gen Fitz John Porter during the battle of Gaines's Mill.

Union lines not far from the house, and a trail leads to Union entrenchments constructed prior to the battle.

Returning to Virginia 156 and heading east takes you to the **Cold Harbor National Park Service Shelter** located at the entrance of a park road that follows the main line of entrenchments built during the 1864 campaign. The amazing closeness of the Union and Confederate trenches may strike you as odd. If you loop through the park road and meet Virginia 633 at Beulah Church, turn south and meet up with Virginia 156 at **Old Cold Harbor**. Heading west will take you to the **Garthright House**, a wartime structure that served as a Union hospital during the battle of Cold Harbor and a Confederate hospital following the battle. Across the road and slightly west is the **Cold Harbor National Cemetery**, which contains the graves of 1,988 Union soldiers. A tomb at the cemetery's north end is a large mass grave that holds the remains of 889 unknown soldiers.

An excursion northward takes you to several ancillary sites. From Old Cold Harbor head northeast on Virginia 632 and turn north where it joins Virginia 628. After five miles you'll reach **Old Church** where you'll see the **Old Church Hotel**. During the Cold Harbor campaign, this stately brick building served as headquarters for Union Maj. Gen. Philip H. Sheridan and Brig. Gens. Alfred T. A. Torbert and Edward Ferrero. Turning west on Virginia 606 and proceeding four and three-fourths miles brings you to the center of **Studley** (pop. 7,321), marked by a general store. Across from the store is the site of **Haws Shop**. Here, on May 29, 1864, a seven-hour battle flared between Sheridan's

ONE OF THE LARGEST MASS GRAVES in a U.S. national cemetery can be found at Cold Harbor National Cemetery. The tomb stands over a burial trench that holds the remains of 889 unknown Union soldiers killed in the 1862 and 1864 campaigns around Richmond.

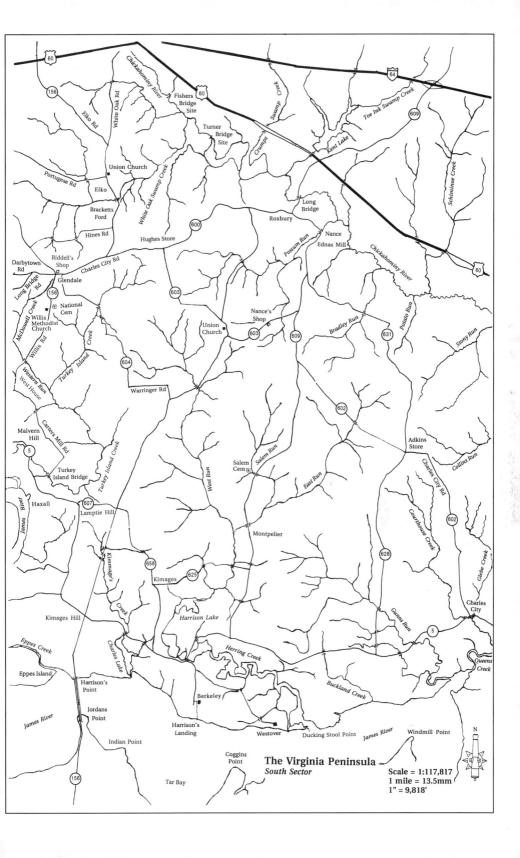

The Virginia Peninsula
South Sector

Scale = 1:117,817
1 mile = 13.5mm
1" = 9,818'

cavalry and the Confederate brigades of Brig. Gens. Thomas L. Rosser and Williams C. Wickham. Armed with Spencer carbines, the Yanks routed the Rebs. One third of a mile west of Studley stands **Salem Church** and another one-half mile west is **Enon Church**, both hospital sites following the battle.

Returning to Salem Church and heading south on Walnut Grove Road (Virginia 615) will take you, after a westward jog on Virginia 627, to the village of **Newman**. About 250 yards east of this intersection, you'll encounter the site of **Bethesda Church**, after which a bloody engagement fought on May 30, 1864, was named.

Now you can return to the Cold Harbor battlefield by heading south on Virginia 615, which becomes Colt's Neck Road (Virginia 1507). Turn east (left) onto Virginia 635 and head south (right) on Virginia 633. This brings you back to the intersection at Old Cold Harbor.

You may wish to head south on Virginia 156 toward the southern part of the Virginia peninsula. After traveling three miles you'll cross the Chickahominy River at **Grapevine Bridge**, the spot where Maj. Gen. Fitz John Porter's men constructed bridges, made partly of swamp foliage, after being pushed south from the Watt House. Later Stonewall Jackson used the same bridges in pursuit. Continue south on Virginia 156, now called Grapevine Road, to a point where the road turns east (left) and is called Meadow Road. About one-half mile east of the turn, south of the road, lies the battlefield of **Savage's Station**, site of the fifth of the Seven Days battles. Continue east and south on Virginia 156 and you can see the remaining sites of the 1862 campaign.

After crossing Interstate 64, the road connects with U.S. 60. Head west (right) on U.S. 60 and proceed three and one-third miles to **Seven Pines National Cemetery**, which contains the remains of 1,407 Union soldiers who died at the battle of Seven Pines or in nearby hospitals. The cemetery marks the position of

the battleground of May 31 and June 1, 1862, when Joe Johnston's Confederates faced McClellan's Federals. To reach the next area, see the Richmond, Virginia, map (p. 123). Head north on Virginia 33 a distance of one and one-fourth miles to see the battlefield of **Fair Oaks**, along the railroad west of the intersection of Virginia 33 and Virginia 156. Here on May 31, Confederates attempted to destroy Brig. Gen. Erasmus D. Keyes's isolated 4th Army Corps. The Confederate attempt failed. During the action their army commander, Joseph E. Johnston, was seriously wounded.

Returning to U.S. 60, travel to the point where Virginia 156 splits off, and take it southward. Now consult the Virginia Peninsula (South Sector) map (p. 127). After about three and one-half miles you'll come to Union Church, the village of Elko, and shortly thereafter White Oak Swamp Creek. The bridge here marks the position of the **White Oak Swamp**, sixth of the Seven Days battles, where Union Brig. Gen. William B. Franklin's skillful artillery work prevented Stonewall Jackson from reuniting with Maj. Gen. A. P. Hill.

Continue south on Virginia 156 as it joins the Charles City Road (Virginia 600). One mile after this intersection you'll arrive in **Glendale**, more ground fought over in the penultimate struggle of the Seven Days. Near the intersection where Virginia 156 heads south is the site of **Riddell's Shop**, a blacksmith's shop that stood at the focus of some of the fighting. Proceeding south on Virginia 156 will, after three-fourths mile, bring you to **Glendale National Cemetery** east of the road, the burying ground of 1,202 Federal soldiers. A short distance farther south, and west of the road, stands **Willis Church**, a rebuilt structure on the site of the wartime building. The church served as a Confederate hospital during the final battle of the Seven Days.

Ironically, the Union army did very well during the last of the Seven Days battles. To see the battlefield, travel south on Virginia 156 one

THE WHITE OAK SWAMP proved difficult for the Union army tramping toward Richmond during the Peninsular campaign in 1862. The swampy terrain brought horses, men, and wagons to a virtual standstill.

and one-half miles and you'll come to **Malvern Hill**. Across from the Park Service pulloff stands the **West House**, headquarters for Federal Brig. Gen. Darius N. Couch during the battle. A few hundred yards south of this spot, on the west side of the road, stands the **Crew House** where the Confederate brigades of Brig. Gens. William Mahone and Ambrose R. Wright concentrated during the battle. From here Lee attempted to hit the retiring Federals hard with a coordinated attack that failed. Nearly 250 Union cannon protected the hill, opening up on July 1 at 1 P.M. and dominating the battle. Lee withdrew toward Richmond and McClellan retired toward Harrison's Landing. The Peninsular campaign was over.

Two summers later Confederate and Union troops constructed substantial forts southeast

THE WEST HOUSE at Malvern Hill was Union Brig. Gen. Darius N. Couch's headquarters during the final clash before McClellan withdrew from the peninsula.

129

of Richmond when Grant's Federals attempted to take the town. To see the best of the remaining earthworks, head south on Virginia 156 and turn west (right) onto New Market Road (Virginia 5). Now you'll need to use the City Point map (p. 132). The area south of the turn is **Strawberry Plains**, a region that witnessed two savage attacks during the 1864 campaign, July 27-29 and August 13-20. After crossing Interstate 295, you'll come into a fortified area where remnants of trenches exist on both sides of the road. About two and three-fourths miles after crossing the interstate, turn south (left) onto Battlefield Park Road. Over the next one and three-fourths miles you'll see the sites of **Fort Alexander, Fort Gilmer, Fort Gregg,** and **Fort Johnson,** all on the west (right) side of the road. During the 1864 campaign these Confederate defensive fortifications were connected by miles of earthworks.

Just over one-half mile past Fort Johnson, turn east (left) onto a small park road and then south (right) onto Varina Road. After traveling 300 yards, you'll come to **Fort Harrison National Cemetery** where 818 Union soldiers lie entombed. Return to the main park road and continue south to reach **Fort Harrison,** a Confederate stronghold captured by Grant on September 29, 1864, during the Petersburg campaign. The fort was thereafter enlarged and heavily reinforced by the Union army.

Continuing south on the park road for just over one-half mile will bring you to the site of **Battery White** (west of the road) and, shortly after that, **Fort Hoke,** both Confederate defensive works. Returning to Fort Hoke and heading south on Hoke-Brady Road takes you past many entrenchments for the Union position at **Fort Brady.** From Fort Brady you can glimpse the James River. Numerous Confederate ships traveled this stretch of the James River as they approached the city, providing a critical supply line for the South.

You may wish to continue your tour by heading north on Hoke-Brady Road and turning east (right) on Kingsland Road, which after three miles connects with Deep Bottom Road. Turning south (right) on this road takes you to an area on the James River known as **Deep Bottom,** where heavy fighting erupted during July and August 1864 as Grant maneuvered toward Petersburg. Return to Kingsland Road and take it eastward to Virginia 5 (New Market Road). Head east past the Malvern Hill area and south as it joins Virginia 156. Now consult the Virginia Peninsula (South Sector) map (p. 127). About four and one-half miles after passing Malvern Hill, you may wish to turn west (right) onto Virginia 608. A one and three-fourths mile trip on this road leads to the **Hill Carter Plantation,** "Shirley," one of the grand plantation houses of Virginia. The house is the birthplace of Anne Hill Carter, Gen. Robert E. Lee's mother. If you look across the James from the house, you'll see the area known as **Bermuda Hundred,** where Butler's Army of the James spent May and June of 1864 pointlessly trying to work its way up river. His men spent the rest of the war digging the **Dutch Gap Canal** to enable warships to move up the James, an exercise that proved of no military value.

To see two more magnificent plantation homes, return to Virginia 5 and head east for two and one-fourth miles, then turn south on a small road that leads to **Harrison's Landing.** After the Seven Days, Union encampments around this area finally drew the Peninsular campaign to a close on August 14, 1862, when McClellan's army began leaving the area by ship from Harrison's Landing. The magnificent house here is the **Benjamin Harrison Plantation,** "Berkeley," which served as McClellan's headquarters during the final stage of the Peninsular campaign. William Henry Harrison was born in the house, and Maj. Gen. Daniel Butterfield's bugler Oliver Norton composed "Taps" nearby. Exiting Berkeley Road, you can travel southeast two miles on Virginia 633 to the **William Evelyn Byrd II Plantation,** "Westover," another lovely house occupied by Union troops before they departed the peninsula.

City Point Tour

Returning to Virginia 156 and heading south, you're now ready to cross the James River. Switch back to the City Point map (p. 132). A prominence in the James, **City Point** served as the center of Union activity—and the largest seaport in the world—during the final ten months of the war. Grant established headquarters at City Point on June 15, 1864, concentrating his efforts on Petersburg and directing a huge volume of supplies that arrived by ship and traveled to the Union lines via the U.S. Military Railroad.

To reach City Point, take Virginia 10 west to **Hopewell** (pop. 23,101), the modern city surrounding Grant's old base of operations. As you enter the town, Virginia 10 will become Randolph Street. Turn northeast (right) onto East Broadway and then north (right) onto Cedar Lane. That will lead to the **City Point Unit** of Petersburg National Battlefield. The central attraction here is the **Eppes House,** "Appomattox Manor," the main structure standing at the time of the war. In 1864 and 1865 these grounds were filled with cabins and tents used by Federal officers and troops. Grant himself did not use the Eppes House as a headquarters—he gave it to his chief quartermaster, Brig. Gen. Rufus Ingalls. Instead, Grant occupied a cabin east of the house. The reconstructed **Grant Cabin** now stands at the position it occupied during the war. A famous wartime series of photographs showing Grant and his staff was made in front of this cabin.

You may wish to return to East Broadway and continue on it as it becomes West Broadway to reach **City Point National Cemetery,** the burial place of 5,158 Union soldiers, many of whom were Black troops in Butler's army. Centrally located in the cemetery, the **Army of the James Monument** was constructed in 1865 under Butler's orders.

To depart City Point, cross the Appomattox River on Virginia 10 and travel six miles to the intersection with Virginia 617, the site of the

Ware Bottom Church. Skirmishes occurred around the church May 9-20, 1864, as Butler attempted to attack the Confederate lines. Some 500 yards south of the intersection on Virginia 617, you'll find the site of **Parker's Battery,** one of the defensive positions from which Confederates fought Butler, eventually "bottling him up" in Bermuda Hundred. You can retrace part of the Confederate **Howlett Line** of defenses by following Virginia 617 south to Woods Edge Road, Howlett Line Drive, Fox Knoll Road, Woodduck Lane, Clear Spring Lane, and Walthall Creek Drive.

Having returned to Virginia 10, continue west 600 yards past the Jefferson Davis Highway (U.S. 1). South of the road stands the **Winfree House,** a prominent landmark during the May 10, 1864, battle of Chester Station. Heading north on Jefferson Davis Highway two miles takes you to the **Halfway House,** Major General Butler's headquarters on May 14 through 16, 1864. About one-half mile north of this structure, you may turn east (right) on Raymet Road, then north (left) on Coach Road, then east (right) onto Willis Road. Some 400 yards east on Willis Road brings you to the **R. A.**

GRANT'S CABIN at City Point is the reassembled structure in which Lieutenant General Grant established headquarters for the final months of the war. The Eppes Mansion, "Appomattox Manor" (background), served as Brig. Gen. Rufus Ingalls's headquarters.

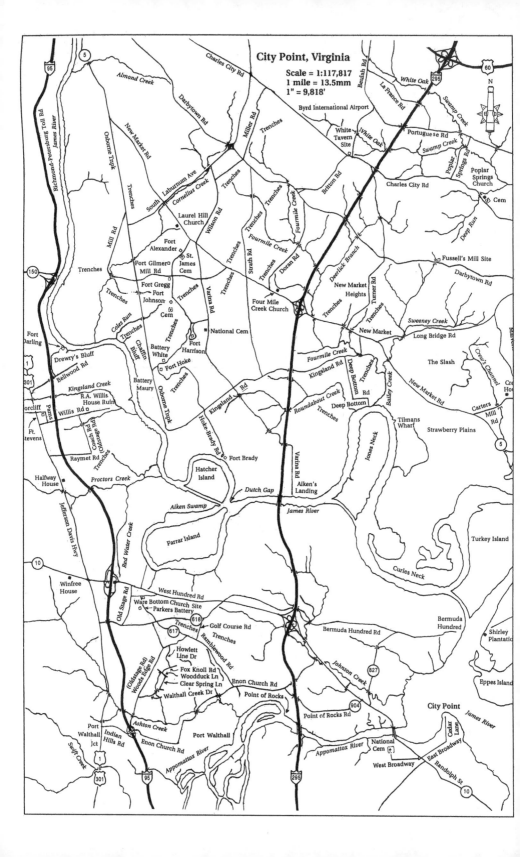

Willis House Ruin, remains of a prominent farmhouse where on May 15, 1864, Maj. Gen. William F. "Baldy" Smith concentrated Union forces close to the Confederate lines. Travel west on Willis Road, turn north (right) on Pams, and stop at the intersection of Pams and Norcliff. You are now at the site of **Fort Stevens**, meeting point of the inner and outer Confederate lines.

To reach the last major site associated with the 1862 campaign, head north on Jefferson Davis Highway until you approach Bellwood Road, a distance of just under half a mile. Turn east (right) onto Bellwood and follow it just over half a mile, then turn north (left) onto Fort Darling Road. This leads to **Drewry's Bluff**, the strategic overlook and fort that provided the most significant defense of the James River south of Richmond. On May 15, 1862, a flotilla of four Union gunboats including the U.S.S. *Monitor* attacked the fort—which Union soldiers called Fort Darling—unsuccessfully. Throughout most of the war the fort and surrounding area served as the Confederate Naval Academy and Marine Corps Camp of Instruction.

Richmond Tour

Now use the Downtown Richmond map (p. 134). Head north on the Jefferson Davis Highway eight miles to return to Richmond. As you cross the James over the Robert E. Lee Bridge, take note of the island below you. It is **Belle Isle**, the largest wartime prison camp in Virginia, where at any given time as many as 10,000 Federal soldiers were incarcerated. As you enter the city, turn west (left) onto Albemarle Street, and after traveling four blocks you'll come to **Hollywood Cemetery**, the most famous of all Confederate cemeteries. About 18,000 Confederate soldiers are buried in Hollywood, including many of the most prominent figures in Confederate history. Two U.S. presidents, James Monroe and John Tyler, also lie within the cemetery's boundaries.

The most important Confederate site in Hollywood is the **Jefferson Finis Davis Grave** honoring the president of the Confederate States, his wife Varina Davis, and other family members. (The tombstone mistakenly names Davis as a U.S. brigadier general.) The **Confederate Memorial Pyramid** honors all Confederate soldiers. Prominent among the Confederate graves are those of general officers Joseph R. Anderson, James J. Archer, Robert H. Chilton, Philip St. George Cocke, Richard B. Garnett, Henry Heth, Eppa Hunton, John D. Imboden, Edward Johnson, David R. Jones, Fitzhugh Lee, John Pegram, George E. Pickett, Isaac M. St. John, John C. C. Sanders, William Smith, Walter H. Stevens, James E. B. Stuart, William R. Terry, Reuben Lindsay Walker, and Henry A. Wise. Hydrographer Matthew

JEFFERSON DAVIS is buried in an honored section of Hollywood Cemetery in Richmond. The Confederate president is accompanied by his wife Varina and other family members.

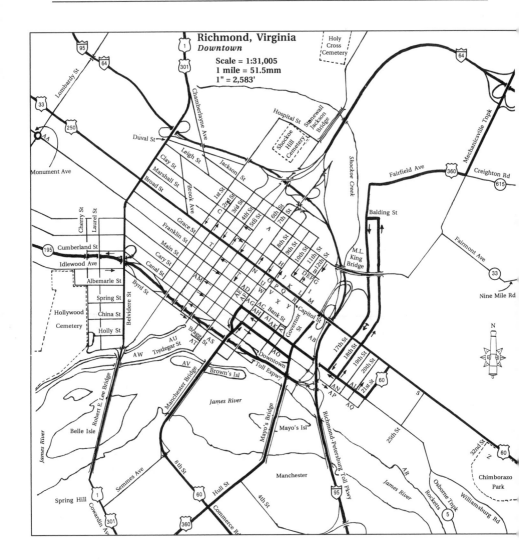

Richmond, Virginia
Downtown

Scale = 1:31,005
1 mile = 51.5mm
1" = 2,583'

Fontaine Maury, military engineer Charles Dimmock, and politicians James A. Seddon and Jabez L. M. Curry are also buried here.

Now consult the Richmond, Virginia, map (p. 123). From Hollywood, head north on Belvidere Street and turn northwest (left) onto Monument Avenue. Over the next two miles you can see some of the finest monuments in the Confederacy, prominently arranged on the

boulevard. You'll encounter the **James Ewell Brown Stuart Monument**, the **Robert Edward Lee Monument**, the **Jefferson Finis Davis Monument**, the **Thomas Jonathan Jackson Monument**, and the **Matthew Fontaine Maury Monument**. You may want to retrace your path to the Jackson Monument and head south on Boulevard Avenue a few blocks. At 428 North Boulevard

Avenue, you'll find the **Virginia Historical Society,** "Battle Abbey," a magnificent building constructed to house the state's Confederate collection. The museum inside contains Confederate murals and an outstanding group of artifacts, including personal memorabilia of Robert E. Lee and Jeb Stuart. Next door to the Virginia Historical Society stands the headquarters of the **United Daughters of the Confederacy.**

Next, you may wish to travel north on Boulevard Avenue, which becomes Hermitage Road, to the intersection with Laburnum Avenue where you'll find the **Ambrose Powell Hill Tomb.** The magnificent equestrian statue of Hill stands atop the general's grave. The final site north of town, the **Yellow Tavern** battle-field, is a significant site associated with Confederate Major General Jeb Stuart.

Reaching Yellow Tavern takes a few changes of road. From Laburnum Avenue go west to Interstate 95, travel north five miles, take Interstate 295 west to U.S. 1, take U.S. 1 north to the Virginia Center Parkway, travel east (right) on the Virginia Center Parkway, and head south (right) on Old Telegraph Road. You'll see the **James Ewell Brown Stuart Mortal Wounding Site Monument** in a residential neighborhood near the intersection of Old Telegraph Road and Harmony Avenue. Here the battle of Yellow Tavern raged on May 11, 1864, and the Confederate cavalry hero was mortally wounded, dying the following day.

THE AMBROSE POWELL HILL MONUMENT
at the intersection of Laburnum Avenue and
Hermitage Road contains the body of this fallen
Confederate hero, who was killed outside
Petersburg on April 2, 1865.

You may wish to head south on Interstate
95 back into town to see the many sites relating to the Confederate government in Richmond. Now consult the Downtown Richmond
map (p. 134). Exit downtown and find Fourth
Street, which you'll take northeast to reach
Hospital Street, where you should turn northwest (left). You'll soon arrive at **Shockoe Hill
Cemetery**, burying ground of 997 soldiers,
most of whom were Federals. The Union spy
and Richmond resident Elizabeth Van Lew is
also buried here. Many of the deceased soldiers
came from the **Alms House**, Confederate General Hospital no. 1, which stands across Hospital Street from the Shockoe Cemetery
entrance.

Continue on Hospital Street to First Street,
which you should take southwest until you
reach Leigh Street. Turn southeast (left) and
proceed until you reach Twelfth Street, where
you should head southwest (right). At Twelfth
and Clay Streets, you'll see a parking garage
available for the **John Brockenbrough
House**, Museum and White House of the Confederacy. This superb museum cannot be
missed. The Brockenbrough House was Jefferson Davis's official residence during the war,
serving as the equivalent of Lincoln's White
House. Lincoln visited Davis's office after the
city fell. A tour guides visitors through the
house into the various rooms where the Davis
family lived and conducted official business.
The adjoining Museum of the Confederacy
houses the greatest collection of Confederate
relics in one place. Included among the displays
are artifacts belonging to the Davis family and
many officers including Simon B. Buckner, John
B. Floyd, John Bell Hood, Stonewall Jackson,
Joseph E. Johnston, Robert E. Lee, John Hunt
Morgan, Raphael Semmes, Jeb Stuart, and
Joseph Wheeler.

Walk northeastward along Clay Street and
you'll encounter several more important buildings. The **Maury House**, located at 1105 East
Clay Street, housed the "Pathfinder of the
Seas," Matthew Fontaine Maury, during the
spring and summer of 1861. Here he conducted
numerous experiments designed to aid Confederate naval warfare. The **James Caskie
House** stands—with a modern storefront
added—near the corner of Eleventh and Clay
Streets. Mrs. Robert Edward Lee lived in this
dwelling during 1862 and part of 1863. During the war the **John Wickham House** on the
southwest corner of Eleventh and Clay Streets
provided lodging for Christopher G. Mem-
minger, Confederate Secretary of the Treasury.
The building now houses the **Valentine Museum** of relics, artwork, and artifacts relating to
Richmond's history. As you walk back to the
White House, you may notice the **Bruce
House** on the northwest corner of Twelfth and

THE WHITE HOUSE OF THE CONFEDERACY is now a superb museum built around the wartime residence of Jefferson Davis. An adjacent building contains the greatest collection of Confederate memorabilia assembled in one spot.

Clay Streets. Confederate Vice President Alexander H. Stephens boarded at this house during 1861 and 1862.

You may wish to continue by heading south on Twelfth Street. At Twelfth and Marshall Streets stands the **Egyptian Building**, a part of the Medical College of Virginia. The institution was the only medical college in the Confederacy that remained open throughout the war. On the northwest corner of Twelfth and Broad Streets, you'll see the **First Baptist Church**, a hospital following the battle of Seven Pines. Turning northwest (right) onto Broad Street will take you past several landmarks. The **Virginia State Library and Archives** faces the First Baptist Church. The building houses an enormous collection of Civil War books and manuscripts. The northeast corner of Tenth and

Broad Streets once supported the **Broad Street Methodist Church**, which was razed in 1968. On April 2, 1865, Confederate Secretary of War John C. Breckinridge was attending services here when he learned the city had to be evacuated. Across the street from this position stood the **Old City Jail** and the **Winder Building**, the headquarters of John H. Winder, Provost Marshal General. Neither building remains. Across the street from the Winder Building stood the old **Richmond City Hall**, which was demolished in 1874.

At the southwest corner of Ninth and Broad Streets is the site of a building occupied by **Hoyer and Ludwig**, lithographers of Confederate documents, stamps, and currency. Two blocks northwest, at the southeast corner of Seventh and Broad Streets, is the site of the

Richmond Theater. After the theater opened on February 9, 1863, many Confederate officials attended shows.

Turning southwest (left) onto Sixth Street and then northwest (right) onto Grace Street will, after three blocks, carry you past the **Samuel Cooper Residence**. The building stands on the northwest corner of Third and Grace Streets and is the second door from Grace Street. Cooper served as adjutant and inspector general of the Confederate States Army and was its ranking general officer. Turn southwest (left) onto Third Street and then southeast (left) onto Franklin Street to continue your tour. You may now wish to park in the vicinity of Eighth or Ninth Street to explore the many significant structures near Virginia's Capitol.

The **Virginia State Capitol**, on the hill's summit, served as the capitol of the Confederacy during the war. The Confederate Congress met inside the building beginning on May 8, 1861, and the old Senate and House chambers can be visited today. Robert E. Lee accepted command of the Virginia State Militia inside the House chamber where you can now see the **Robert Edward Lee Monument**. Also in this room the bodies of Lee, Stonewall Jackson, and Jeb Stuart lay in state. On February 22, 1862, Jefferson Davis took the oath here as president of the Confederate States of America. Outside the house chamber you can see the Houdon **George Washington Monument**, the only statue for which Washington posed. On the capitol's grounds you can see the **George**

THE VIRGINIA STATE CAPITOL hosted the Confederate Congress throughout the Civil War. Besides serving the current state government, the magnificent structure holds statues and artifacts relating to heroic Confederates.

Washington Monument, a famous equestrian statue that stood during the war, the **Thomas Jonathan "Stonewall" Jackson Monument**, the **William Smith Monument**, and the **Hunter Holmes McGuire Monument**. On the southeast side of the capitol's grounds, you'll find the **Governor's Mansion**, a stately building occupied by wartime governors John Letcher and William Smith. The southwest corner of the grounds contains the **Richmond Tocsin**, the bell tower constructed in 1824, whose three quick taps signaled an enemy approach and a need for defense.

The area of Richmond from the capitol's grounds down to the James River burned in the evacuation fire of April 2, 1865. Lt. Gen. Richard S. Ewell's troops, abandoning the city, set the fire to prevent ammunition and other military supplies from falling into Federal hands. Hence, most of the wartime structures in this area no longer stand. Walking down to the southeast corner of the grounds and out to Bank Street will bring you to the sites of the following buildings. At the southeast corner of Twelfth and Bank Streets stood the **Confederate States Post Office**. At the northwest corner of Twelfth and Main Streets is the site of the **Confederate States Telegraph Office**. On the north side of Main Street, between Tenth and Eleventh Streets, the **Confederate States Treasury Buildings**, which housed many of the government's principal offices, once existed. Now part of the U.S. Post Office, the Treasury Building complex is still visible as the component with five arches. On Bank Street between Ninth and Tenth Streets, across from the Tocsin, is the site of the **Confederate States Army Headquarters**. On the west side of Ninth Street, near the intersection of Bank Street, you'll find the site of the **Virginia Mechanics Building**, which housed the Confederate States War and Navy Departments.

Five more buildings and sites are in the immediate area. On the southwest corner of Eighth and Franklin Streets is the **Baskerville House**, where Confederate Vice Pres. Alexan-

der H. Stephens stayed from 1863 to 1865. Several doors northwest of here is the site of the **George Wythe Randolph Residence**, where the Confederate war secretary lived. On the north side of Franklin Street, midway between Seventh and Eighth Streets, is the **Stewart House**, residence of Mrs. Robert E. Lee from 1864 to 1865. The famous photograph of General Lee after Appomattox was made on the porch of this house. **St. Peter's Roman Catholic Cathedral** stands on the northwest corner of Eighth and Grace Streets. Worshipers here included Pierre G. T. Beauregard, Stephen R. Mallory, and John H. Reagan. At the outbreak of war, the church raised a unit that became part of the 1st Virginia Infantry. **St. Paul's Episcopal Church** stands on the southwest corner of Ninth and Grace Streets. The quasi-official church of the Confederacy, St. Paul's was attended by Jefferson Davis and Robert E. Lee. Richard S. Ewell, Seth M. Barton, and John Pegram were married at this church during the war. In pew sixty-three of St. Paul's President Davis received the evacuation news on April 2, 1865.

Returning to your car will enable you to view the remaining sites of wartime Richmond. Head northwest on Main Street. On the south side of the street, between Third and Fourth Streets, is the site of the **Stephen R. Mallory Residence**, which housed the Confederate Secretary of the Navy. Turn southwest (left) on Third Street, southeast (left) on Byrd Street, and southwest (right) on Tredegar Street. As you pass Bragg Street, you'll come to the site of the **Confederate States Arsenal and Ordnance Shops** on the northwest side of the road. Straight ahead is the site of the **Confederate States Ordnance Laboratory**. As the road winds west along the river, you'll come to the **Tredegar Iron Works Ruins**. Here Brig. Gen. Joseph Reid Anderson, operating the principal iron foundry of the Confederacy, produced the material for cannon and small arms desperately needed by the South. The buildings, nicely preserved since the evacuation fire,

THE TREDEGAR IRON WORKS supported the Confederacy's great need for iron manufacturing during the war. In 1994 the site opened as the Valentine Riverside Museum.

opened in 1994 as the Valentine Riverside Museum of Civil War, Richmond, and industrial history.

Turning around and heading to Cary Street will take you to the next sites. Turn southeast (right) on Cary Street. When you reach Eleventh Street, you'll enter the **Shockoe Slip Historic District**. The **Shockoe Warehouse** was the first building set ablaze in the evacuation fire. Turn northeast (left) on Fourteenth Street and as you pass Franklin Street, east of the road, is the site of **Lumpkin's Jail**, "Castle Godwin." This warehouse specialized in confining political prisoners during the war. Turn southeast (right) onto Broad Street, southwest (right) onto Seventeenth Street, and southeast (left) onto Cary Street. On the north side of Cary Street between Eighteenth and Nineteenth Streets stood **Castle Thunder**

Prison, a converted factory that held spies, deserters, and soldiers who committed serious crimes. Another facility, **Castle Lightning Prison**, stood across the street.

At the intersection of Cary and Twentieth Streets is the site of the most famous lockup in the Confederacy, **Libby Prison**. This converted warehouse building was reserved for Union officers and boasted high security, yet on February 9, 1864, 109 Federal officers escaped from Libby after tunneling their way across the street. In 1889 the building was dismantled and shipped, piece by piece, to Chicago for the 1892 World's Fair. There it stood for a short time as a museum until it was demolished. A surviving piece of the structure is now in the Chicago Historical Society.

From the site of Libby Prison you can look southeast to the sites of the **Confederate**

States Navy Yard on the James and **Rocketts**, the city's principal landing where numerous ships loaded and unloaded soldiers and supplies.

To return to the quiet solitude of Chimborazo Park, head northeast (left) on Twenty-first Street and turn southeast (right) on Broad Street. As you pass the southwest corner of Broad and Twenty-fifth Streets, you'll see **St. John's Episcopal Church**, the city's oldest church, where Patrick Henry in 1775 proclaimed, "Give me liberty or give me death." During the war the church was a minor structure because Richmond high society had migrated to the other side of Shockoe Valley. After several more blocks, you'll rediscover the pretty building that houses the museum at Chimborazo Park.

Richmond National Battlefield Park
Mailing address: 3215 East Broad Street, Richmond, Virginia 23223
Telephone: (804) 226-1981
Park established: March 2, 1936
Area: 2,508 acres

City Point National Cemetery
Established: 1866
Area: 6.6 acres
Civil War interments: 5,158

Cold Harbor National Cemetery
Established: April 30, 1866
Area: 1.4 acres
Civil War interments: 1,988

Fort Harrison National Cemetery
Established: May 1866
Area: 1.7 acres
Civil War interments: 818

Glendale National Cemetery
Established: July 14, 1866
Area: 2.1 acres
Civil War interments: 1,202

Hollywood Cemetery
Established: 1847
Area: 135 acres
Civil War interments: about 18,000

Richmond National Cemetery
Established: September 1, 1866
Area: 9.7 acres
Civil War interments: 6,670

Seven Pines National Cemetery
Established: June 27, 1866
Area: 1.9 acres
Civil War interments: 1,407

Shockoe Hill Cemetery
Established: April 10, 1822
Area: 14 acres
Civil War interments: 997

Richmond accommodations
Richmond contains sixty hotels and motels, with nearly 8,000 rooms, and the surrounding area has many more, making a place to stay relatively easy to find no matter what time of year you visit.

Chapter 9

❂   ❂   ❂

The Shenandoah Valley

From New Market Jackson disappeared so suddenly
that the people of the Valley were again mystified.
He crossed the Massanutten Mountain, and, passing Luray,
hurried toward Front Royal. He sometimes
made thirty miles in twenty-four hours with his entire army,
thus gaining for his infantry the sobriquet of
"Jackson's Foot Cavalry."

—Col. John Daniel Imboden, 62nd Virginia Infantry,
describing Stonewall Jackson's Valley Campaign of 1862.

The rich, fertile plains of northwestern Virginia, stretching from Staunton in the south to Harpers Ferry in the north, are collectively known as the **Shenandoah Valley**. Lying between the Blue Ridge and Allegheny mountains, the valley offered a natural corridor through which Confederate troops could march north to Maryland and Pennsylvania undaunted by the Union buildup around Washington. The lofty peaks in the Blue Ridge offered a natural protection threatened only by a few defensible, high-elevation gaps. An important Confederate resource early in the war because of its protection and transportation value, the valley also contained productive farms, mills, and natural goods so abundant that it garnered the name "Breadbasket of the Confederacy." The valley was strategically important only to the Confederates during the first two years of war; as the conflict dragged on, however, the area became vital for the contin-

uance of the Confederate army and, therefore, its destruction became a serious military objective of the Union army.

We drove into the valley from Harpers Ferry, proceeded up the Valley Turnpike (which rises in altitude as one moves south) and toward the many battle sites to the south. The Shenandoah Valley can be divided into three regions. The Lower (Northern) Valley extends from Winchester in the north to New Market in the south and contains the important Civil War towns of Middletown, Strasburg, Toms Brook, Front Royal, Edinburg, Mount Jackson, and New Market. The Central (Middle) Valley extends from New Market in the north to Port Republic in the south and contains Harrisonburg, Cross Keys, Port Republic, and Piedmont. The Upper (Southern) Valley extends from just south of Cross Keys in the north to Lexington in the south and contains the strategic wartime town of Staunton.

Unlike most of the other major regions of Civil War battle, none of the land in the expansive Shenandoah Valley has been preserved in a park funded and operated by the federal government. As of the early 1990s, however, Congress had at least studied the prospects for purchasing lands for a Shenandoah National Battlefield. Scenic land has been preserved: **Shenandoah National Park** offers mountain views of the region from Skyline Drive, which follows the summit of the Blue Ridge parallel to the valley. Despite the relatively small number of markers and monuments in the valley, it is possible to see important landmarks and areas of the two major campaigns that occurred here: Maj. Gen. Thomas J. "Stonewall" Jackson's Valley campaign of 1862, and Maj. Gen. Philip H. Sheridan's Valley campaign of 1864.

In November 1861 Major General Jackson arrived in Winchester to command the Confederate forces in the valley district. His mission was to guard the valley from Federal Maj. Gen. Nathaniel P. Banks, who was instructed to push Jackson out of the area. Threatened by the forward movement of Banks and his subordinate Brig. Gen. James Shields, Jackson in March withdrew to Strasburg, then to Mount Jackson. On March 23 he fought back, however, at the battle of Kernstown, where he was driven back and routed by the Yankees. On May 8 the Federal brigades of Brig. Gen. Robert C. Schenck and Brig. Gen. Robert H. Milroy engaged Jackson at McDowell, west of Staunton, and here Jackson repulsed the more numerous Federals. On May 23 Jackson attacked the Union army in force at Front Royal, forced Banks to retreat, but failed to follow up his victory with an effective pursuit. Banks withdrew to Winchester where Jackson attacked him on May 25, an action known as the first battle of Winchester. Jackson's Confederates hit the Federals hard, gaining another victory that Jackson was unable to follow up.

Jackson's Valley campaign gained momentum at the end of May 1862, when McClellan's Peninsular campaign was heating up to the southeast. President Lincoln sent Maj. Gen. Irvin McDowell and Maj. Gen. John Charles Frémont toward Strasburg, hoping to cut off Jackson's route of escape to the south. Through decisive action, however, Jackson escaped the trap. The Federals pursued up the Valley Turnpike, clashing with the Confederate rear guard, one result of which was the death of Jackson's trusted cavalry commander, Col. Turner Ashby, near Harrisonburg.

By June 7 Jackson occupied the fields near Cross Keys and Port Republic. The following day Union Major General Frémont attacked Jackson at Cross Keys, a battle skillfully won by Jackson. Early the next day Jackson attacked Union Brig. Gen. James Shields at nearby Port Republic, a mismanaged affair during which Federal troops had ample opportunities to demolish the Confederate lines, but failed due to piecemeal efforts. As the battle waned, Jackson seized the initiative and forced the Yankees to retreat, gaining the day once again.

Facing greater numbers, Jackson fought a brilliant campaign in the Shenandoah Valley in 1862, thwarting the Union attempts at overall control and leaving Washington in complete frustration. On August 9, 1862, as part of the Second Bull Run campaign, Jackson clashed with Banks again at Cedar Mountain south of Culpeper, crushing the Federal eastern flank with a sweeping counterattack.

Another spring, summer, and autumn would pass before the Shenandoah Valley was again a decisive battlefield. In early 1864 Jackson was gone, a casualty of the battle of Chancellorsville. With the Confederacy substantially weakened and supplies running low, the initiative now belonged to a Union officer, Maj. Gen. Philip Henry Sheridan. July and August 1864 brought a large scale raid on Washington by Confederate Lt. Gen. Jubal A. Early. The bold Rebel damaged the northern spirit by burning the town of Chambersburg, Pennsylvania, fighting a vigorous battle at Monocacy Creek, Maryland, and nearly reaching Washington. Alarmed Federal authorities again needed to control the

Shenandoah Valley. Sheridan, a particular favorite of Lt. Gen. Ulysses S. Grant, was assigned the task of clearing out the valley, controlling it, and destroying anything within it of military value to Confederate troops.

On August 16, 1864, a small clash occurred at Front Royal. On September 19 a great battle commenced at Winchester, the third battle of Winchester, wherein Sheridan blasted Early back to Fishers Hill near Strasburg. Sheridan quickly pursued and again defeated the Confederates at the battle of Fishers Hill on September 22, pushing Early to Mount Jackson. Sheridan now proceeded to move back to Winchester to reinforce Grant with surplus troops. During the movement, a vicious cavalry battle took place on October 9 at Toms Brook, in which the Confederates were routed. Sheridan now believed the valley was safely in control and concentrated his army at Middletown.

Meanwhile, Early was not about to concede defeat. At the battle of Cedar Creek on October 19, he drove the Federals back along several positions, creating a confused Federal retreat down the Valley Turnpike. When Sheridan received the news at Winchester, he rode furiously toward the battle, rallied the weary lines, and created a monstrous counterattack that sent the Confederates reeling. This decisive battle marked the end of major military operations in the valley.

Several small engagements also occurred in and around the valley in the intervening year, 1863. The most important of these was the great cavalry battle at Brandy Station, east of Culpeper, which is within reasonable driving distance.

Shenandoah Valley Tour

Due to the relatively small number of complex and abundantly marked battlefields in the valley, many small buildings and monuments are described in the following text but not plotted individually on the maps. Following the directions will take you to them. For the first part of the tour consult the Lower (Northern Sector) Shenandoah Valley map (p. 149). Should you approach the valley from the north, as we did, the first place of importance you'll reach is **Winchester** (pop. 21,947), the key stronghold in the northern Shenandoah Valley. You can reach Winchester by taking the Berryville Avenue exit from Interstate 81. Winchester changed hands seventy times during the war, and hosted eight battles: March 23, 1862; May 24–25, 1862; June 12–14, 1863; August 11, 1864; August 17, 1864; September 5, 1864; September 19, 1864; and October 25, 1864.

You may wish to visit the **Winchester-Frederick County Visitor Center**, 1340 South Pleasant Valley Road, to orient yourself and obtain information on the area. You'll find the **Lewis T. Moore House** at 415 North Braddock Street. In this house, now a museum of Civil War artifacts, Stonewall Jackson established headquarters in November 1861 and stayed through the beginning of his Valley campaign. Continuing south on Braddock Street will bring you to the **Lloyd Logan House**, now the Elks Club, at the southwest corner of Braddock and Picadilly Streets. Here Sheridan established his headquarters in 1864 during his stay at Winchester, and from this point he embarked on his ride to Cedar Creek. Earlier in the war the structure served as a headquarters for Union Maj. Gen. Nathaniel P. Banks (in 1862) and Brig. Gen. Robert H. Milroy (in 1863). One block south of the Logan House, on the northeast corner of Braddock and Amherst Streets, is the **Hunter Holmes McGuire House**, home of Stonewall Jackson's staff surgeon.

About one block east of the McGuire House in the Loudoun Street Mall is the **Old Frederick County Court House**, a structure that switched allegiance almost monthly as the town was captured and recaptured. The **Old Stone Presbyterian Church**, at 306 East Picadilly Street, served as a chapel and a stable for Union troops occupying Winchester. **Winchester National Cemetery**, located on National Avenue east of the church, contains the graves

THE LEWIS T. MOORE HOUSE served as Stonewall Jackson's headquarters in Winchester from November 1861 to March 1862. The house now contains a museum.

of more than 4,000 Union soldiers, half of whom are unknowns. Nearby **Stonewall Cemetery**, on Cork Street, contains the remains of about 3,000 Confederate soldiers killed in battles around Winchester. The cemetery lies within **Mount Hebron Cemetery**, the local burying ground. Notable Confederate officers buried in Stonewall Cemetery include Maj. Gen. John G. Walker, Brig. Gen. Robert D. Johnston, and Col. Turner Ashby.

Few of the battlefields around Winchester and **Kernstown**, four miles to the south, are identified by markers. The first battle, Kernstown, occurred on March 23, 1862, between the modern roads Virginia 622 (the Cedar Creek Pike) and U.S. 11, the Valley Turnpike. Traveling south on the Valley Turnpike,

you'll reach the center of the battlefield about two miles south of Winchester as you pass **Pritchard's Knob** on the west side of the turnpike. From this area Union troops attacked the Confederates positioned two miles west on **Sandy Ridge**. On Pritchard's Knob the **Pritchard House** still stands, but is private.

You may wish to proceed on the Valley Turnpike about two miles south of the intersection with Virginia 622. After you cross **Hogg Run**, and immediately after passing Shawnee Drive on your left, turn right on a small road. This leads you to the reconstructed **Opequon Church**, a structure that survived the battle, though damaged by artillery fire. It burned in 1873. The engagement at

WINCHESTER NATIONAL CEMETERY contains the graves of 4,459 Union soldiers, half of which are unknowns.

Winchester from June 13 to 15, 1863, occurred on much the same ground as the May 25, 1862, engagement, though it spread due south of town over the plank road to Front Royal. The vicious battle on September 19, 1864, raged northeast of town, south of **Redbud Run** and north of **Abraham's Creek**. The Confederates moved through town on their retreat up the Valley Turnpike.

Having seen Winchester and Kernstown, you may wish to travel to **Berryville** (pop. 3,097), an eight-mile trip on Virginia 7. Shortly before reaching this town, you'll see a marker commemorating the clash on September 3, 1864, between Brig. Gen. George Crook's Union troops and Lt. Gen. Richard H. Anderson's Confederates. Crook's men at first fumbled

THE FIRST BATTLE in Jackson's Valley campaign of 1862 occurred at Kernstown on March 23. Here Maj. Gen. Nathaniel P. Banks's Federals routed Confederates under Maj. Gen. Thomas J. "Stonewall" Jackson.

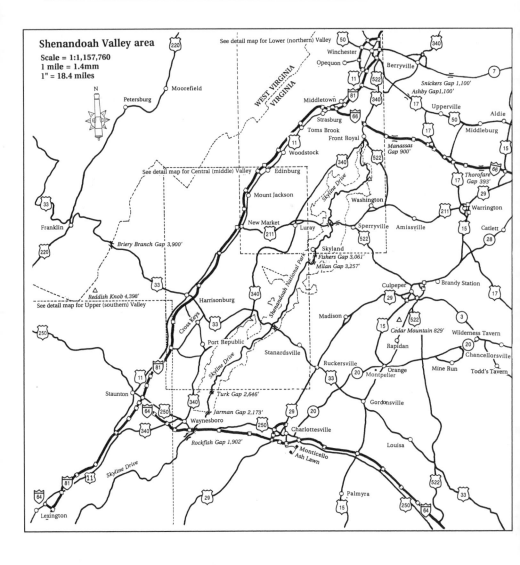

Shenandoah Valley area

Scale = 1:1,157,760
1 mile = 1.4mm
1" = 18.4 miles

and retreated only to mount a counterattack that drove Anderson's troops back toward Winchester. In Berryville you'll see the **Old Clarke County Courthouse**, a wartime hospital. One mile north of town on U.S. 340, you'll find a sign marking the Lee-Longstreet Camp, where the two Confederate generals stayed on June 18 and 19, 1863, on their way to Gettysburg. You are now also on the ground where on August 13, 1864, Confederate Col. John S. Mosby captured a Federal supply train along with 200 prisoners. Continuing east of town on Virginia 7 will bring you to markers, four and one-half and seven and one-half miles distant, describing Crook's attack on Early on July 16, 1864, following Early's Washington Raid.

If you return to Winchester, you can continue your tour. You'll want to move up the

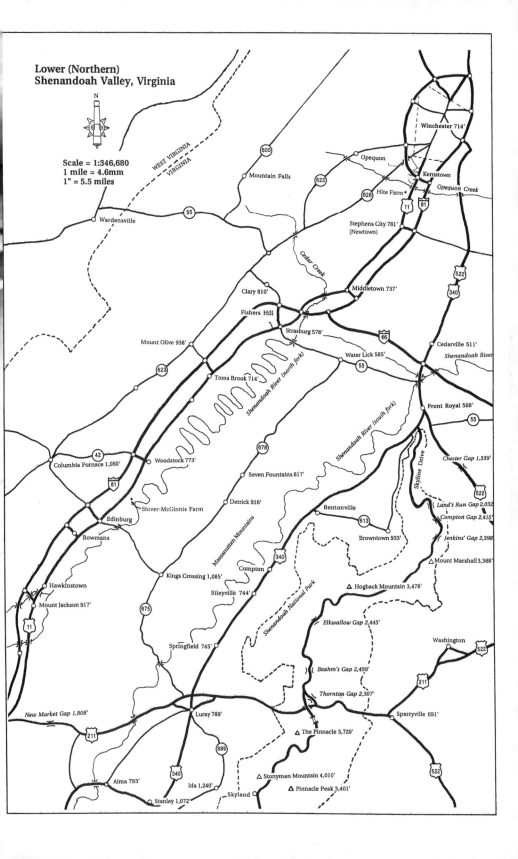

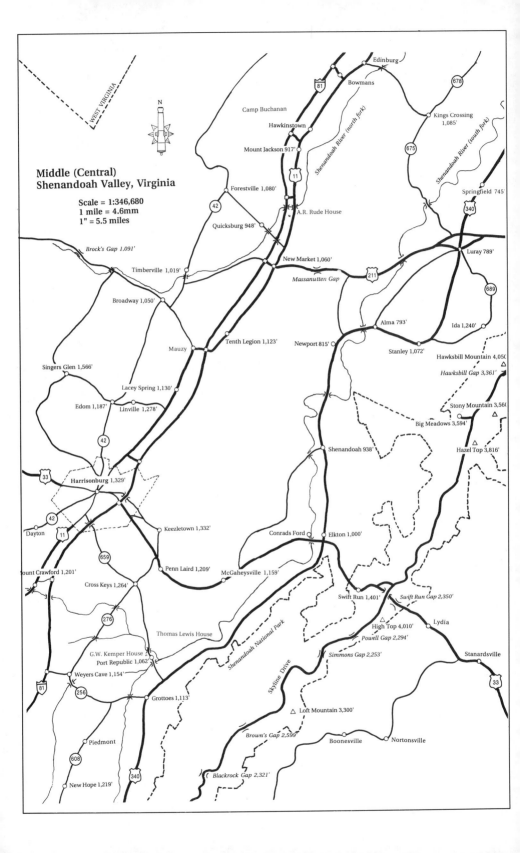

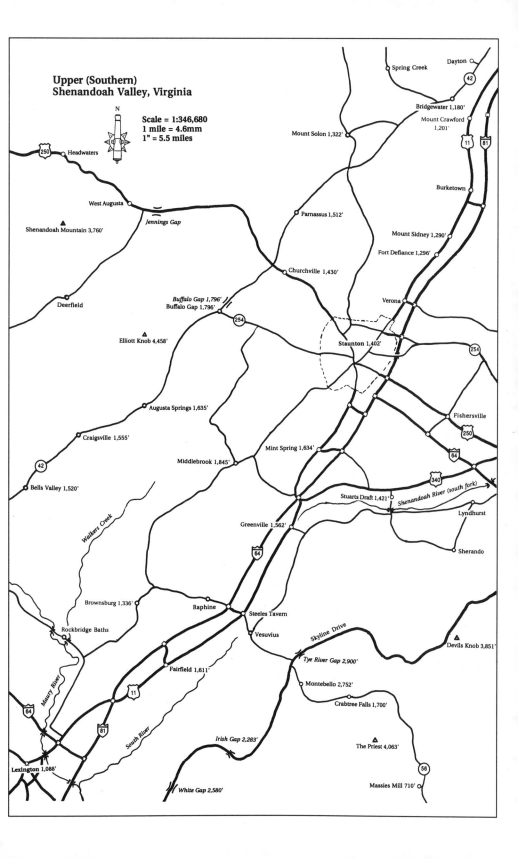

Upper (Southern)
Shenandoah Valley, Virginia

N

Scale = 1:346,680
1 mile = 4.6mm
1" = 5.5 miles

Spring Creek
Dayton
42

Bridgewater 1,180'
Mount Crawford 1,201'

Mount Solon 1,322'

11 81

250 Headwaters

Burketown

West Augusta

Shenandoah Mountain 3,760'

Jennings Gap

Parnassus 1,512'

Mount Sidney 1,290'

Fort Defiance 1,296'

Churchville 1,430'

Deerfield

Buffalo Gap 1,796'
Buffalo Gap 1,796'

Verona

254

Elliott Knob 4,458'

Staunton 1,402'

254

Augusta Springs 1,635'

Fishersville

Craigsville 1,555'

250

42

Mint Spring 1,634'

Middlebrook 1,845'

64

Bells Valley 1,520'

340

Stuarts Draft 1,421'

Shenandoah River (south fork)

Lyndhurst

Walkers Creek

Greenville 1,562'

Sherando

64

Brownsburg 1,336'

Raphine

Steeles Tavern

Skyline Drive

Devils Knob 3,851'

Rockbridge Baths

Vesuvius

Tye River Gap 2,900'

Fairfield 1,611'

Montebello 2,752'

11

Crabtree Falls 1,700'

Maury River

81

South River

Irish Gap 2,283'

The Priest 4,063'

64

Lexington 1,088'

56

White Gap 2,580'

Massies Mill 710'

Valley Turnpike (U.S. 11), heading south across **Opequon Creek,** site of heavy fighting on several occasions, and toward **Middletown** (pop. 1,061). You are now on the road traveled many times by soldiers on both sides during the war. Along this road, Sheridan rallied his retreating troops and sent them back to victory at Cedar Creek. Travel eight miles from Kernstown and you'll reach Middletown where you may see **St. Thomas's Chapel,** a country church used as a Confederate hospital during the war. One mile south of Middletown, you'll want to turn northwest onto Virginia 727, which leads to the **Belle Grove Plantation.** At the junction you'll see the **Stephen Dodson Ramseur Monument** honoring a Confederate brigadier general mortally wounded at Cedar Creek. Ramseur died the following day at Belle Grove. On the short drive in you will

see the **Cedar Creek Battlefield Foundation Visitors Center,** which contains a small museum. On October 19, 1864, the battle of Cedar Creek raged around Belle Grove and its grounds, which served as Sheridan's headquarters, and extended several miles south to **Cedar Creek** itself. Graffiti scribbled by Union soldiers during their stay is visible in the attic of the house. The wartime **Heater House** lies east of Belle Grove. North of the intersection of the Valley Turnpike and Virginia 840 lies the **128th New York Infantry Monument,** a memorial to a regiment with heavy losses at Cedar Creek. The **D. Stickley House** lies north of the Cedar Creek Bridge on the Valley Turnpike. The structure was hit by small arms and artillery fire during the battle.

Two miles south of Belle Grove, you may wish to turn east onto Interstate 66, travel

BELLE GROVE PLANTATION served as Maj. Gen. Philip Sheridan's headquarters during the Valley campaign of 1864. The battle of Cedar Creek flared around the house.

seven miles, then head south on U.S. 340/U.S. 522 for three miles. This brings you to **Front Royal** (pop. 11,880), site of five engagements during the war. The battles occurred on May 23, 1862; May 30, 1862; July 25, 1864; August 15, 1864; and September 29, 1864. You may wish to stop at the **Main Street Station Visitor's Center** to obtain local information. In the center of town you'll come to a monument honoring the county's soldiers and the new **Warren County Courthouse**, which stands on the location of the wartime structure. Northeast of the Courthouse, at 95 Chester Street, you'll see the **Warren Rifles Confederate Museum**, which contains a collection of Civil War artifacts. Next door you'll see the **Belle Boyd Cottage**, a Civil War hospital now used as a museum honoring the South's most famous spy whose aunt and uncle owned the structure dur-

ing the war. During the engagement on May 23, 1862, Union Col. John R. Kenly used the house as headquarters. A marker at the junction of Chester Road and U.S. 340 commemorates the battle. **Prospect Hill Cemetery**, located south of the town center on U.S. 340, contains the remains of 276 Confederate soldiers and a monument honoring Col. John S. Mosby's Rangers.

You may wish to return to the Valley Turnpike by heading north on U.S. 340/U.S. 522 and then west on Interstate 66 to continue the tour southward. Once you're back on the turnpike, travel about one-half mile. The rise east of the road is **Hupp's Hill**, which contains entrenchments built by Sheridan's troops in 1864 to control the Valley Turnpike. After traveling another one and one-half miles, you'll come to **Strasburg** (pop. 3,762). Lying at the

PROSPECT HILL CEMETERY in Front Royal contains a soldier's circle with the remains of 276 Confederates and a monument erected in 1899 by the survivors of Mosby's rangers.

base of Massanutten Mountain, Strasburg was the scene of bloody fighting thrice during the war, on May 24–25, 1862; September 29, 1864; and October 8–9, 1864. As you enter Strasburg you'll see a prominent hill west of the road now topped by a water tower. This is **Banks's Fort**, built by Union troops in 1862 and fought around in several of the Strasburg battles. In Strasburg you can find the **Presbyterian Church** whose cemetery contains 137 unknown Confederate soldiers. On King Street you can visit the **Strasburg Museum**, which displays a collection of Civil War artifacts from the battles nearby.

Less than a mile south of town on the turnpike, you'll see **Fishers Hill**, which lies east of the road. Fishers Hill is the site of three battles, on September 22, 1864; September 29, 1864; and October 8–9, 1864. The first followed Early's defeat at Winchester. A week later Sheridan's Yankees routed the Confederates here and sent them retreating south. The final battle was a cavalry clash known as Toms Brook wherein the Federal cavalry smashed the Rebels and sent them south across Toms Brook and on to Woodstock. The event was afterward known as the Woodstock Races.

You may wish to continue south on the turnpike, taking you past **Toms Brook**, **Woodstock**, and on to **Edinburg** (pop. 860). Two and one-half miles south of Woodstock, you'll pass the **Stover-McGinnis Farmhouse** east of the Turnpike. Jackson established headquarters in this house while his army camped on the grounds. Many troops passed in and out of Edinburg on their way to battle, and Confederate Col. Turner Ashby set up headquarters in Edinburg in 1862. At **Stony Creek** at the western end of Edinburg, you can see the rebuilt **Edinburg Mill**, which was set ablaze by Sheridan's troopers in the 1864 Valley campaign. A trip south on the turnpike another four miles brings you to **Red Banks** on the east side of the turnpike. Jackson established headquarters in this house early in the Valley campaign and set up **Camp Buchanan** west of the turnpike for his command. Another two and one-half miles brings you to **Mount Jackson** (pop. 1,583), site of engagements on April 17, 1862; November 17, 1863; September 29, 1864; November 22, 1864; and March 7, 1865. In town the **Mount Jackson Confederate Cemetery** contains the graves of 500 soldiers. Two miles south of town, the turnpike passes **Rude's Hill**, site of the March 7, 1865, engagement when Confederate Brig. Gen. Thomas L. Rosser attacked Yankee cavalry. Jackson established headquarters in the **A. R. Rude House**, "Locust Grove," at the base of the hill (west of the turnpike) for a time during the 1862 Valley campaign.

Now in the Middle (Central) Shenandoah Valley, you're gaining altitude as you progress southward. Consult the Middle (Central) Shenandoah Valley map (p. 150). Continuing on the turnpike seven miles brings you to **New Market** (pop. 1,435), site of the **New Market Battlefield Historical Park**. Engagements occurred at New Market on May 15, 1864, and September 29, 1864. The first was a large, pitched battle that happened when Union troops under Maj. Gen. Franz Sigel, who were moving toward Staunton, faced Confederate Maj. Gen. John C. Breckinridge. The latter, short on manpower, enlisted a battalion of 247 cadets from the Virginia Military Institute (VMI) in Lexington. The Confederates pushed Sigel back to Strasburg, the Union retreat taking place during a heavy rainstorm.

At the park you'll see the **Hall of Valor**, a circular building containing a superb museum of Civil War artifacts. Nearby lies the **Jacob Bushong Farm**, around which the battle flared and which served as a hospital after the engagement. The farm is nicely preserved. In addition to the main house, you may see the **Wheelwright Shop, Blacksmith's Shop, Summer Kitchen, Meat and Loom House, Oven, Hen House**, and **Ice House**. On the northeastern edge of the adjoining field, you'll see

THE JACOB BUSHONG FARMHOUSE was the focal point of fury at the battle of New Market on May 15, 1864. Here cadets from the Virginia Military Institute charged and broke the Federal ranks.

the **Woodson's Rangers Monument**, a pile of stone honoring the First Missouri Cavalry, C.S.A., commanded by Col. Charles H. Woodson. The VMI cadets charged the Union lines north of the Bushong Farm, many of them without shoes after crossing a muddy gully. The **Field of Lost Shoes** contains a walking path that takes you past several cannon, to the site of a sixty-foot white oak tree (a prominent landmark during the battle), and to a scenic overlook on **Bushong Bluff**, above the North Fork of the **Shenandoah River**. In the town of New Market you may see the **John Strayer House** (Lee-Jackson Hotel) on the southeast corner of the Valley Turnpike and the Lee Highway (U.S. 211). This structure served as Early's headquarters in 1864.

Having seen New Market, you may wish to travel seventeen and one-half miles south on the Valley Turnpike to **Harrisonburg** (pop. 30,707) where a battle occurred on September 29, 1864. In town you can see the **Warren-Sipe Museum** at 301 North Main Street (three blocks south of Court House Square), which contains exhibits on Stonewall Jackson and the Civil War.

Nine miles north of town on Virginia 42, near Broadway, you may wish to visit the **Lincoln Homestead and Cemetery**, where Abraham Lincoln's great-grandfather John settled in 1768. The president's great-uncle Jacob built the present structure about 1800. The cemetery, situated on the hill behind the house, contains the graves of five Lincoln generations,

THE INCONCLUSIVE BATTLE of Cross Keys took place on June 8 and 9, 1862, when Stonewall Jackson met and tangled with troops under Union Maj. Gen. John Charles Frémont and Brig. Gen. James Shields.

including those of John and Jacob. A marker on the Valley Turnpike near Lacey Spring describes the nearby birthplace of Thomas Lincoln, the president's father.

From Harrisonburg, travel south on the Valley Turnpike until you reach Virginia 659, where you should turn southeast (left). After four and one-half miles you'll reach **Cross Keys**, site of the first part of the bloody battle of June 8, 1862, that ended the first Valley campaign. Here Stonewall Jackson halted Federal Maj. Gen. John C. Frémont's advance before turning the next day to attack Brig. Gen. James Shields's force at **Port Republic**, four miles south of Cross Keys on Virginia 659. A marker on U.S. 340 three and one-half miles north of the town Grottoes describes the action. Jackson delivered a knockout punch to the two Union armies and stymied Frémont by burning the North River Bridge at Port Republic. The Federals threatened the Valley no more in 1862. At the western end of Port Republic, you can see the **G. W. Kemper House**, "Madison Hall," Jackson's headquarters during the battle. Three miles east-northeast of the Kemper House, on the Shenandoah River (south fork), is the **Thomas Lewis House**, "Lynnwood,"

around which heavy fighting occurred during the battle.

After seeing the hamlets of Cross Keys and Port Republic, you may wish to travel one and one-half miles south on Virginia 659 to the town of Grottoes, then continue just over two miles west on Virginia 256. This brings you to a junction where you may turn south on Virginia 608 and travel three miles to **Piedmont**. Here on June 5, 1864, a clash erupted following the battle of New Market. Federal Maj. Gen. David Hunter had replaced Maj. Gen. Franz Sigel, and Hunter's men, moving south on Staunton, encountered Brig. Gen. William E. "Grumble" Jones's Confederates. After several attacks and counterattacks, the Union army routed the Confederates, killing Jones in the process. They marched into Staunton the following day unopposed.

Resume the Valley Turnpike tour by returning to Harrisonburg. If you return via U.S. 33 you'll see a marker describing the battle of Cross Keys about five miles southeast of Harrisonburg. Travel south on the Valley Turnpike. One and one-half miles south of town, a small road leads to the **Turner Ashby Monument** on **Chestnut Ridge**, which marks the spot where this Confederate colonel, a favorite of Stonewall Jackson's, was killed on June 6, 1862. About two miles south of this spot, you'll come to **Mount Crawford** where you'll see a marker on the highway describing Sheridan's raid on the town on March 1, 1865.

Continue up the Valley Turnpike sixteen miles to reach **Staunton** (pop. 24,461) where you can find **Staunton National Cemetery**. You are now in the Upper (Southern) Shenandoah Valley. You can use the Upper (Southern) Shenandoah Valley map (p. 151). Among the many fine buildings in this city is the **Jedediah Hotchkiss House**, "The Oaks," located at 437 East Beverly Street. This well-preserved home belonged to Stonewall Jackson's military cartographer. From Staunton, you may wish to make the thirty-two-mile trip on the Valley Turnpike to **Lexington** (pop. 6,959), a site

A LONE MONUMENT near Harrisonburg marks the spot where Confederate Col. Turner Ashby was killed on June 6, 1862.

filled with magnificent Confederate landmarks.

The best place to start in Lexington is the **Stonewall Jackson House** at 8 East Washington Street. The only house ever owned by Jackson (he bought it in 1858), the dwelling is filled with Jackson artifacts. From the Jackson House you can see the impressive form of the **Virginia Military Institute** (VMI), the foremost military academy in the South, where Jackson was employed as a professor before the war. On its grounds you can see the **Thomas J. "Stonewall" Jackson Statue**, the **New Market Statue**, and the **Cadet Battery**. The rebuilt **Old Hospital** served as a Civil War hospital but is now used as office space. The **VMI Museum**, housed in **Jackson Memorial Hall**, contains an outstanding collection of Civil War relics, including Jackson's horse Little Sorrel, Alexander S. Pendleton's uniform, the Rockbridge Artillery flag, jackets worn by VMI cadets

at New Market, and Stonewall Jackson's bullet-pierced raincoat from Chancellorsville.

In town the **Stonewall Jackson Memorial Cemetery** on the east side of Main Street contains the grave of Lieutenant General Jackson. The central Jackson monument stands over the general's remains; his earlier burial site was the family plot nearby. Many other Confederate officers and politicians lie buried in this cemetery, including Virginia Governor John Letcher, Brig. Gen. Edwin G. Lee, Brig. Gen. Elisha F. Paxton (killed at Chancellorsville), Brig. Gen. William N. Pendleton, Lt. Col. Alexander S. "Sandie" Pendleton (killed at Fishers Hill), and John Mercer Brooke, chief of ordnance and hydrography for the Confederate States Navy.

The nearby campus of **Washington and Lee University** (Washington College during the war), on the western end of Henry Street, contains important sites relating to General Lee,

THE STONEWALL JACKSON HOUSE in Lexington memorializes the eccentric professor from the Virginia Military Institute who became one of the great generals in American history.

who became its president after the war. The **Lee Chapel and Museum**, located near the intersection of Jefferson Street and Letcher Avenue, contains the Lee family tombs, including the remains of Robert E. Lee, his wife Mary Custis Lee, his father Henry "Light-Horse Harry" Lee, his sons Maj. Gen. George Washington Custis Lee and Maj. Gen. William Henry Fitzhugh "Rooney" Lee, and other relatives. Above the crypt in the chapel, you can see the **Robert Edward Lee Statue**, Edward Valentine's famous recumbent figure. The adjacent museum contains a collection of Lee family relics. Outside the chapel, near an exit door, a small stone marks the burial spot of Traveller, Lee's favorite war horse.

When finished with Lexington, you've seen the greater part of the Shenandoah Valley. If

time permits, you may wish to visit a few other Civil War towns nearby that offer exceptional remembrances of the war. From Lexington, travel seven miles east on U.S. 60 until you reach the Blue Ridge Parkway, known as Skyline Drive, which you should take north. After a forty-mile drive you'll reach **Rockfish Gap**, an overlook affording a spectacular view of the valley below. Just beyond Rockfish Gap in the vicinity of **Waynesboro** (pop. 15,329), you can turn east on Interstate 64, which after twenty miles reaches **Charlottesville** (pop. 40,341).

In Charlottesville you can see the **Albemarle County Court House** and the adjacent **Stonewall Jackson Monument**. On Jefferson Street between First and Second Streets, you'll find the **Robert E. Lee Monument**. On the campus of the **University of Virginia** at the western end of Main Street, the Jeffersonian **Rotunda** was used as a Confederate hospital during the war. Located south of town, off the Monticello exit on Interstate 64, is the **Thomas Jefferson Visitor Center**, which offers information on local sites. East of the visitor center is **Monticello**, Jefferson's magnificent and storied home. Among the dead buried alongside the third president is Brig. Gen. George Wythe Randolph, Confederate secretary of war. Not far from Monticello stands **Ash Lawn**, home of President James Monroe.

From Charlottesville you may wish to travel east on Interstate 64 and, after thirteen miles, turn north on U.S. 15. Continuing a distance of eleven miles will bring you to **Gordonsville** (pop. 1,351), a strategically important railroad town. On South Main Street next to the railroad junction, you will find the **Exchange Hotel**, an important Confederate hospital site that received more than 23,000 wounded soldiers during the war.

Continuing on U.S. 15 north from Gordonsville brings you, after a jaunt of eight miles, to **Orange** (pop. 2,582). The **Orange County Courthouse**, at the intersection of North Main Street and Madison Road, was a prominent Civil War landmark. Nearby **St. Thomas's**

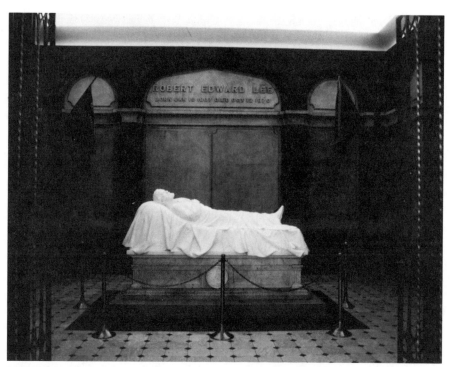

R. E. LEE rests in recumbent sleep in Edward Valentine's famous statue placed above the Lee family crypt in the Lee Chapel at Washington and Lee University.

Episcopal Church at 119 Caroline Street served as a Confederate hospital throughout much of the war. Just west of town near Montpelier Station stands impressive **Montpelier,** home of James Madison. On the grounds are the graves of the fourth president and his wife Dolly Madison. A marker one and one-half miles east of town on Virginia 20 denotes the position where General R. E. Lee encamped during the winter of 1863–1864. Continuing north on U.S. 15 from Orange brings you past the town of Rapidan and to a marker commemorating the battle of Cedar Mountain fought on August 9, 1862. After the Valley campaign Jackson received an attack from Union Maj. Gen. Nathaniel P. Banks that drove the Confederates south. As he would later at Antietam, Maj. Gen. A. P. Hill slammed into the

ROCKFISH GAP on Skyline Drive affords one of the most magnificent views of the Shenandoah Valley. The corridor served as an always active route during several Civil War campaigns.

Federals with a crushing counterattack that drove them from the field. About ten miles north of Orange on the west side of the road, you can see **Cedar Mountain** where the heaviest fighting occurred. One mile north of this site, you'll see **Clark's Mountain** where one week after Cedar Mountain General Lee wearily watched Union Maj. Gen. John Pope's army from a signal tower. The battle that did not happen here occurred two weeks later at Second Bull Run.

Some six and one-half miles north of Cedar Mountain, you'll reach **Culpeper** (pop. 8,581), another Virginia town that changed hands frequently during the war. **Culpeper National Cemetery** contains the graves of 1,376 Union soldiers who perished in several nearby battles. **Culpeper County Court House** at 118 West Davis Road replaces the earlier structure that was once a familiar sight to thousands of soldiers. In the same block, at 102 North Main Street, is the **Ambrose Powell Hill Boyhood Home** where Lieutenant General Hill grew up before leaving for West Point. At 302 North Main Street you'll find the **William Green House Site**. Now occupied by the U.S. Post Office, the building was used as headquarters by U. S. Grant from March 26, 1864, until the beginning of Grant's Overland campaign. The **Hill Mansion** can be found at 501 South East Street. Early in the war this structure was a Confederate hospital; later it served as a headquarters for Union officers. The **John Williams Green House**, "Greenwood," at 1913 Orange Road, was occupied by Federal troops who built gun emplacements on the front lawn. The **Culpeper Cavalry Museum** at 113 West Davis Street has a collection of Civil War relics relating to local battles.

Having toured Culpeper, you may wish to proceed to the final target in the Shenandoah Valley region, **Brandy Station**. An important railroad depot, Brandy Station became a battlefield early in the Gettysburg campaign when, on June 9, 1863, Union Brig. Gen. Alfred Pleasonton's cavalry attacked that of Maj.

Gen. James E. B. "Jeb" Stuart. Infantry was present on both sides, but Brandy Station was predominantly a cavalry battle, the largest fought in North America. Although Stuart retained the field, strong charges by the Yankees stunned the southern horsemen, who were used to completely dominating their northern counterparts. Stuart was humiliated, and the battle marked a turning point for Union cavalry operations in the war.

To reach Brandy Station, simply head north on U.S. 29 some six and one-half miles. The rise north of the station is **Fleetwood Hill**, the central area of fighting. Heading north on Virginia 663 for three-fourths of a mile brings you to the **James Barbour House**, "Beauregard," used late in 1863 as a Union headquarters and hospital site. Just under two miles north of this house stands the **Franklin P. Stearns House**, "Farley," used as Union Maj. Gen. John Sedgwick's headquarters during the battle. Travel south toward Brandy Station on Virginia 663 until reaching Virginia 665, where you should head west (right). Continuing one and one-half miles will bring you close to the **John Minor Botts House**, "Auburn," located southwest of the road. Botts was a prominent Virginian who remained loyal to the Union throughout the war. At the time of the battle Major General Stuart conducted an extensive review of his cavalry south of the home.

Next, turn south (left) on Virginia 665 and then east (left) on U.S. 29. Head south (right) on Virginia 663 at Brandy Station. After one and one-half miles, before crossing **Jonas Run**, you'll see the **Pembroke Thom House**, "Glen Ella," on the west side of the road. The house was occupied by officers of the Union 2nd Corps during the battle. Another two miles brings you to Stevensburg, where you should head east on Virginia 3. After three-fourths mile you'll see **"Salubria,"** an impressive mansion where Massachusetts cavalry pushed Virginians off the field. Return to Brandy Station by heading north (left) on Virginia 669. You have now visited not only the sites associated with the Shenandoah Valley battles of 1862 and 1864, but also a few places associated with the campaigns focused on Richmond and Petersburg when the war dragged on unrelentingly.

New Market Battlefield State Historical Park

Mailing address: P.O. Box 164, New Market, Virginia 22844
Telephone: (866) 515-1864
Established: 1964
Area: 260 acres

Culpeper National Cemetery

Established: 1867
Area: 17.8 acres
Civil War interments: 1,376

Prospect Hill Cemetery

(Front Royal)
Established: 1865
Area: 60 acres
Civil War interments: 168

Staunton National Cemetery

Established: 1867
Area: 1.2 acres
Civil War interments: 1,175

Stonewall Cemetery

(Winchester, within Mt. Hebron Cemetery)
Established: 1866
Area: 0.3 acre
Civil War interments: about 3,000

Stonewall Jackson Memorial Cemetery

(Lexington)
Established: 1796
Area: 11 acres
Civil War interments: 144

Winchester National Cemetery

Established: April 8, 1866
Area: 4.9 acres
Civil War interments: 4,459

Shenandoah Valley accommodations

Plentiful accommodations exist throughout the Shenandoah Valley. Charlottesville leads other towns in the valley with twelve hotels, motels, and resorts. You'll also find places to stay in Front Royal (which has five establishments), Harrisonburg (six), Lexington (five), Luray (three), Middletown (two), New Market (three), Staunton (six), Waynesboro (two), and Winchester (eight).

Chapter 10

✪   ✪   ✪

Shiloh

Fill your canteens, boys.
Some of you will be in hell before night
and you'll need water.

—Col. Isaac C. Pugh, 41st Illinois Volunteer Infantry,
during the battle of Shiloh, April 6, 1862.

The Civil War would be won or lost in the west. Although the great eastern battles—Gettysburg, Petersburg, Fredericksburg, Chancellorsville—attracted far more attention during the war, strategically the west was critically important. For the Confederacy, it meant a huge pool of resources and free transportation on the Mississippi River. For the Union, controlling the river would cut the Confederacy in two, reducing the enormity of the task of militarily conquering the entire south. Few realized the importance of the west early in the war, but as the years rolled on its value grew in significance. The issue of occupying Kentucky and Tennessee, geographically important states divided in sentiment, became paramount.

The winter of 1862 ushered in the first Union military success in the west when a little-known brigadier general, Ulysses S. Grant, captured Forts Henry and Donelson on February 6 and February 16. The fall of these fortifcations shifted control of the Tennessee and Cumberland Rivers to the Yankees. This allowed Grant, now a major general of volunteers, to move his 35,000-man Army of the Tennessee south along the Tennessee River. Maj. Gen. Don Carlos Buell stationed his Army of the Ohio at Nashville. The Confederate forces, meanwhile, were scattered from Memphis to Corinth, Mississippi, to Murfreesboro. On March 11 Maj. Gen. Henry W. Halleck, in command of the area, ordered Buell to reinforce the Army of the Tennessee at Pittsburg Landing, Tennessee.

By April 5 Grant and his army were encamped at Pittsburg Landing near a little wooden church called Shiloh, a Hebrew word meaning place of peace. The area of encampment was triangular and circumscribed by avenues of water, most prominently the Tennessee River to the east. Difficult terrain and a feeling that Confederates would not launch an immediate attack may have contributed to the Union army's lax attitude toward security. By the evening of April 5, some 40,000 Confederates under Gen. Albert Sidney Johnston approached the Union encampment from the southwest. Johnston had been encouraged to move north on the offensive by Confederate Gen. Pierre G. T. Beauregard at Corinth. The Confederate attack had been delayed for nearly two days due to difficult road travel between Corinth and Pittsburg Landing. The Confederate army slept only two miles from the southernmost Union camps, unobserved by the Federals. They planned a surprise attack for the following morning.

The battle of Shiloh, the bloodiest encounter of the war up to that time, erupted on April 6, 1862. At 6 A.M. Johnston drove into the Federal left flank, hoping to push them northward into Snake and Owl Creeks and away from Pittsburg Landing. The strength of the Confederate attack was insufficient, however, and a raging battle escalated along the entire front of the east-west lines. Johnston left overall control of the battle to Beauregard and rode forward to lead an assault.

As the morning developed, the Union right softened. Brig. Gen. William T. Sherman's division fell back, only to be supported by Maj. Gen. John A. McClernand. By mid-morning Brig. Gen. Benjamin M. Prentiss, whose division received much of the force of the opening attack, fell back to a field and held it stubbornly. The intensity of the firefight at this position gave rise to the nickname "Hornet's Nest." Grant arrived from his Savannah headquarters at 8:30 A.M. and quickly and cooly tried to stabilize a dangerous situation for the Army of the Tennessee.

By noon, relentless Confederate attacks began to push the Union defenders east toward the Tennessee River. Confederate brigades became intermingled and the corps commanders, Maj. Gens. Braxton Bragg, William J. Hardee, and Leonidas Polk, and Brig. Gen. John C. Breckinridge, issued commands along the line without regard to technical organization. As one Union unit was forced to withdraw, Confederate artillery and infantry assaults pushed back the adjacent unit, effectively moving the entire Union line. But the Confederate soldiers were tired and hungry when the battle began, and many of them were now becoming exhausted. While Confederates were using all available troops, the Union army had reserves in waiting. And Buell was supposedly on the way from Columbia with the Army of the Ohio, some 50,000 strong.

Throughout the afternoon of April 6, the battle continued. The Union lines pulled back farther toward the river and the Federal left flank was crumbling. Meanwhile, Prentiss stubbornly held his ground at the Hornet's Nest, withstanding incredible firepower and turning back twelve separate assaults. Shortly after 2 P.M. Johnston, the overall Confederate commander, received a leg wound. Refusing medical attention, the general bled to death in a few minutes' time. Word of Johnston's death dampened morale among the Confederate troops.

At the close of the first day of Shiloh, the Yankees, caught off guard as the battle began, found themselves in a precarious position with their backs near the Tennessee River. A stormy night developed and the armies dug in and waited for the morning. By evening two important arrivals had bolstered the Union prospects for a second day of battle. Maj. Gen. Lew Wallace arrived with a division from Crump's Landing. And, on the opposite bank of the Tennessee River, the first elements of Buell's Army of the Ohio arrived and began to ferry across the river to Pittsburg Landing.

At dawn on April 7 Grant's three fresh divisions made a great difference. Now the Federals took the initiative and attacked at 5 A.M. and again at 9 A.M. Confederate resistance was stiff, and by 10 A.M. the entire battle line had exploded. Beauregard's Confederates, now faced with 20,000 new attackers, were driven back. The sting of a massive Federal assault forced Beauregard to issue orders for a retreat and an hour later at 3:30 P.M. the Confederates began marching south on the road to Corinth. The unparalleled bloodbath may have contributed to Grant's unwillingness to follow the Confederate army south. Grant later wrote that some fields at Shiloh were so covered with dead that it was possible to walk over them without touching the ground. Some 62,282 Federals and 40,335 Confederates were engaged over the two days. The casualties stunned the nation—3,477 men lay dead on the fields and another 20,264 were wounded or missing.

Shiloh Tour

Shiloh National Military Park lies isolated from large towns, in a wooded, brushy area ninety miles east of Memphis and twenty-five miles north of Corinth, Mississippi. When we arrived from Memphis we traveled on U.S. 64 to Bolivar and Selmer, and then took Tennessee 142 to Stantonville, Hurley, and the park. We stopped first at the **Visitor Center** on Grant Road to see its museum of Shiloh-related artifacts. The visitor center is located near the Tennessee River, northwest of Pittsburg Landing, in the area of Grant's concentration on the first day of the battle. This Shiloh tour follows the northern areas of the battlefield held by the Union, regions of intense battle throughout the central part of the park, and the southern lines held by the Confederacy.

From the visitor center, turn right on Confederate Drive. At the fork bear right, then turn left onto Grant Road. This area marks **Grant's Last Line**, where the Federal commander established a strong defensive work while troops farther south held the Confederate advance. You'll see many monuments including the **William Harvey Lamb Wallace Headquarters Monument**. This Federal brigadier general commanded the Second Division of the Army of the Tennessee. Nearby you'll see the **Iowa Monument**, honoring Iowa's soldiers who fought at Shiloh. Continuing west brings you to the **5th Ohio Cavalry Monument** and the **68th Ohio Infantry Monument**. Also along this road you'll find the **James Madison Tuttle Headquarters Monument**, position of

the First Brigade in Wallace's division, and the **Thomas William Sweeny Headquarters Monument**. Colonel Sweeny commanded the Third Brigade in Wallace's division. The field south of Grant Road opposite these positions is the **Samuel Chambers Field**. Many fields at Shiloh now bear the names of farmers whose houses stood in the area during the battle. None of the houses are extant.

At the intersection with River Road you'll see the **John McArthur Headquarters Monument,** where the brigadier general commanding Wallace's Second Brigade was stationed. A trail (Crump's Landing Road) leads 350 yards northwest to the **4th U.S. Cavalry Monument**. The ground directly south of the intersection is the **James A. Perry Field**. You may wish to turn southeast (left) onto River Road, cross **Tilghman Branch** (Glover Branch) and continue 600 yards to the **Abraham M. Hare Headquarters Monument,** east of the road (and labeled the Oglesby-Hare Headquarters Monument). This Federal colonel commanded the First Brigade of Maj. Gen. John A. McClernand's First Division. The ground east of the road at this point is **Jones Field**, the position of heavy fighting on the battle's second day. Generals Grant and Sherman met in Jones Field on the first day. It was the first time the two had discussed military strategy face to face on a battlefield. Continue southwest 500 yards to a picnic area road that heads west, where you may wish to turn around. The ground immediately north of you is the **George Sowell (Sewell) Field**, where fighting occurred on the seventh.

To continue the tour, retrace your route back to the visitor center and this time head south (right) on Confederate Drive just west of the museum and left at the fork. About 500 yards south of the point where the road arcs south is the **James Clifford Veatch Headquarters Monument**, about 140 yards west of the road. This Union colonel lead the Second Brigade of Brig. Gen. Stephen A. Hurlbut's Fourth Division. At the intersection with Johnston Road, you'll find the **Michigan Monument**.

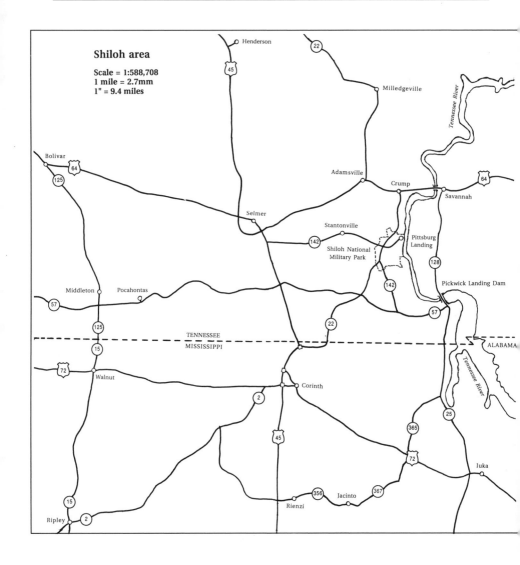

Shiloh area

Scale = 1:588,708
1 mile = 2.7mm
1" = 9.4 miles

Some 400 yards northwest of this spot, along a trail (Cavalry Road), is a **Confederate Burial Trench**. Five such sites exist on the battlefield, repositories of dead Confederates collected after the battle. Continue south to see the **United Daughters of the Confederacy Monument**. Pass Gladden Road (Hornet's Nest Road), and shortly thereafter note the **William Harvey Lamb Wallace Mortal Wounding Monument**. While pulling his men out of a dangerous situation at this spot on April 6, the Federal brigadier general was shot through the left eye, hideously wounding him. The general remained alive for four days, dying at Savannah.

Continue 175 yards past the Wallace Monument to the **2nd Iowa Infantry Monument**. Across the road you'll see the **58th Illinois**

Infantry Monument. About 200 yards northeast of this monument are the **15th, 16th, and 19th U.S. Infantry Monument** and the **1st Ohio Infantry Monument.** You've now reached the northern end of the crucial area known as the **Hornet's Nest** which stretches south of the road down to the Bloody Pond. Here Federal troops under Brig. Gen. Benjamin M. Prentiss held off waves of Confederate attacks on the first day, preventing Grant's army from possible disaster. From the 2nd Iowa Monument, you can walk southeast along the **Sunken Road**, a makeshift rifle pit for Union soldiers who weathered extensive cannon fire from the western end of the field. If you walk the Sunken Road down to Gladden Road, you'll see the **12th Iowa Infantry Monument** and the **1st Minnesota Artillery Monument.** In

this area Prentiss finally surrendered, along with 2,100 of his men, after six hours and twelve Confederate attacks.

Returning to Confederate Drive and heading west brings you to **Ruggles' Battery** on the western end of the Hornet's Nest. Outraged at the lack of success against Prentiss, Confederate Brig. Gen. Daniel Ruggles wheeled up sixty-two cannon and opened fire repeatedly. Nearby stands the **Julius Raith (Leonard Fulton Ross) Headquarters Monument.** Although the monument shows Ross's headquarters here, the Union brigadier general was absent from Shiloh and the Third Brigade of McClernand's division was commanded by Colonel Raith. The ground south of this point is the **Joseph Duncan Field**, heavily fought over throughout the two-day battle.

SURRENDER IN THE HORNET'S NEST occurred at this spot when Union Brig. Gen. Benjamin M. Prentiss could no longer hold off repeated Confederate assaults. The hot fight here bought valuable time for the Union high command.

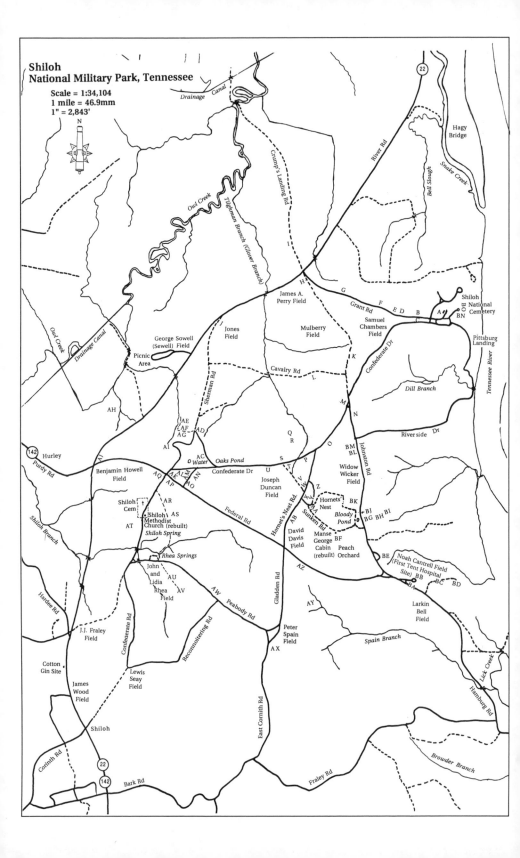

Key to Features on Shiloh Map

A NPS Visitor Center and Museum
B William Harvey Lamb Wallace HQ
   Monument
C Iowa Monument
D 5th Ohio Cavalry Monument
E 68th Ohio Infantry Monument
F James Madison Tuttle HQ
   Monument
G Thomas William Sweeny HQ
   Monument
H John McArthur HQ Monument
I 4th U.S. Cavalry Monument
J Abraham M. Hare HQ Monument
K James Clifford Veatch HQ
L Confederate Burial Trench
M Michigan Monument
N Stephen Augustus Hurlbut HQ
   Monument
O United Daughters of the
   Confederacy Monument
P William Harvey Lamb Wallace
   Mortal Wounding Monument
Q 15th, 16th, and 19th U.S.
   Infantry Monument
R 1st Ohio Infantry Monument
S 58th Illinois Infantry Monument
T 2nd Iowa Infantry Monument
U Julius Raith (L. F. Ross) HQ
   Monument

V 12th Iowa Infantry Monument
W 1st Minnesota Artillery Monument
X Arkansas Monument
Y 14th Iowa Infantry Monument
Z Wisconsin Monument
AA 8th Iowa Infantry Monument
   5th Ohio Artillery Monument
AB 14th Wisconsin Infantry (J. D.
   Putnam) Monument
AC John Alexander McClernand HQ
   Monument
AD 81st Ohio Infantry Monument
AE Confederate Burial Trench
AF 13th Missouri (22nd Ohio)
   Infantry Monument
AG 40th Illinois Infantry Monument
AH 78th Ohio Infantry Monument
AI Confederate Monument and
   Burial Trench
AJ John A. McDowell HQ
   Monument
AK Julius Raith Mortal Wounding
   Monument
AL 15th Illinois Infantry Monument
AM Illinois Monument
AN 14th Ohio Artillery Monument
AO 15th Ohio Infantry Monument
AP 2nd Illinois Artillery Monument
AQ 6th Indiana Artillery Monument
AR William Tecumseh Sherman HQ
   Monument
AS Confederate Burial Trench

AT 2nd Pennsylvania Infantry
   Monument
AU 53rd Ohio Infantry Monument
AV Confederate Burial Trench
AW Everett Peabody Death
   Monument
AX Adley Hogan Gladden Mortal
   Wounding Monument
AY Benjamin Mayberry Prentiss HQ
   Monument
AZ 24th Louisiana Infantry (Crescent
   Regiment) Monument
BA David Stuart HQ Monument
BB 71st Ohio Infantry Monument
BC 55th Illinois Infantry Monument
BD 54th Ohio Infantry Monument
BE Albert Sidney Johnston Mortal
   Wounding Monument
BF 44th Indiana Infantry Monument
BG 6th Ohio Infantry Monument
BH 24th Ohio Infantry Monument
BI 36th Indiana Infantry Monument
BJ 4th U.S. Artillery Monument
BK 9th Indiana Infantry Monument
BL Joseph Wheeler Monument
BM Alabama Monument
BN Ulysses Simpson Grant HQ
   Monument
BO Wisconsin Color Bearers'
   Monument

Bear right and head north where the road splits. Just beyond the split you'll see the **John Alexander McClernand Headquarters Monument**, position of the commander of Grant's First Division. After 450 yards you'll come to the **81st Ohio Infantry Monument** at the intersection of Sherman Road, now a trail that leads north. A short distance west of this position you can see a **Confederate Burial Trench**. South of the trench stand the **13th Missouri (22nd Ohio) Infantry Monument** and the **40th Illinois Infantry Monument**. The former unit consisted of Ohioans who traveled to Missouri to form a regiment. South of these monuments you'll see the **Confederate Monument and Burial Trench** honoring all Confederate soldiers who died at Shiloh. The

WELKER'S MISSOURI BATTERY, designated Battery H and commanded by Capt. Frederick Welker of the 1st Missouri Light Artillery, composed part of Grant's Last Line near the river landing.

trench here is the largest on the field, containing the bodies of more than 700 soldiers.

Continuing southward you'll come to **Water Oaks Pond** where the Confederate counterattack on April 7 pushed the Union line but failed to break it, causing General Beauregard to order the Confederate retreat to Corinth. Making a loop east (left) on Confederate Road, then south (right), then west (right) on Federal Road, takes you past several more monuments. You'll see the **Julius Raith Mortal Wounding Monument** where the Federal colonel, commanding McClernand's Third Brigade, was hit in the right leg by a minié bullet. The leg was shattered, later amputated, and Raith died on April 11. The **15th Illinois Infantry Monument** and the **Illinois Monument** stand nearby. East of the connecting road, you'll find the **14th Ohio Artillery Mon**

ument and the **15th Ohio Infantry Monument**. Southeast of the intersection of Federal Road and Confederate Drive is the **2nd Illinois Artillery Monument**. Southwest of the intersection stands the **6th Indiana Artillery Monument**.

Head west on Federal Road from this point to the intersection with River Road (Tennessee 142, Tennessee 22) to see the **John A. McDowell Headquarters Monument**, northeast of the intersection. Colonel McDowell commanded the First Brigade of Brig. Gen. William T. Sherman's Fifth Division. About 500 yards north of this spot is the **78th Ohio Infantry Monument**. The ground south of the intersection is the **Benjamin Howell Field**.

Returning to Confederate Drive and heading south (right) leads after 400 yards to the **Shiloh Methodist Church**, a brick structure

THE REBUILT SHILOH CHURCH stands near the wartime structure that gave the battle its name. Ironically, Shiloh means place of peace. The surrounding burying ground contains gravestones present during the battle.

built in 1949 that stands near the site of the wooden cabin church that existed during the battle. **Shiloh Cemetery,** spreading north of the church, contains tombstones that were present during the battle. The battle flared over this ground throughout the two days. Important sites exist in the area, most notably the **William Tecumseh Sherman Headquarters Monument,** 275 yards northeast of the church, a **Confederate Burial Trench,** 350 yards east, and the **2nd Pennsylvania Infantry Monument,** 200 yards southwest.

Head south and cross **Shiloh Branch,** a small creek. Turn east (left) onto Peabody Road and a small parking area in the **John and Lidia Rhea Field** where Confederates held positions during the initial attack. From here you may wish to walk north to see **Rhea Springs,** an important water source for many powder-caked soldiers, or south to the **53rd Ohio Infantry Monument** and the fifth **Confederate Burial Trench.**

Turn around and return to Confederate Drive and continue south (left). Proceed one-half mile to the **J. J. Fraley Field,** west of the road, and the **James Wood Field,** south. At 5:15 A.M. on April 6 Federal scouts spotted approaching Confederate lines. Shortly thereafter the opening shots of the battle rang out as Confederates attacked the southernmost camps of Union soldiers. At the point where Confederate Drive turns sharply east, note the area southeast of the road. This is the **Lewis Seay Field,** ground east of Fraley Field that also witnessed the opening battle actions.

Continue along the tour route, now called Reconnoitering Road, to the position where the road bends north. This marks the **Union Defense Line** where Prentiss established his line of battle to halt the Confederate advance. Prentiss and his command were pushed back nearly one and one-half miles to their position at the Hornet's Nest before they held off the attack. At the junction of Reconnoitering Road and Peabody Road, you'll find the **Everett Peabody Death Monument,** where the Federal colonel, in command of Prentiss's First Brigade, was shot in the head and killed instantly early on the sixth. Peabody sent the patrol that discovered the Confederate advance and attempted to alert Prentiss. He formed a battle line but was killed soon after.

South of the intersection of Peabody Road and Gladden Road stands the **Adley Hogan Gladden Mortal Wounding Monument.** The Confederate brigadier general was leading a brigade of mixed troops early on April 6 when he was hit by a shell fragment. His arm was amputated on the field. He died on April 12. The area east of the intersection is the **Peter Spain Field,** scene of intense fighting during the opening attacks. About 500 yards northeast of the intersection is the **Benjamin Mayberry Prentiss Headquarters Monument** where the Federal division commander collected his forces before retreating northward.

Continue north on Gladden Road, which becomes Hornet's Nest Road, beyond the intersection with Federal Road. The ground immediately east of you is the **David Davis Field.** You'll see a number of monuments along this stretch, including a particularly unusual one. The **14th Wisconsin Infantry (J. D. Putnam) Monument** is a stone tree stump built in the place of a real one. Private Putnam of Company F of the 14th Wisconsin carved his initials into the stump as he lay dying. Traveling northward brings you to the center of the Sunken Road, which you saw earlier from the northwestern end. East of the road you'll find the **Arkansas Monument** and the **14th Iowa Infantry Monument.** A short loop road from this position leads to the **Wisconsin Monument,** the **8th Iowa Infantry Monument,** and the **5th Ohio Artillery Monument.**

Returning to Federal Road and heading east takes you to more monuments including the **24th Louisiana Infantry (Crescent Regiment) Monument** and the **Texas Monument.** Continue east past the intersection with Johnston Road, bearing left where the road splits, and you'll come to the **Noah Cantrell**

Field, site of one of the first Union tent field hospitals. Among the monuments here are the **David Stuart Headquarters Monument,** where the Federal colonel commanded Sherman's Second Brigade, and the **71st Ohio Infantry Monument.** A wooded path leads east to the **55th Illinois Infantry Monument** and the **54th Ohio Infantry Monument.** The ground south of the road at this position is the **Larkin Bell Field.**

Now you may wish to head north on Johnston Road to a pullout 500 yards northwest of the hospital site. Here you'll see the **Albert Sidney Johnston Mortal Wounding Monument.** Commander of the Army of Tennessee, Johnston nonetheless exposed himself in a desperate charge against the Hornet's Nest and was shot behind the knee. Refusing medical help, Johnston rested under a tree and bled to death after a few minutes' time. The preserved tree stump under which Johnston died stands a few feet away from the monument. Though he was revered as one of the greatest generals of the south, Johnston lost the only battle he commanded and was mortally wounded as well.

Proceeding north 300 yards takes you to the eastern end of the Sunken Road. You may wish to walk westward to the rebuilt **Manse George Cabin,** the only reconstructed building on the Shiloh battlefield. Near the cabin you'll see the **44th Indiana Infantry Monument.** During the battle the ground south and east of the cabin was the **Peach Orchard,** in full bloom during the action. A short walk north of the Sunken Road, immediately west of Johnston Road, leads to **Bloody Pond,** the most infamous of all bodies of water associated with Civil War battlefields.

After the first day's action soldiers from both sides crawled to Bloody Pond to quench their

ALBERT SIDNEY JOHNSTON, considered by some an exceptionally able general, was mortally wounded at Shiloh while commanding his first battle. The Confederate general bled to death under a tree whose trunk is preserved (right background).

THE PEACH ORCHARD surrounding the rebuilt Manse George Cabin (background) witnessed intense fighting throughout both days at Shiloh.

thirst, staining the water deep red. Many of the soldiers died near the pond or drowned, unable to keep their heads above the water once they began to drink. Monuments north and east of Bloody Pond include the **4th U.S. Artillery Monument,** the **6th Ohio Infantry Monument,** the **36th Indiana Infantry Monument,** the **24th Ohio Infantry Monument,** the **9th Indiana Infantry Monument,** and the **Missouri Monument.** Continue north on Johnston Road to pass the **Widow Wicker Field** west of the road (another scene of brutal carnage), the **Joseph Wheeler Monument,** and the **Alabama Monument.**

If you head north past the intersection with Riverside Drive you'll come to the **Stephen Augustus Hurlbut Headquarters Monument,** the position occupied by the brigadier general who commanded Grant's Fourth

BLOODY POND served wounded and dying soldiers from both sides who crawled to the watering hole for a drink. The numerous injured men stained the water blood red, giving the pond its gruesome nickname.

AT PITTSBURG LANDING on the Tennessee River, Maj. Gen. Don Carlos Buell's Army of the Ohio arrived on steamers after the battle's first day. The massive reinforcement turned the tide and helped Grant push back the Confederate attacks that threatened to pin Union forces against the river.

Division. Continue until you reach Confederate Drive, where you should turn northeast (right). Now proceed to the area of **Pittsburg Landing** on the **Tennessee River**. Here thousands of Grant's troops stood with their backs against the Tennessee River late in the day on April 6. Here also, Maj. Gen. Don Carlos Buell's Army of the Ohio ferried across the water and reinforced Grant, enabling him to attack early on the seventh. The subsequent Federal assaults swept the Confederates from the field.

From Pittsburg Landing you may wish to climb the hill to see **Shiloh National Cemetery**, a ten-acre burying ground established in 1866 to hold the Union dead from the battle. In total, 6,831 soldiers are buried in the cemetery. Among the monuments within the cemetery grounds are the **Ulysses Simpson Grant Headquarters Monument,** marking the base for the Army of the Tennessee, and the **Wisconsin Color Bearers' Monument,** which overlooks the river. Six color bearers from Wisconsin regiments, shot down during the battle, are buried here side by side.

Touring Shiloh reminds us of the awful scale of the destruction that happened here. Because it happened early in the war, Shiloh seems not so fearsome as battles that took place later—Gettysburg, Antietam, the Wilderness, Fredericksburg, Petersburg. But at the time the incredible loss of life stunned the nation, North and South. The cost in dead and wounded had been greater than the sum of all American battles before it. Shiloh proved beyond the shad-

SHILOH NATIONAL CEMETERY contains the graves of six color bearers from Wisconsin regiments who were killed during the battle. The cemetery holds a total of 6,831 dead Union soldiers.

ow of a doubt that the Civil War would be a long, bloody affair, and that many Shilohs were still to come.

Shiloh National Military Park

Mailing address: 1055 Pittsburg Landing Road, Shiloh, Tennessee 38376
Telephone: (731) 689-5696
Park established: December 27, 1894
Area: 5,048 acres

Shiloh National Cemetery

Established: 1866
Area: 10.1 acres
Civil War interments: 6,831

Shiloh accommodations

The closest large city to Shiloh is Memphis, which lies ninety miles away and offers plentiful accommodations. Memphis contains twenty-four major hotels and motels with more than 3,500 rooms. The outlying area has more motels. You can stay closer to Shiloh in Savannah (ten miles away, two motels), Pickwick (fifteen miles, three motels), or Corinth, Mississippi (twenty-five miles, eight motels).

Chapter 11

✪   ✪   ✪

Stones River, Franklin, and Spring Hill

A bitter cold night was now on us.
We were masters of the field. The sheen of a bright moon revealed
the sad carnage of the day, and the horrors of war
became vividly distinct. . .[General Bragg] announced to Richmond by telegraph:
"God has granted us a happy New Year."

—Col. David Urquhart describing the evening of December 31, 1862,
on the Stones River battlefield.

Stones River is a nearly forgotten battlefield. Although the U.S. government established a national battlefield on a portion of the ground at Stones River, few memorials stand on this spot where one of the bloodiest contests of the western theater took place. Nevertheless, visiting the important site clarifies much about the Civil War in Tennessee. Additionally, the nearby towns of Franklin and Spring Hill contain significant areas of Civil War history.

The battle of Stones River, or Murfreesboro, occurred on the frigid days of December 31, 1862, through January 2, 1863. Following the gigantic clash at Shiloh in April 1862 (see chapter 10), the western armies underwent a period of reorganization. Maj. Gen. Henry W. Halleck's Federals advanced on Corinth, Mississippi. Gen. Braxton Bragg's Confederates invaded Kentucky and on October 8 fought the inconclusive battle of Perryville against Union Maj. Gen. Don Carlos Buell. Unpursued, Bragg headed south to the rail center of Murfreesboro,

Tennessee, and faced a new opponent, Union Maj. Gen. William S. Rosecrans, who occupied Nashville.

During the final weeks of 1862, Rosecrans began implementing his orders to capture eastern Tennessee. On December 26 Rosecrans's Army of the Cumberland marched south from Nashville, checked by Confederate cavalry, fog, and steady rains. On the twenty-ninth one of Rosecrans's corps finally approached Murfreesboro. Bragg's Army of Tennessee would stay and fight at Murfreesboro, concentrating its lead forces north and west of the town along the west fork of Stones River.

The armies positioned on December 30, the Confederate corps under Maj. Gen. William J. Hardee occupying the east bank of the river and the corps under Lt. Gen. Leonidas Polk on the west bank of the river. Polk's forces stood between the Yankees and the river, but the bridges and fords provided ample means of escape if needed. The Union left wing under

Maj. Gen. Thomas L. Crittenden and the center under Maj. Gen. George H. Thomas marched southeast parallel to the Old Nashville Highway. The right wing under Maj. Gen. Alexander M. McCook approached from the west.

Bragg anticipated a Union attack on the thirtieth. It did not come. He issued orders for a Confederate attack on the Union right flank at dawn on the thirty-first. Meanwhile, Rosecrans planned to attack the Confederate right flank. While shifting troops north, Rosecrans had McCook's corps build lines of campfires to simulate a great body of troops to the south.

The deception failed. At 6 A.M. Hardee's corps hit the Union right, driving the Yankees from their breakfast before meeting steadfast resistance. Bragg heightened the Confederate attack but could not break the Union line. After nearly two hours of heavy fighting, Hardee began to push the Union troops northward. Union Brig. Gen. Philip H. Sheridan, however, offered a vicious fight and finally surprised the onrushing Confederates with a stinging counterattack. Then Sheridan fell back and his men ran low on ammunition; however, the delay in the Confederate attack allowed the Union lines to re-form along the highway. There they repulsed subsequent Confederate attacks.

Throughout the afternoon Polk's Confederates attacked along the Nashville and Chattanooga Railroad, smashing into Col. William B. Hazen's brigade in the Round Forest. Hazen's men held the position, however, freezing Bragg's hope of a decisive victory crushing the Union left. The battle stabilized and the armies settled in for the night. Rosecrans, disagreeing with those subordinates who felt defeated, decided to stay and fight. Bragg, certain he had won a victory, had his troops dig in. Fighting erupted in small areas on New Year's Day 1863, but the armies were mostly silent.

On January 2 Bragg sent Maj. Gen. John C. Breckinridge to move the Union left back across Stones River. Late in the afternoon Breckinridge pushed Union troops across the river only to meet heavy Union batteries massed above McFadden's Ford. The batteries delivered a devastating artillery barrage. The following day Bragg retreated to Tullahoma, and Rosecrans, who occupied the battlefield, made no attempt to follow him. During the action at Stones River, Rosecrans engaged 41,400 troops, Bragg 34,739. The casualties in killed, wounded, or missing amounted to 24,645 men.

The Army of Tennessee met its match in late 1864. The force was now commanded by Gen. John Bell Hood, who had been unable to stop Maj. Gen. William Tecumseh Sherman from marching through Georgia. In one of the poorest campaigns of the war, Hood turned his army north and invaded Tennessee. Rather than heading north to defend Nashville, however, Sherman gave the task to the Army of the Cumberland under Maj. Gen. George H. Thomas, hero of Chickamauga. Command of the forces in the field facing Hood fell to Maj. Gen. John M. Schofield.

During November 1864 Hood chased Schofield's men north and had the opportunity to close a trap on them at Spring Hill. The heavy fighting at Spring Hill on the twenty-ninth favored the Confederates, but Schofield effortlessly used a main road to withdraw to Franklin. Schofield's army arrived at Franklin at dawn on November 30 and encountered difficulty in crossing the Harpeth River. Schofield would have to fortify and defend the town from any immediate attack.

In one of the bloodiest one-day battles of the war, Hood attacked at Franklin. The results were disastrous for the Army of Tennessee. The Confederate frontal attacks toward hastily entrenched positions exposed the onrushing Rebels to devastating fire. In one afternoon much of Hood's army was cut to pieces. Of the 27,939 Federals and 26,897 Confederates engaged, the casualties were astounding— 8,578 were dead, wounded, or missing, three-fourths of whom were Confederates, including six general officers dead or mortally wounded. Before Hood's army was defeated, it would face

178

Thomas at Nashville, but in one afternoon Hood had substantially ruined the fighting ability of what had been the premier Confederate army of the west.

Stones River Tour

Solemn reminders at Stones River, Franklin, and Spring Hill recall these terrible battles. As we arrived in **Murfreesboro** (pop. 44,922), my father and I headed first to the **Stones River National Battlefield** and its **Visitor Center** on the Old Nashville Highway. See the Stones River detail map (p. 180). The museum at the visitor center contains artifacts relating to the Civil War and the battle of Stones River. The park itself consists primarily of a single loop road between the Old Nashville Highway and the

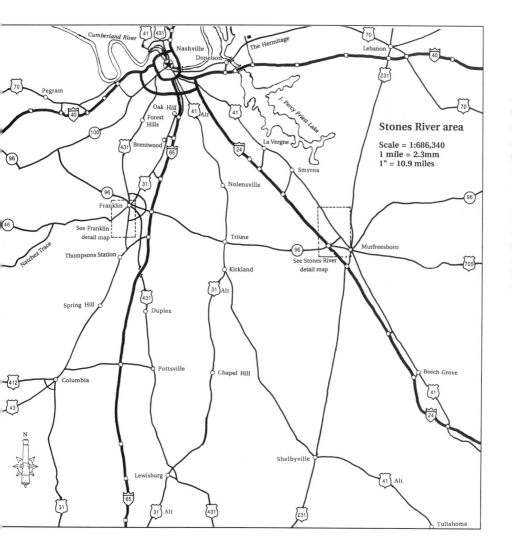

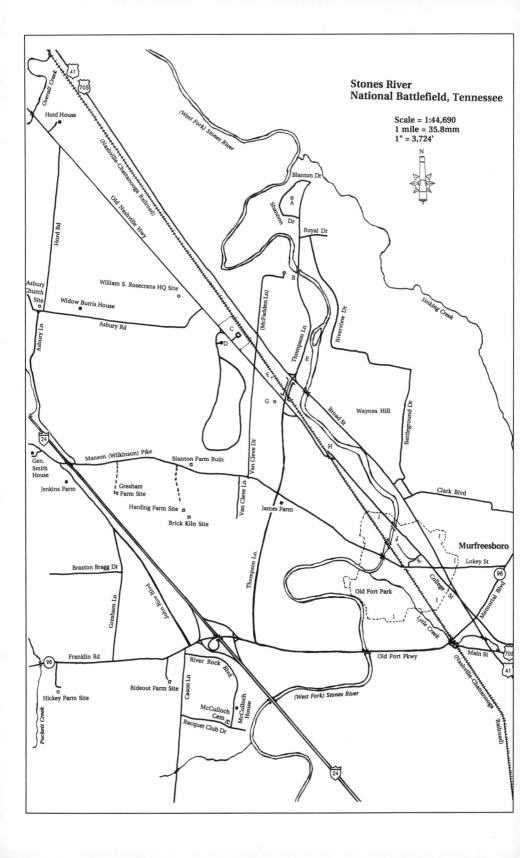

Manson (Wilkinson) Pike, an area covering only about one-tenth of the battlefield. The first stop on the circuit is the **Chicago Board of Trade Battery Site** where at 10 A.M. on December 31, 1862, the Illinois artillerists helped to repel a Confederate attack that had driven back thousands of Union troops. The Chicago battery's six guns, along with those of another battery, checked the Confederate assault on this part of the field.

Continuing south 250 yards brings you to the **Fight for the Cedars Site** where at 10 A.M. on the thirty-first Confederates drove deep into the Union line near this position. Rosecrans switched plans because of the Confederate attack and did not press an attack on the Confederate right. Follow the loop south 500 yards from this point and you'll come to the **Waters's Alabama Battery Site** where at 12:30 P.M. on the thirty-first Capt. David D. Waters brought his Company B, 2nd Alabama Artillery into position to fire north into the Union lines. The limestone outcrops and thick cedar forest prevented placing the guns properly to support the Confederate infantry attacks along the Nashville Highway. Without this support, the Confederates could not break the Union lines.

As the loop road bends east, you'll approach the site of **Sheridan's Stand**, the position where Brig. Gen. Philip H. Sheridan and Maj. Gen. George H. Thomas fought off stubborn Confederate attacks during the morning of the thirty-first. Confederates fired round after round of artillery into Sheridan's troops from a

distance of only 200 yards, yet failed to break the Union line. Sheridan and Thomas ultimately abandoned their positions, but their resistance allowed Rosecrans to regroup the army along the Nashville Highway. A superb display in the woods near this spot simulates Wiard guns demolished by artillery fire.

Travel along the loop road another 500 yards to see the site of the **Confederate High Tide**. During the afternoon of the thirty-first Confederates attacked the area held by Maj. Gen. Thomas L. Crittenden without success. A Confederate attack finally broke the line in this area around 4 P.M., but the retreating Federals regrouped behind a stone wall and poured a volley back at the onrushing Confederates. The attackers succeeded in pushing the Federals away from the position an hour later. About 175 yards north of this spot is the area of **Rosecrans's New Line**. The commanding general established a formidable line of Union infantry along the Nashville Highway and in the Round Forest about 5 P.M. on the thirty-first. The Confederates fell back into the cedars and awaited an opportunity, but the next day was relatively quiet. The battle did not flare intensely until January 2, 1863.

You've now seen the greater portion of the battlefield owned by the federal government. Apart from the loop road, the Park Service owns ancillary sites, and you can also see several buildings and positions not in government hands. Exit the park, turn northwest (left) on the Old Nashville Highway, and head southwest (left)

A DEMOLISHED CANNON lies in the thick woods where Brig. Gen. Philip H. Sheridan's brigade stalled waves of Confederate attacks, buying time so the Union army could re-form along the Nashville Highway (background).

and also hosted Maj. Gen. Thomas's wagon train.

Head southeast on the Old Nashville Highway about one and one-half miles to the site of the **General Headquarters, Army of the Cumberland (Rosecrans) Monument,** southwest of the road. Rosecrans established headquarters in a cabin near this spot (probably farther south of the road).

Continue southeast past the park entrance and turn northeast (left) into **Stones River National Cemetery.** This twenty-acre burying ground was established in June 1865 and holds the remains of about 6,100 Federal soldiers who were killed at Stones River or later died of disease. Several monuments stand on these grounds, including a stone erected in 1865 by the 43rd Wisconsin Infantry to honor its dead comrades, those of the 180th Ohio Infantry, and "Tennessee Union soldiers, railroad employees, etc." You'll also see the **United States Regulars Monument,** which honors the 15th, 16th, 18th, and 19th U.S. Infantry and the 5th U.S. Artillery.

Near the southeast corner of the cemetery, you'll see a small sign beside the tracks of the

on Asbury Road. After traveling one mile you'll pass the **Widow Burris House,** north of the road, a structure that is difficult to see. A Confederate attack under Maj. Gen. Patrick Cleburne attempted to push Federals north, but it was stopped by heavy fighting from Maj. Gen. Thomas L. Crittenden's Union left wing. Continuing west one-half mile brings you to the intersection of Asbury Lane and Hord Road. On the northwest corner is the **Asbury Church Site,** a prominent structure on the battlefield and hospital following the battle. Heading north on Hord Road, turning northwest onto the Old Nashville Highway, and traveling 225 yards brings you to the **Hord House,** north of the road at 5722 Old Nashville Highway. This impressive structure served as the principal Union hospital during and after Stones River,

STONES RIVER, after which the battle was named, flows serenely past McFadden's Ford 125 years after the battle. Here on January 2, 1863, Maj. Gen. John C. Breckinridge's Confederates attacked the Federals in the final phase of the contest.

old Nashville and Chattanooga Railroad running between the cemetery and Van Cleve Lane. This marks the position where Lt. Col. Julius P. Garesché, Rosecrans's chief of staff, was decapitated by a cannonball during the battle.

Now head southeast on the Old Nashville Highway, turn north (left) on Van Cleve Lane (McFadden Lane), and proceed three-fourths mile to **McFadden's Ford** on the west fork of **Stones River**. Here you'll see the **Union Artillery Monument** that marks the position where, on January 2, Confederate Maj. Gen. John C. Breckinridge attempted to drive the Union troops across the river. The intense Union artillery barrage that ensued killed or wounded 1,800 Confederates in less than one hour, thwarting the resumption of the battle. Confederate Brig. Gen. Roger W. Hanson was mortally wounded in the fight. About one-half mile north is the **Hoover Farm Site**, the position of Union Col. William Grose's reserve brigade.

Now you may wish to return to the Old Nashville Highway. At the southeast corner of the intersection of Van Cleve Lane and the highway, you'll see the **Toll Gate House Site**. Nothing of this wartime structure remains. Now head southeast 230 yards to the **Round Forest** where you can find the **William Babcock Hazen Brigade Monument**. This is the position where Hazen's brigade stubbornly held the Round Forest on the thirty-first against Confederate attacks. The position was dubbed "Hell's Half Acre" by the troops after they experienced the ferocity of the combat. The Hazen Brigade Monument is the oldest surviving Civil War memorial, having been erected in 1863 by members of Hazen's command. Fifty-six veterans of Hazen's brigade killed in the forest are buried around the base of the monument. Strangely, when the monument was opened in 1985, park officials found relics including shells and longarms—now on display in the museum—inside the sealed monument, perhaps simply an indication of the vast amount of discarded junk lying about the field in the wake of the battle.

About one-third mile northeast of the Hazen Brigade Monument is the site of **Harker's Crossing**, on the west fork of Stones River. A Union reconnaissance by Col. Charles Garrison Harker's command on December 29th probed the Confederate lines before the battle commenced.

Continuing southeast on the highway 270 yards brings you to the **Cowan Farm Site**, south of the road. The prominent farmhouse that once stood here burned shortly before the battle. Both sides fought around the ruins and outbuildings during the struggle for the Round Forest.

Just over one-half mile southeast on the highway, near the railroad crossing, you'll find the **General Headquarters, Army of Tennessee (Bragg) Monument** north of the road. A short drive leads to the monument. Farther southeast, where the highway crosses the west fork of Stones River, is the site of **Brannan's Redoubt**, south of the road. The overgrown earthworks mark the position where Union Brig. Gen. John M. Brannan constructed defensive positions east of the river. Remains of **Old Fort Park**, a line of earthworks constructed around the town following the battle of Stones River, can still be seen.

Heading southeast on the highway, now turn southwest (right) on Rosebank Drive and west (right) on Lokey Street, which becomes the Manson (Wilkinson) Pike. Follow the road just over one mile and you'll come to the **James Farm**, south of the road but difficult to see. This house served as Confederate Lt. Gen. Leonidas Polk's headquarters. Continue three-fourths mile to the **Blanton Farm Ruin**, another prominent battlefield structure, north of the road. South of this area are the **Harding Farm Site** and the **Brick Kiln Site**. In this area Confederate Col. Arthur Middleton Manigault attacked Union forces under Brig. Gen. Joshua Woodrow Sill. Confederates overran the position and Sill was killed, his body taken to the **Gresham Farm Site**, some 900 yards to the west, at 1556 Gresham Road. The Gresham Farm Site, which served as Maj. Gen. Alexander McDowell

THE FIRST CIVIL WAR MONUMENT stands along the Nashville and Chattanooga Railroad near the center of the Stones River battlefield. Erected in 1863 by members of Col. William B. Hazen's brigade, the monument commemorates this unit's heroic stand in the Round Forest. One face of the monument reads, "The veterans of Shiloh have left a deathless heritage of fame upon the field of Stones River"

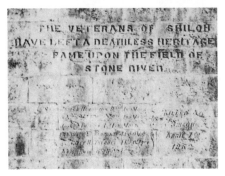

McCook's headquarters during the battle, is now marked by a tall silo.

Continue west on the Manson Pike 500 yards past the point where you cross Interstate 24. You'll then find the **General Smith House**. Federal wagon trains were passing by this structure on the thirty-first when Confederate cavalry struck a blow. Escaping capture, the wagon trains (under Major General McCook) headed north along Asbury Lane.

Travel south along Gresham Lane to see the **Jenkins Farm**, another wartime structure, then proceed south to Franklin Road. The **Hickey Farm Site** and the **Rideout Farm Site** were busy farms during the battle. By turning south on Cason Lane, east on Racquet Club Drive, and north on River Rock Boulevard, you can reach the **McCulloch House**. This building served as Confederate Lt. Gen. William J. Hardee's headquarters. The nearby **McCulloch Cemetery** is a local burying ground.

You may now wish to head back into Murfreesboro to see several sites within the town. The **James Maney House**, "Oaklands," at the end of North Maney Avenue (at Roberts

Street), was headquarters for Union Col. William W. Duffield of the 9th Michigan Infantry during part of the Federal occupation of Murfreesboro. **Evergreen Cemetery** contains a mass grave of about 2,000 Confederate soldiers who died in and around Murfreesboro. Only 156 are identified. The burying ground also contains the grave of Brig. Gen. Joseph Benjamin Palmer. Not far from Evergreen Cemetery, at 434 East Main Street, you may find the **Joseph B. Palmer House**, home of

the Confederate general officer. The **Confederate Monument** in Court House Square, paying tribute to Rutherford County's Confederate troops, is typical of the thousands of such memorials erected after the war.

Franklin and Spring Hill Tour

Having seen the battleground reminders of Stones River, you may wish to travel twenty-eight miles to **Franklin**, Tennessee (pop.

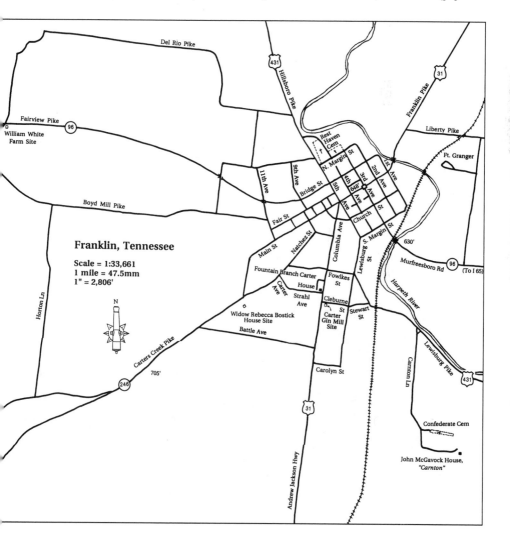

20,098), to visit the several sites associated with the battle of Franklin. See the Franklin detail map (p. 185). We traveled west to Franklin on Tennessee 96. Upon arriving in the town we visited the **Confederate Monument**, in the town square, which honors Williamson County's Confederate soldiers.

Now head south on Columbia Avenue one-half mile to the intersection with Strahl Avenue. Here, at 1140 Columbia Avenue, you'll find the **Fountain Branch Carter House**, a beautifully preserved wartime structure. (You may reach the Carter House parking lot by turning into Fowlkes Street.) Now a museum, the Carter House and its outbuildings stood at the storm center of the Union lines during the battle on November 30, 1864. The house received the central thrust of the ill-fated frontal attack that partially destroyed Hood's army. The Carter family huddled inside the house as bullets whizzed past and struck the walls. Small arms damage remains visible on several of the Carter outbuildings, the most significant from Confederate fire at the south-facing walls of the **Farm Office Building** and the **Smokehouse**. During the battle the Carter House served as headquarters for the Union field commander, Brig. Gen. Jacob Dolson Cox.

The Federal lines at Franklin stretched east-west along the southern end of the town. The Union commander, Maj. Gen. John McAlister Schofield, stayed at **Fort Granger** across the **Harpeth River**, commanding the battle from a position that would have been more utilitarian had the Union center been pushed back. Winstead Hill, south of town, served as Gen. John Bell Hood's headquarters. Heavy fighting rolled over the **Carter Gin Mill Site**, across Columbia Avenue southeast of the Carter House. The Gin Mill, a hauntingly familiar land-

THE FOUNTAIN BRANCH CARTER HOUSE in Franklin marks the storm center of the battle that occurred on November 30, 1864. The structure served as Union Maj. Gen. Jacob D. Cox's headquarters.

THE CARTER FARM OFFICE shows clapboards damaged by small arms fire from Confederate units that charged the center of the Union line. The thickness of the musketry during the battle becomes evident through a close examination of the wooden ediface (above and at right).

mark for many soldiers who fought at Franklin, no longer stands.

Two other house sites, the **Widow Rebecca Bostick House** and the **William White Farm**, are southwest and northwest of the Carter House area. Nothing remains of these wartime structures. If you wish to see the White Farm Site, turn north on Columbia Avenue, bear northwest (left) on Fifth Avenue, then turn west (left) onto Bridge Street, which becomes Fairview Pike. The White Farm Site lies at the intersection of Fairview Pike and Boyd Mill Pike.

Returning to town, head south on Columbia Avenue and turn east (left) on Cleburne Street. Southeast of this intersection is the site of the Carter Gin Mill. Follow Stewart Street east, turn right on Lewisburg Avenue, then right onto Carnton Lane, which you may follow south. After one mile you'll come to the **John McGavock House**, "Carnton." Although the fighting swept as far south as the McGavock House, this wartime structure is best known for its porch. Following the bloody afternoon of fighting, four dead Confederate general officers were laid out on the porch, under the white columns. They were Maj. Gen. Patrick Cleburne, beloved as one of the greatest Confederate generals in the west, and Brig. Gens. John Adams, Otho F. Strahl, and Hiram B. Granbury. Two other Confederate brigadier generals, John C. Carter and States Rights Gist, died fighting at Franklin. Gist was killed instantly and Carter mortally wounded.

Northwest of the McGavock House you'll find the **Confederate Cemetery**, originally the McGavock Family Cemetery. As the McGavock House transformed into a hospital, the residents began to bury in their cemetery Confederate soldiers found on the nearby fields. The two-acre plot now holds 1,484 Confederate dead including Brig. Gen. Johnson Kelly Duncan, who died of fever at Knoxville in 1862.

Franklin's terrible battle had badly depleted the Confederate Army of Tennessee. A month later, the army's fighting effectiveness was crushed by Maj. Gen. George H. Thomas's Union men at the battle of Nashville. Before Franklin, however, Confederates had run wild at **Spring Hill** (pop. 1,464), thirteen miles south of Franklin on U.S. 31. See the Stones River area map (p. 179). Now famous as an automobile manufacturing town, the area was first renowned for its Civil War reminders. On the way to Spring Hill, you may see **Winstead Hill**, some two miles south of Franklin. From this spot Hood commanded the Confederate side of the battle. An observation tower here affords a splendid overlook of the town. You will also see the **Patrick Ronayne Cleburne Monument** and the **Confederate Soldiers Monument** near the **Winstead Hill Observation Tower**.

Several more structures are visible along the way to Spring Hill. Just over a mile south of Winstead Hill, you'll encounter the **Harrison House** on the west side of U.S. 31. This residence served as Hood's headquarters prior to the battle of Franklin. Following the battle, Confederate soldiers brought the body of Brig. Gen. John C. Carter to the house. Earlier in the war another mortally wounded brigadier general, John H. Kelly, was transported to this house. Continue south nearly six miles to the **Francis**

FOUR CONFEDERATE GENERALS lay dead on the porch of the John McGavock House, "Carnton," after the battle of Franklin. The victims were Maj. Gen. Patrick R. Cleburne and Brig. Gens. John Adams, Hiram B. Granbury, and Otho F. Strahl. Two more brigadiers, John C. Carter and States Rights Gist, were killed or mortally wounded during the battle.

Giddens House, "Homestead Manor," a prominent landmark and hospital during the nearby battle at Thompson's Station. Travel just under half a mile south to see a marker describing the action at **Thompson's Station** itself.

Continuing south nearly three and one-half miles takes you into Spring Hill where you'll see the **William McKissack House** on the west side of Main Street, between Duplex Road and Depot Street. This structure was a prominent wartime landmark during Schofield's movement toward Franklin. You'll see a marker on Main Street describing the **Richard Stoddert Ewell Farm,** which still stands two miles to the west. Here the Confederate commander lived his last years. Some 500 yards south of the McKissack House, also on Main Street, is the **Martin Cheairs House.** In the spring of 1863 Confederate Maj. Gen. Earl Van Dorn headquartered in this house. At this time he entertained Jessie Peters, a local married woman. In retaliation, on May 7, 1863, Dr. George Peters entered the Martin Cheairs House and shot Van Dorn in the head, killing him.

Continue south on Main Street as it becomes the Columbia-Franklin Turnpike (U.S. 31). About one and one-half miles south of the Martin Cheairs House is the **Nathaniel Cheairs House,** General Hood's headquarters during the battle at Spring Hill. Continuing south on the pike, turning east (left) on Denning Road, and proceeding two and one-half miles brings you to the **Absalom Thompson House,** north of, but not easily visible from, the road. This house also served, briefly, as headquarters for Hood.

Worn from our travels through the Tennessee countryside, we packed up at Spring Hill and proceeded back to Franklin, passing the Carter House and imagining the carnage that occurred around the mill. We made it back to Nashville and wondered when we might again come back to the peaceful fields and cemeteries of Civil War Tennessee.

Stones River National Battlefield

Mailing address: 3501 Old Nashville Highway, Murfreesboro, Tennessee 37129
Telephone: (615) 893-9501
Park established: March 3, 1927
Area: 709 acres

Stones River National Cemetery

Established: June 1865
Area: 20.1 acres
Civil War interments: about 6,100

Confederate Cemetery

(Franklin)
Established: 1864
Area: about 2 acres
Civil War interments: 1,484

Evergreen Cemetery

(Murfreesboro)
Established: 1873
Area: about 100 acres
Civil War interments: about 2,000

Stones River accommodations

Staying close to the Stones River National Battlefield is relatively easy, as Murfreesboro contains six hotels and motels with a total of more than 600 rooms. You might also stay in Lebanon (twenty-four miles away, two motels), Franklin (twenty-eight miles, three motels), or Nashville (thirty-one miles, fifty-eight motels).

Franklin accommodations

Franklin's three motels offer travelers 325 rooms, so you may find staying here convenient unless the city is unusually busy. You can also stay at Nashville (sixteen miles away, fifty-eight motels), Columbia (twenty-four miles, one motel), or Murfreesboro (twenty-eight miles, six motels).

⭐ ⭐ ⭐

Chapter 12

Vicksburg

The slow shelling of Vicksburg goes on all the time,
and we have grown indifferent. It does not at present interrupt or interfere
with daily avocations, but I suspect they are only getting
the range of different points; and when they have them all complete,
showers of shot will rain on us all at once.

—anonymous, Vicksburg, Mississippi,
March 20, 1863.

Vicksburg, Mississippi (pop. 20,908), is one of the most charming cities associated with Civil War history. Standing high atop a bluff overlooking the Mississippi River, the city proved to be the Confederacy's last powerful bastion in control of the strategic waterway. Because of this, Vicksburg became the target of an all-out Union effort between late 1862 and mid 1863. The fall of Vicksburg would prove to be the decisive event in the Civil War's western theater.

For the Confederacy, Vicksburg was doubly important. It prevented Union ships from navigating downriver and allowed Confederate communication and the passage of supplies to and from the vast open spaces west of the waterway. Because Vicksburg was built on a high bluff overlooking a significant bend in the river, it was heavily fortified and served as a daunting military objective for any Federal army.

Early in 1862, after the fall of New Orleans, Capt. David G. Farragut moved upriver and demanded the surrender of Vicksburg. But Farragut lacked sufficient troops to assault the position. During June and July 1862 further naval attacks succeeded primarily in encouraging the Confederates to strengthen the city's defenses and shift thousands more men to the Vicksburg area. Now a rear admiral, Farragut returned to New Orleans without the prize.

As Vicksburg continued to fortify, the armies in the area clashed in October at Corinth, Mississippi, south of the old Shiloh battlefield. Federal Maj. Gen. William S. Rosecrans occupied Corinth and was attacked by Confederates under Maj. Gen. Earl Van Dorn. The Confederate attacks proved unsuccessful, however, and no sizeable clashes took place in the area until year's end.

One day after Christmas 1862, Maj. Gen. William T. Sherman's Union forces began a campaign to take Vicksburg by moving up the Yazoo River and assaulting southward. Sherman was now working under the direction of Maj. Gen.

U. S. Grant, while the Confederate forces in Mississippi had now been consolidated under Lt. Gen. John C. Pemberton, northern born but a favorite of Jefferson Davis. Sherman's attack at Chickasaw Bluffs on December 29 was easily repulsed by Pemberton, who anticipated the move. A subsequent action at Hayne's Bluff also failed. Sherman then moved back to Milliken's Bend to assess the situation.

Grant and his Army of the Tennessee, meanwhile, were north at Oxford, where raids cut off his supply routes and forced his 40,000 men to live off the land. Grant's plan of attacking Vicksburg by land had to be abandoned; he was now forced to move down the river to support the troops opposite Vicksburg. After arriving at the Union staging area, Grant made four successive attempts to reach high ground east of Vicksburg during March 1863. All four were unsuccessful. During this period Col. Benjamin H. Grierson, a daring cavalryman, led a raid from La Grange, Tennessee, to Baton Rouge that significantly confused the Confederate cavalry about Grant's motives, tying them up and scattering them for two weeks.

During April Grant hatched the bold strategy of crossing the Mississippi south of Vicksburg, relying on long and imperiled communication and supply lines, and attacking the stronghold by land from the east. Grant now had 41,000 men versus Pemberton's heavily entrenched 32,000. The Federal army massed at Hard Times before battles erupted at Port Gibson and Grand Gulf, areas captured by the first week of May. Pemberton now began collecting his scattered forces into the formidable works surrounding Vicksburg on three sides.

Before Grant could concentrate on Vicksburg, however, he determined to march on Jackson and defeat the Confederate force assembled there under Gen. Joseph E. Johnston. During this period in mid May, Pemberton spread a heavy force along the Big Black River between Vicksburg and Jackson. On May 14 Sherman captured Jackson. Grant immedi-

ately began a westward assault on Vicksburg, and the Confederates were in disarray. Johnston fled northward, while Pemberton planned an attack on Grant's supply line which he erroneously believed was southeast of the Big Black River.

Events now accelerated. On May 16 the armies clashed at Champion's Hill northwest of the town of Raymond. After a vigorous afternoon of fighting, Grant inflicted severe casualties on Pemberton's men but failed to block their retreat toward Vicksburg. Skirmishing erupted along the Big Black River as both Rebels and Yankees marched on the Vicksburg defenses. By May 18 Grant reached the outer lines east of Vicksburg and arrayed his army into position. He attacked the next day but could not break through into the city.

Fearful of a siege, Grant tried one last grand assault on May 22. Union gunboats lobbed thousands of shells into the Confederate lines. The Union assault force reached the Confederate fortifications at only a handful of places and could not capture significant positions. By nightfall it was clear to Grant that the attack had failed.

The siege began. Sniping, artillery bombardments, heavy reinforcements, trench and mine digging, and a hot, humid, blistering summer occupied the troops. By July 1 Grant had 71,000 troops investing the city's forts, and Pemberton's soldiers were slowly starving. As Grant planned a final, decisive assault, Pemberton sent word of a surrender, and the two generals met and discussed the situation. As Lee's army retreated southward from Gettysburg on July 4, Pemberton surrendered the city to Grant. It marked the end of any reasonable hope for Confederate military success, although the war would drag on for nearly two years more.

Vicksburg Tour

As we entered the city of Vicksburg from the east we located the National Park Service **Visitor Center**, at 3201 Clay Street. Exits to reach

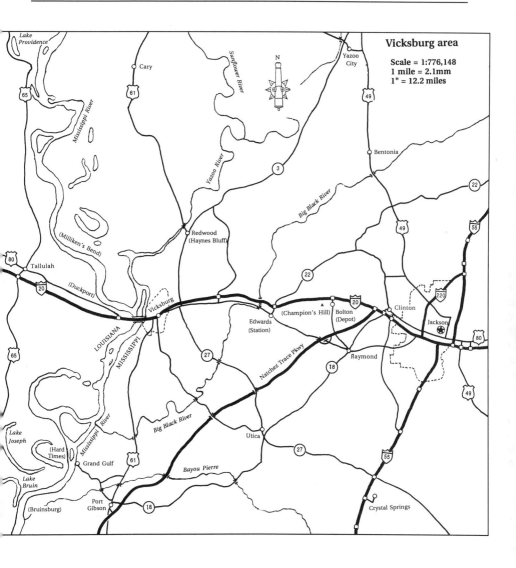

Vicksburg area
Scale = 1:776,148
1 mile = 2.1mm
1" = 12.2 miles

Vicksburg National Military Park are clearly marked on Interstate 20. The museum inside the visitor center contains examples of firearms and other Civil War relics relating to the Vicksburg campaign, as well as several dioramas depicting the siege. Outside the museum you can see a superb display of gun tubes showing the range of cannon used in the siege. You may also see the **96th Ohio Infantry Monument**

and the **16th, 60th, and 67th Indiana Infantry Monument.**

Although these regimentals are prominently located near the park headquarters, you may be surprised at the number of monuments honoring commanders rather than commands in the Vicksburg park. Many bronze statues, busts, and bas-relief plaques commemorate officers who played key roles during the Vicksburg

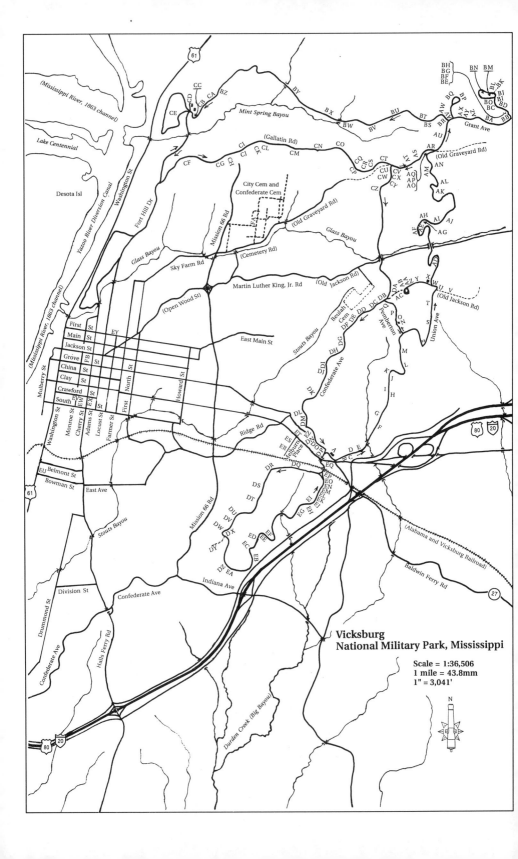

**Vicksburg
National Military Park, Mississippi**

Scale = 1:36,506
1 mile = 43.8mm
1" = 3,041'

Key to Features on Vicksburg Map

A NPS Visitor Center and Museum
B 96th Ohio Infantry Monument
C 16th, 60th, and 67th Indiana Infantry Monument
D Stephen G. Burbridge Monument
E 83rd Ohio Infantry Monument
F William J. Landram Monument
G 48th Ohio Infantry Monument
H John B. Sanborn Monument
I Minnesota Monument
J Green B. Raum Monument
K U.S. Battery Archer
L Isaac F. Quinby Monument
M Charles L. Matthies Monument
N 1937 NPS Headquarters Building
O John D. Stevenson Monument
P Grant-Pemberton Surrender Interview Monument
Q Flag of Truce Meeting Site Monument
R Michigan Monument
S Samuel DeGolyer Battery (8th Michigan Artillery Monument)
T 2nd Illinois Artillery Monument
U John A. Logan Monument
V 68th Ohio Infantry Monument
W 20th Ohio Infantry Monument
X James Shirley House, "White House" (restored), and cemetery
John E. Smith Monument
Manning F. Force Monument
Y Illinois Monument
Z Mortimer D. Leggett Monument
AA Andrew Hickenlooper Monument
AB Melancthon Smith Monument
AC Mine Road
AD 23rd Indiana Infantry Monument
AE John McArthur Monument
AF Ransom's Gun Path
AG Thomas E. G. Ransom Monument
AH Wisconsin Monument
AI Marcellus M. Crocker Monument
AJ Alexander Chambers Monument
AK Giles A. Smith Monument
AL West Virginia Monument
AM 47th Ohio Infantry Monument
AN Hugh Ewing Monument
AO Stockade Redan Attack Point
AP Joseph R. Cockerill Monument
AQ Francis P. Blair Jr. Monument
AR Joseph A. J. Lightburn Monument
AS Thomas K. Smith Monument
AT Joseph A. Mower Monument
AU 57th Ohio Infantry Monument
AV Cadwallader C. Washburn Monument
AW 53rd Ohio Infantry Monument
AX Elias S. Dennis Monument
AY Isaac F. Shepard Monument
AZ Hugh T. Reid Monument
BA Kansas Monument
BB Cyrus Bussey Monument
BC New York Monument

BD Rhode Island Monument
BE Robert B. Potter Monument
BF William Sooy Smith Monument
BG Nathan Kimball Monument
BH Edward Ferrero Monument
BI Cyrus B. Comstock Monument
7th Rhode Island Infantry Monument
Frederick E. Prime Monument
James H. Wilson Monument
John A. Rawlins Monument
BJ Simon G. Griffin Monument
9th Corps HQ Site (John G. Parke)
BK Pennsylvania Monument (Andrew G. Curtin and John G. Parke)
BL Thomas Welsh Monument
BM New Hampshire Monument
BN Ulysses S. Grant Monument and HQ Site
BO Massachusetts Monument
BP 12th Indiana Infantry Monument
BQ William T. Sherman HQ Site
BR 22nd Ohio Infantry Monument
BS James M. Tuttle Monument
BT Ralph P. Buckland Monument
BU William L. McMillen Monument
BV 4th Ohio Artillery Monument
BW Thayer's Approach and Tunnel (reconstructed)
BX John M. Thayer Monument
BY Bernard G. Farrar Monument
BZ U.S. Navy Monument (David G. Farragut, Andrew H. Foote, Charles H. Davis, and David D. Porter)
CA Thomas O. Selfridge Jr. Monument
CB Alfred W. Ellet Monument
CC Charles R. Woods Monument
Frederick Steele Monument
CD Ironclad Gunboat U.S.S. Cairo and Cairo Museum
CE Vicksburg National Cemetery
CF Fort Hill
CG Jeptha V. Harris Monument
CH John C. Vaughn Monument
CI Tennessee Circle
CJ John Adams Monument
CK Randal W. MacGavock Monument
CL Tennessee Monument
CM William E. Baldwin Monument
CN 17th and 31st Louisiana Infantry Monument
CO Defense Against Thayer's Approach
CP Francis A. Shoup Monument
CQ Allen Thomas Monument
CR John S. Bowen Monument and HQ Site
CS William Wade Death Monument
CT Martin L. Smith Monument
CU Francis M. Cockrell Monument
CV Stockade Redan
CW Thomas P. Dockery Monument
CX Martin E. Green Monument
CY Missouri Monument
CZ Arkansas Monument

DA 3rd Louisiana Infantry Redan
DB Great Redoudt
DC Louis Hébert Monument
DD Louisiana Monument
DE Daniel W. Adams Monument
DF Lloyd Tilghman Monument
DG John H. Forney Monument
DH Mississippi Monument
DI John C. Pemberton Monument
DJ Dabney H. Maury Monument
DK William T. Withers Monument
DL Jefferson F. Davis Monument
DM John C. Moore Monument
DN Thomas J. Lucas Monument
DO Peter C. Haines Monument
DP William F. Vilas Monument
DQ Railroad Redoubt
DR Texas Monument
DS Thomas N. Waul Monument
DT Stephen D. Lee Monument
DU Alabama Monument
DV Edward D. Tracy Monument
DW Isham W. Garrott Monument
DX Square Fort (Isham W. Garrott Death Site)
DY Georgia Monument
DZ George F. McGinnis Monument
EA Indiana (Oliver H. P. T. Morton) Monument
EB Alvin P. Hovey Monument
EC Hovey's Approach
ED William T. Rigby Monument
EE James R. Slack Monument
EF Theophilus T. Garrard Monument
EG Peter J. Osterhaus Monument
EH Lionel A. Sheldon Monument
EI Samuel J. Kirkwood Monument
EJ Iowa Monument
EK Edward O. C. Ord Monument
EL John A. McClernand Monument and HQ Site
EM Michael K. Lawler Monument
EN David Shunk Monument
EO Eugene A. Carr Monument
EP William P. Benton Monument
EQ Andrew J. Smith Monument
ER Matthew D. Ector Monument
ES John Gregg Monument
ET William H. T. Walker Monument
EU William Lum House, U. S. Grant Post-Siege HQ Site
EV Louisiana Monument
EW Sydney House, Carter L. Stevenson HQ
EX Willis-Cowan House, John C. Pemberton HQ
Dr. William T. Balfour House, James B. McPherson Post-Siege HQ
EY Duff Green House
EZ Anshe Chesed Hebrew Cemetery
FA Soldier's Rest Confederate Cemetery
FB Old Vicksburg Courthouse and Museum

campaign. The first part of this tour takes you far north to the river along the siege lines and includes many Union memorials. The second part takes you south of Fort Hill and includes many Confederate monuments. The third part incorporates important sites in the city of Vicksburg.

Unfortunately, the Vicksburg park has not had a sterling history of preserving its original holdings. Many of the important areas located in the original southern part of the park, including many Confederate monuments, have not been preserved. The land has been sold and many monuments isolated or moved.

When you're ready to begin touring the park, head north on Union Avenue through the **Memorial Arch**, and immediately you'll see monuments and markers to explore. Northwest of the road is the **Stephen Gano Burbridge Monument** honoring the brigadier general who commanded the First Brigade in Andrew J. Smith's division of the 13th Corps. Nearby stands the **83rd Ohio Infantry Monument**. Crossing a stream and continuing north will take you to the **William Jennings Landram Monument** which recognizes the colonel who commanded Smith's Second Brigade. As the road winds north, you'll see the **John Benjamin Sanborn Monument**. Colonel Sanborn commanded the First Brigade of the Seventh Division under James B. McPherson's 17th Corps. Nearby stands the impressive **Minnesota Monument**. Continuing north to a bend in the road takes you to the **Green Berry Raum Monument**, honoring the commander of the Second Brigade of McPherson's Seventh Division, and **U.S. Battery Archer**.

Two more monuments honoring Union commanders can be found north of Battery Archer. They are the **Isaac Ferdinand Quinby Monument** and the **Charles Leopold Matthies Monument**. Quinby commanded the Seventh Division in McPherson's 17th Corps while Matthies commanded the Third Brigade of that division.

When you reach Pemberton Avenue, turn northwest (left) to explore this short stretch of road. You'll see several important structures here, including the **1937 National Park Service Headquarters Building**, the former museum and welcome center. Nearby stands the **John Dunlap Stevenson Monument**, which honors the Federal commander of the Third Brigade in John A. Logan's Third Division of the 17th Corps. Midway along Pemberton Avenue, you'll encounter the **Grant-Pemberton Surrender Interview Monument**, an upturned cannon. His command starving to death and the city crumbling in decay, Pemberton met Grant here on July 3, 1863, to discuss the possibility of surrender. Pemberton capitulated the following day. Nearby you'll see the **Flag of Truce Meeting Site Monument** where Union troops met Pemberton's flag of truce on the afternoon of July 3.

Now you may wish to turn around and head north again on Union Avenue to continue the tour. At the point where the road bends south, you'll come to the **Michigan Monument** and, shortly thereafter, the **Samuel DeGolyer Battery**. Here artillery units including DeGolyer's 8th Michigan Artillery bombarded the Great Redoubt, visible from Battery DeGolyer. Captain DeGolyer was mortally wounded during a bombardment and died on August 8, 1863. North of this position you'll see the **2nd Illinois Artillery Monument**.

When you reach a sharp turn in the road, you'll want to park and explore the surrounding terrain. The Old Jackson Road that heads east from this position, now just a footpath, contains many monuments including the **20th Ohio Infantry Monument**, the **John Alexander Logan Monument**, and the **68th Ohio Infantry Monument**. Major General Logan was considered by many the greatest citizen-soldier in the Union army. At Vicksburg he commanded the Third Division in McPherson's 17th Corps.

After you see the remains of Old Jackson Road, note the prominent white house north-

THE ILLINOIS MONUMENT, the largest and most elaborate state memorial in the park, records the names of the Illinois regiments and commanders who participated in the siege.

west of the intersection. It is the **James Shirley House**, the only wartime structure surviving within the Vicksburg National Military Park. The house, a prominent battlefield landmark during the siege, was mentioned by many soldiers and officers in accounts of the fighting and often called "the White House." Restored to approximate its wartime appearance, the Shirley House served for a time as headquarters for the 45th Illinois Infantry, whose colonel was Jasper A. Maltby. Members of the regiment constructed numerous bombproofs in the ground surrounding the house, particularly on the southeast side of the house that slopes down into a steep ravine. Famous wartime photos of the house show these numerous underground shelters.

Many monuments are scattered around the Shirley House. In the back yard you can see the **James and Adeline Shirley Grave**. In the front yard you may see the **John Eugene Smith Monument** and the **Manning Ferguson Force Monument**. Brigadier General Smith commanded the First Brigade of Logan's division of the 17th Corps. Colonel Force commanded the 20th Ohio Infantry and later the Second Brigade of Logan's division.

Head west on the paved portion of the Old Jackson Road to see the most spectacular state memorial on the battlefield, the **Illinois Monument**. West of this position you'll encounter the **Mortimer Dormer Leggett Monument**, which honors the brigadier general who commanded the Second and (later) First Brigades

THE JAMES SHIRLEY HOUSE is the only surviving wartime structure in the Vicksburg National Military Park. During the siege dugout caves surrounded the house and provided shelter for Union troops.

of Logan's Third Division. At the turning circle you'll see the **Andrew Hickenlooper Monument**. Hickenlooper served as McPherson's chief engineer and later chief of artillery for the Army of the Tennessee.

You may walk a slight distance to the west along a path that was once part of the old Mine Road. The area you are now standing in is the **Third Louisiana Infantry Redan**, one of the principal Confederate forts blocking access to the city from the Old Jackson Road. Here Grant ordered mines dug, and the first was exploded on June 25, 1863, the second six days later. Neither broke the Confederate line at this position. Along the earthworks here, you'll find the **Melancthon Smith Monument**, remembering the lieutenant colonel of the 45th Illinois who was mortally wounded during the mine explosion on June 25. Smith died three days later.

You should now return to the Shirley House and turn north (left) on Union Avenue to continue the tour. You'll pass monuments including the **23rd Indiana Infantry Monument**, cross over the Old Jackson Road, and encounter several structures as the road makes several curves. These include the **John McArthur Monument**, which honors the brigadier general who commanded the Sixth Division in McPherson's 17th Corps. Continue northward to the **Thomas Edward Greenfield Ransom Monument**. Ransom commanded McArthur's Second Brigade. Next you'll encounter **Ransom's Gun Path**, where artillery and infantry under Brig. Gen. Thomas E. G. Ransom dragged two guns to within 100 yards of the Confederate line, assembled them, and opened up on the Confederate defenses. As the road bends east, you'll see the impressive **Wisconsin Monument**, one of the most ornately embellished monuments on the field. East of this area stand the **Marcellus Monroe Crocker Monument** and the **Alexander Chambers Monument**. Brigadier General Crocker commanded McPherson's Seventh Division, Colonel Chambers the Third Brigade of the Sixth Division.

Continuing north will bring you to the **Giles Alexander Smith Monument** honoring the Union colonel who commanded the First Brigade of Blair's division in the 15th Corps. Shortly thereafter you'll come to the **West Virginia Monument**, the **47th Ohio Infantry Monument**, and the **Hugh Ewing Monument**. An adoptive brother of Sherman's, Ewing commanded the Third Brigade in Blair's division. As you approach the intersection of Union Avenue and Old Graveyard Road, you'll come to an important site. The **Stockade Redan Attack Point** was a Union staging area from which Sherman launched a massive attack on May 19 on the Stockade Redan, a heavily fortified Confederate position in view to the west. The attack failed, as did a similar effort three days later. Near the Attack Point you'll find the **Joseph Randolph Cockerill Monument** and the **Francis Preston Blair Jr. Monument**. Major General Blair commanded the 15th Corps's Second Division, Colonel Cockerill the Third Brigade of Smith's division of the 16th Corps.

You may now wish to turn west (left) onto Old Graveyard Road to explore the area. Near the intersection you'll find the **Joseph Andrew Jackson Lightburn Monument**, which honors the brigadier general who commanded the Second Brigade of Blair's division. Continue on to see the **Thomas Kilby Smith Monument** in remembrance of the brigadier general who earlier commanded the same brigade. Near the end of the road, you'll spot the **Joseph Anthony Mower Monument** honoring the brigadier general who commanded the Second Brigade, Tuttle's division, 15th Corps.

Next, return to Union Avenue and continue north. After a short stretch the road will intersect Grant Avenue where you should turn east (right). Along the way you'll see the **57th Ohio Infantry Monument**, the **Cadwallader Colden Washburn Monument**, the **53rd Ohio Infantry Monument**, and the **Elias Smith Dennis Monument**. Major General Washburn commanded the 16th Corps, Brigadier General Dennis the District of Northeast Louisiana. Two more memorials stand along the southern stretch of Grant Avenue, the **Isaac Fitzgerald Shepard Monument** and the **Hugh Thompson Reid Monument**. Colonel Shepard commanded the African Brigade of the district of Northeast Louisiana. Brigadier General Reid commanded the First Brigade of McArthur's division of the 17th Corps.

Continuing along Grant Avenue brings you to one of the most unusual state memorials at any battlefield park, the **Kansas Monument**. As the road bends north, you'll see the **Cyrus Bussey Monument**, which honors the colonel who commanded the unattached cavalry of the Army of the Tennessee. Shortly thereafter you'll find important memorials of commanders, including the **Robert Barnwell Potter Monument** and the **William Sooy Smith Monument**. Brigadier General Potter commanded the Second Division of the 9th Corps, Brigadier General Smith the First Division of the 16th Corps. Nearby stand the **Nathan Kimball Monument** and the **Edward Ferrero Monument**. Brigadier General Kimball commanded the Provisional Division of the 16th Corps, Brigadier General Ferrero the Second Brigade of Potter's division.

Continuing along takes you to the grounds of the General Headquarters, Army of the Tennessee, where Grant directed the Yankee assaults. You'll see the **7th Rhode Island Infantry Monument** and a quartet of monuments honoring important Grant staff officers, the **Cyrus Ballou Comstock Monument**, the **Frederick Edward Prime Monument**, the **James Harrison Wilson Monument**, and the **John Aaron Rawlins Monument**. Captain Comstock served as chief engineer for the Army of the Tennessee. Captain Prime preceded Comstock in the same capacity. First Lieutenant Wilson served as chief topographical engineer under Grant. Lieutenant Colonel Rawlins was Grant's assistant adjutant general and chief advisor. You'll also see the **New York Monument**.

As you enter Grant Circle, you'll see a number of monuments including the **Simon Goodell Griffin Monument**. Colonel Griffin commanded the First Brigade in Potter's division of the 9th Corps. Nearby is the **9th Corps Headquarters Site** where Maj. Gen. John Grubb Parke commanded. Continuing around the circle brings you to the elaborate **Pennsylvania Monument**, which incorporates statues of Major General Parke and Governor Andrew G. Curtin. West of this monument you'll see the **Thomas Welsh Monument**, which honors the brigadier general who commanded Parke's First Division.

Inside the island of land in the circle are three important memorials including the equestrian **Ulysses Simpson Grant Monument**, which marks the position of the Federal commander's headquarters during the Vicksburg siege. East of the Grant monument, you'll find the **New Hampshire Monument** and the **Massachusetts Monument**.

Heading west on Grant Avenue and turning north (right) at the first opportunity takes you to the Sherman Circle, site of the **15th Corps Headquarters**, commanded by Maj. Gen. William Tecumseh Sherman. You'll also see the **12th Indiana Infantry Monument** at this location.

As you return from Sherman Circle, head west on Union Avenue. You'll pass the **22nd Ohio Infantry Monument** near the intersection. Shortly thereafter you'll come to the **James Madison Tuttle Monument** and the **Ralph Pomeroy Buckland Monument**.

ULYSSES S. GRANT established headquarters northeast of the city and bore down on the Confederate lines during the long siege. The Grant headquarters site is marked by this equestrian statue of the commanding general.

Brigadier General Tuttle commanded the Third Division in Sherman's corps. Brigadier General Buckland commanded the First Brigade of Tuttle's division. Continue along to the **William Linn McMillen Monument,** which honors the colonel who succeeded Buckland in command of his brigade. As the road bends, you'll see the **4th Ohio Artillery Monument.**

The next area you'll encounter is a significant site, **Thayer's Approach and Tunnel.** The imposing hill south of this position was heavily defended by Confederates. On May 22, 1863, troops under Brig. Gen. John M. Thayer stormed the hill and were hurled back with heavy casualties. The men then resorted to digging a deep trench to approach the Confederate lines, using the tunnel under the roadway (reconstructed since the war) to avoid enemy fire. You'll see the receiving end of Thayer's Approach later in the tour.

After crossing Mint Spring Bayou, your next destination is the **John Milton Thayer Monument.** Brigadier General Thayer commanded the Third Brigade of Steele's division of the 15th Corps. Continue along to see the **Bernard Gains Farrar Monument,** which honors the commander of the First Brigade in Steele's division. Traveling a considerable distance as the road bends south will bring you to the most imposing obelisk on the field, the **United States Navy Monument.** Built overlooking the Mississippi, the Navy Monument contains four superb sculptures of the top commanders involved with the Vicksburg bombardment, Rear Adm. David Glasgow Farragut, Rear Adm. Andrew Hull Foote, Rear Adm. Charles Henry Davis, and Acting Rear Adm. David Dixon Porter.

A short distance west of the Navy Monument stands the **Thomas Oliver Selfridge Jr. Monument,** built on the site of **Battery Selfridge.** The battery placed here consisted of naval guns that pounded southward into Confederate lines. Lieutenant Commander Selfridge was stationed here after his ship, the ironclad gunboat U.S.S. *Cairo,* sank when it struck

THE U.S. NAVY MONUMENT honors the significant contribution of naval gunboats to the reduction of the fortress at Vicksburg. The obelisk incorporates bronze statues of Rear Adm. David G. Farragut, Rear Adm. Andrew H. Foote, Rear Adm. Charles H. Davis, and Acting Rear Adm. David Dixon Porter.

a mine in the Yazoo River on December 12, 1862. The battery was therefore named for Selfridge. A century after the ship's sinking, National Park Service personnel raised the gunboat, restored it in part, and displayed it at Vicksburg. It is visible from Battery Selfridge, covered by a large roof, several hundred yards to the southwest. The exceptional exhibit of the gunboat and the accompanying museum of artifacts is a highlight of Civil War tourism.

Before heading to the *Cairo,* however, take a look at the **Alfred Washington Ellett Monument,** the **Charles Robert Woods**

VICKSBURG NATIONAL CEMETERY contains the graves of about 17,000 Union soldiers who fell during the siege of Vicksburg. The cemetery's grounds cover forty acres.

Monument, and the **Frederick Steele Monument**. Brigadier General Ellett commanded the Marine Brigade. Colonel Woods commanded the Second Brigade of Steele's division. Major General Steele commanded the First Division of Sherman's 15th Corps.

Now you may wish to proceed downhill to the parking lot at the **Ironclad Gunboat U.S.S. *Cairo* and Cairo Museum**. The reconstructed ship (many original pieces were damaged or destroyed in raising the ship) provides an amazing insight into a Civil War Mississippi River gunboat. The fact that the ship sank quickly (in about twelve minutes, with no fatalities) and settled into ice-cold mud, helped, not only to preserve it well, but prevented crewmen from removing many artifacts. Because of these circumstances, the museum holds exam-

RAISED FROM THE YAZOO in the mid 1960s, the sunken Federal ironclad gunboat U.S.S. *Cairo* was painstakingly reassembled and put on display at the Vicksburg park. The boat is the only extant example of a city class Civil War Mississippi gunboat.

202

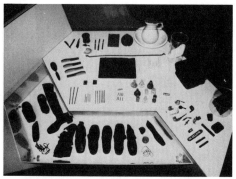

ARTIFACTS ABOUND in the U.S.S. *Cairo* Museum, located adjacent to Vicksburg National Cemetery. Because the gunboat sank quickly, after hitting a torpedo, and settled in cold mud, the ship's goods stayed on board for a century until recovered. The museum's vast collection includes personal goods such as shoes, inkwells, pens, combs, razors, pipes, and eyeglasses.

ples of nearly the entire spectrum of Civil War naval relics, from the ship's bell, tools, lanterns, buckets, arms and ammunition, to a wide range of personal effects belonging to the sailors.

Having seen the gunboat, you may want to drive into **Vicksburg National Cemetery** across the road. Established in 1866, the burying ground covers forty acres and is one of the largest Civil War cemeteries, holding some 17,000 Federal dead. Along with the many officers buried here lies Bvt. Brig. Gen. Embury D. Osband.

Next you may wish to head south on the connecting avenue to **Fort Hill**, positioned high above the river. This position, marking the left flank of the Confederate lines, was never attacked by Union forces. As you head east along Confederate Avenue (the old Gallatin Road), you'll now be tracing the path of the Confederate defense lines north of the city. The monuments you'll now see commemorate Confederates rather than Federals. Continue along Confederate Avenue to the **Jeptha V. Harris**

Monument. Harris was a brigadier general of Mississippi State Militia. Traveling a considerable distance past this spot brings you to the **John Crawford Vaughn Monument**, remembering the brigadier general who commanded a brigade in Smith's division.

Continue east to see more Confederate monuments. You'll come to the **Tennessee Circle** and the **John Adams Monument** next. Brigadier General Adams led a brigade under Gen. Joe Johnston at Raymond and Jackson. East of this position you'll find the **Randal W. MacGavock Monument** and the **Tennessee Monument**. MacGavock, colonel of the 10th Tennessee Infantry, was killed at Raymond on May 12, 1863. Along this stretch of road, you'll find the **William Edwin Baldwin Monument** and the **17th and 31st Louisiana Infantry Monument**. Brigadier General Baldwin commanded a brigade in Smith's division.

As you reach a point in the road where it begins to arc southward, you'll come to the **Defense Against Thayer's Approach**, the overlook hill that was the receiving end of Thayer's attack. You can now see the hillside, road, and tunnel below you, and appreciate the desperate nature of an attack up this slope. As the road again bends eastward, you'll come to several sites of interest including the **Francis Asbury Shoup Monument**, the **Allen Thomas Monument**, and the **John Stevens Bowen Monument and Headquarters Site**. Brigadier General Shoup commanded a brigade in Smith's division. Colonel Thomas commanded the 28th Louisiana in Shoup's brigade. Major General Bowen commanded a division under Pemberton. Bowen's health declined during the siege, and he died near Raymond, a paroled prisoner, on July 13, 1863.

After Bowen you'll come to the **William Wade Death Monument**. Colonel Wade, chief of artillery for Bowen's division, was killed April 29, 1863. You'll also see the **Martin Luther Smith Monument**, honoring the major general who commanded a division under Pemberton.

As you reach the intersection of Confederate Avenue and the Old Graveyard Road, you'll see a large group of sites. The most significant of these is the **Stockade Redan**, the impenetrable Confederate position guarding the approach to Vicksburg via Old Graveyard Road. Federal attacks concentrated on this position, most importantly the assaults of May 19 and May 22, 1863. These two unsuccessful attempts helped Grant decide to lay siege to the town.

Near the Stockade Redan you'll see the **Francis Marion Cockrell Monument**, the **Martin Edwin Green Monument**, and the **Thomas Pleasant Dockery Monument**. Colonel Cockrell commanded the First (Missouri) Brigade in Bowen's division and Brigadier General Green the Second Brigade in Bowen's division. Green was killed while walking the parapet on June 27, 1863, and Colonel Dockery took over his command. A short distance south of this area, you'll find the **Missouri Monument** and the **Arkansas Monument**.

Heading south three-fourths mile brings you to the intersection of Confederate Avenue and Pemberton Avenue. Bear southwest (right), staying on Confederate Avenue. You'll direct-ly see the **Great Redoubt**, a huge Confederate earthwork that guarded the Old Jackson Road. After a devastating attack on May 22 when Union soldiers were hurled back, the Federal artillery blasted this fortification throughout the remaining weeks of the siege. South of the Great Redoubt, you'll see the **Louis Hébert Monument**. This brigadier general commanded a brigade in Forney's division. Continue south to the **Louisiana Monument**, the **Daniel Weisiger Adams Monument**, and the **Lloyd Tilghman Monument**. Brigadier General Adams was not present during the siege but is memorialized nonetheless. Brigadier General Tilghman was killed on May 16, 1863, at Champion's Hill.

More Confederate monuments are scattered along this stretch of the Confederate defense line. Continue to see the **John Horace Forney Monument**, the **Mississippi Monument**, and the **John Clifford Pemberton Monument**. Major General Forney commanded a division under Pemberton. Lieutenant General Pemberton, though northern born and mistrusted by some Confederates, commanded the garrison and defense forces in Vicksburg. He ultimately surrendered the city

THE STOCKADE REDAN on Graveyard Road marks the site of the final vicious assaults in which the Federals failed to break the Confederate center. The offensives on May 19 and 22, 1863, led Grant to cease direct attacks.

GRANT AND PEMBERTON met at the Surrender Interview Site on July 3, 1863. Grant demanded, and eventually received, unconditional surrender of the city from the beleaguered Confederate chief.

to Grant on July 4, 1863, feeling he could get better terms from the Yankees on Independence Day. The lieutenant general was never again respected in the South. Vicksburg itself did not celebrate the holiday for eighty-three years after the surrender.

Just south of Pemberton is the **Dabney Herndon Maury Monument**, which commemorates the major general who helped fortify Vicksburg before Grant's army marched on it. Continue on to the **William Temple Withers Monument** honoring the colonel who commanded the 1st Mississippi Light Artillery. South of this position, after the road bends gently southeast, you'll come to the **Jefferson Finis Davis Monument**, which honors the president of the Confederate States of America and stands on the site of the **Second Texas Lunette**. You'll also see the **John Creed Moore Monument**. Brigadier General Moore commanded a brigade in Forney's division. Continue along to the **Thomas John Lucas Monument**, the **Peter Conover Haines Monument**, and the **William F. Vilas Monument**. You've now crossed back into the Union line (temporarily) and are viewing Federal monuments. Colonel Lucas commanded the 16th Indiana Infantry at Vicksburg. First Lieutenant Haines served as chief engineer of the 13th Corps. Lieutenant Colonel Vilas commanded the 23rd Wisconsin Infantry.

Having now returned to the area of the visitor center, you're ready to make the southern loop to see both Confederate defense lines and Union siege lines. Cross under Clay Street and head south, bearing right at the split. The first thing you'll come to is the **Railroad Redoubt**, a massive earthwork built by Confederate troops to protect the Southern Railroad. An attack on this position on May 22 at first scattered the Rebels, but a decisive Confederate counterattack retook the position. South of the redoubt stand the **Texas Monument**, the **Thomas Neville Waul Monument**, and the **Stephen Dill Lee Monument**. Colonel Waul's Texans finally drove the Yankees from

the Railroad Redoubt. Brigadier General Lee commanded Pemberton's artillery during the siege.

Continuing south brings you to the **Alabama Monument**, the **Edward Dorr Tracy Monument**, and the **Isham Warren Garrott Monument**. A brigade commander in Stevenson's division, Tracy was killed instantly on May 1, 1863, during the battle at Port Gibson. Colonel Garrott, who took charge of the brigade following Tracy's death, was himself shot down on June 17, 1863, in the earthwork you're now approaching, called the **Square Fort** (now also called Fort Garrott). A short trail south of the Square Fort leads to the **Georgia Monument**.

As the road bends eastward and then north, you'll approach several Union markers, including the **George Francis McGinnis Monument**, the **Indiana (Oliver Hazard Perry Throck Morton) Monument**, and the **Alvin Peterson Hovey Monument**. Brigadier General McGinnis commanded the First Brigade in Hovey's division of the 13th Corps. The Indiana Monument features a statue of the state's wartime governor, Morton. Brigadier General Hovey commanded a division in the 13th Corps. The next site you'll see is **Hovey's Approach** where a restored trench depicts how Hovey's men attempted to reach the Confederate lines.

Monuments honoring still more Union commanders dot the road as it loops north back toward the visitor center. Among these are the **William T. Rigby Monument**, the **James R. Slack Monument**, and the **Theophilus Toulmin Garrard Monument**. Rigby, a second lieutenant in the 24th Iowa Infantry, was for many years the park commissioner at Vicksburg. Colonel Slack commanded the Second Brigade of Hovey's division in the 13th Corps. Brigadier General Garrard commanded the First Brigade of Osterhaus's division of the 13th Corps.

After crossing a branch of **Durden Creek**, you'll come to the **Peter Joseph Osterhaus Monument**, which honors the commander of a division in the 13th Corps. Just north of this position are the **Lionel Allen Sheldon Monument** and the **Samuel Jordan Kirkwood Monument**. Colonel Sheldon commanded the Second Brigade in Osterhaus's division of the 13th Corps. The Kirkwood Monument honors Iowa's wartime governor.

From this spot northward to the closure of the loop, you'll pass a large number of monuments east of the road. These include the **Iowa Monument**, the **Edward Otho Cresap Ord Monument**, and the **John Alexander McClernand Monument and Headquarters Site**. Major Generals McClernand and Ord commanded the 13th Army Corps during the siege, and the McClernand Monument marks the position of the corps's headquarters. North of this area are the **Michael Kelly Lawler Monument**, the **David Shunk Monument**, and the **Eugene Asa Carr Monument**. Brigadier General Carr commanded a division in the 13th Corps. Brigadier General Lawler commanded Carr's Second Brigade, Colonel Shunk his First Brigade. The final pair of monuments on this road consists of the **William Plummer Benton Monument** and the **Andrew Jackson Smith Monument**, located across Clay Street from the visitor center. Brigadier General Benton preceded Shunk in his command, and Brigadier General Smith commanded a division in the 13th Corps.

You've now completed the tour of the park itself. You may wish to continue with a tour of additional important sites, some of which are outside the government's land ownership. To do so, head west (right) on Clay Street and travel a short distance to Melburn Place, where you should turn southwest (left). Here you'll see the **Matthew Duncan Ector Monument**, the **John Gregg Monument**, and the **William Henry Talbot Walker Monument** (across Clay Street). Brigadier Generals Gregg and Walker commanded brigades under Gen. Joe Johnston. Brigadier General Ector was not present during the siege.

Continuing west on Clay Street brings you to Mission 66 Road, where you may wish to turn south (left) and proceed to Confederate Avenue. The stretch of Confederate Avenue south of the park contains many Confederate memorials—this land was once part of the park—but the busy road offers no safe stopping points. Among the most important monuments in this area are the **North Carolina Monument**, the **Florida Monument**, the **South Carolina Monument**, and monuments honoring the following commanders: Maj. Gens. Samuel Gibbs French and William Wing Loring, Brig. Gens. Seth Maxwell Barton, Abraham Buford, Alfred Cumming II, Nathan George Evans, Winfield Scott Featherston, States Rights Gist, William Hicks Jackson, Samuel Bell Maxey, Evander McNair, Marcellus Augustus Stovall, and John Wilkins Whitfield, and Cols. Alexander Welch Reynolds, Arthur E. Reynolds, Lawrence Sullivan Ross, and Clement Hoffman Stevens. Because of the traffic density along this road, examine these monuments with caution.

You may now wish to head south on Confederate Avenue by turning right onto North Frontage Road, which leads to Washington Street. A southward (left) drive on Washington Street takes you to the **Louisiana Circle**. Here you'll see a small preserve of land owned by the Park Service. This was once a heavily fortified position where naval guns protected the river approach. You can see a famous gun, the "Widow Blakely," in position at this fort. The 7.44-inch Blakely rifle's barrel exploded, after which Confederate artillerists converted the gun into a mortar. Continuing south a short distance on Washington Street takes you to **South Fort**, another battery position protecting the river. (To see the fort, you must park and walk into the grounds.) Heading south one-fourth mile from this spot leads to the **Navy Circle**, another gun position close to the river.

To see several sites within the city of Vicksburg, head north on Washington Street. Between Bowman and Belmont Streets, in the parking lot at the Blackburn Chrysler dealership, is the position of the William Lum House, the **U. S. Grant Post-Siege Headquarters Site**.

Continue north on Washington Street until you reach South Maison Street, where you should turn east (right). Turn north (left) on Monroe Street and then east (right) onto Crawford Street. Near the intersection of Crawford and Monroe Streets, in the median, you'll see the **Louisiana Monument**. On the corner stands the **Sydney House**, a part of which served as Confederate Maj. Gen. Carter L. Stevenson's headquarters. Just down the street, at 1002 Crawford Street, is the **Dr. William T. Balfour House**, a bed and breakfast inn which served as Union Maj. Gen. James B. McPherson's headquarters following the siege. Next door, at 1018 Crawford Street, stands the

Willis-Cowan House, headquarters of Confederate Lieutenant General Pemberton during the siege.

Heading north on Adams Street and turning east (right) onto First East Street takes you to the **Duff Green House**, a bed and breakfast inn at 1114 First East Street, which during the war served as a Confederate hospital and then a Union hospital. Across the street a small house provided quarters for the town's nurses.

Heading north on Farmer Street and northeast on Sky Farm Road brings you to the **Vicksburg City Cemetery**, burial place for many Confederate veterans. **Soldier's Rest Confederate Cemetery** lies within the City Cemetery and contains the graves of 1,600 Confederate soldiers, many of whom were

CITY CEMETERY and its Confederate section, "Soldier's Rest," holds the remains of three important Confederate officers, Maj. Gen. John S. Bowen, Brig. Gen. Martin E. Green, and Col. Isham W. Garrott. All three gravestones wrongly elevate these men by one grade.

killed or died during the siege. Near the access road you can see the graves of three important Confederate officers, Maj. Gen. John S. Bowen (incorrectly labeled a lieutenant general), Brig. Gen. Martin E. Green (incorrectly labeled a major general), and Col. Isham W. Garrott (incorrectly identified as a brigadier general). Garrott was appointed a brigadier general posthumously but his commission was never confirmed.

To complete your Vicksburg tour, you'll definitely want to see the central building of wartime Vicksburg, the **Old Vicksburg Courthouse and Museum**, located at 1008 Cherry Street. Symbol of the town's resistance, this magnificent building was a target of Federal shelling and housed many Confederate officers during the siege. The museum within contains

THE VICKSBURG *DAILY CITIZEN*, wallpaper edition, shows how difficult the siege was for civilians caught in the city. Shortages of all goods were severe; the final newspaper had to be printed on wallpaper. The Old Court House displays a rare authentic copy of this paper.

VICKSBURG'S OLD COURT HOUSE was the defiant Confederate stronghold during the siege. It housed Union prisoners and served as a signal station for Confederate forces. The building now houses a superb museum of Civil War artifacts.

many wartime artifacts including a collection of Jefferson Davis items, Grant's chair from the Lum House, and superb collections of artillery shells, plates, buckles, and other relics. Soaking in such a collection in the richly historic building is the perfect way to cap off an exploration of the battlefield.

Vicksburg National Military Park

Mailing address: 3201 Clay Street, Vicksburg, Mississippi 39182
Telephone: (601) 636-0583
Park established: February 21, 1899
Area: 1,762 acres

Soldier's Rest Cemetery

(Within Vicksburg City Cemetery)
Established: 1840
Area: 2 acres
Civil War interments: about 1,600

Vicksburg National Cemetery

Established: 1865
Area: 40 acres
Civil War interments: about 17,000

Vicksburg accommodations

Vicksburg has thirteen hotels, motels, and inns, with a total of more than 2,000 rooms, and nine bed and breakfast inns offering an additional 100 rooms. Nearly all of the inns stood at the time of the siege and were used as Confederate hospitals or Union offices after the siege.

Index